The Intimate Economies of Bangkok

The Intimate Economies of Bangkok

Tomboys, Tycoons, and Avon Ladies in the Global City

Ara Wilson

UNIVERSITY OF CALIFORNIA PRESS

Berkeley   Los Angeles   London

Portions of chapter 5 appeared as a slightly different version
in "The Empire of Direct Sales and the Making of Thai
Entrepreneurs." *Critique of Anthropology* 19(4) 1999: 401–22.

University of California Press
Berkeley and Los Angeles, California

University of California Press, Ltd.
London, England

Library of Congress Cataloging-in-Publication Data

Wilson, Ara.
    The intimate economies of Bangkok : tomboys,
tycoons, and Avon ladies in the global city / Ara Wilson.
        p.   cm.
    Includes bibliographical references and index.

ISBN 978-0-520-23968-5 (pbk. : alk. paper)
    1. Sex role—Thailand—Bangkok   2. Capitalism—
Social aspects—Thailand—Bangkok.   3. Globalization.   4. Women—Thailand—Social conditions.
5. Women—Thailand—Economic conditions.   I. Title.

HQ1075.5.T5 W54   2004
381'.1'09593—dc21   2003012772

Manufactured in Canada

13   12   11   10   09   08   07
11   10   9   8   7   6   5   4   3

The paper used in this publication is both acid-free and
totally chlorine-free (TCF). It meets the minimum
requirements of ANSI/NISO z39.48–1992 (R 1997)
(*Permanence of Paper*).♾

To Gaye, Nit, and Tang
and especially to Chompoo

CONTENTS

ILLUSTRATIONS

FIGURES

MAPS

ACKNOWLEDGMENTS

Over a good number of years, diverse sources of funds underwrote the research for and preparation of this book, including support from the following: a Foreign Language and Area Studies (FLAS) award; the City University of New York (CUNY) Women's Faculty and Staff Development Fund; a grant from the Ph.D. Program in Anthropology at the Graduate School of the City University of New York; Sigma Xi; the Kenneth B. and Mamie Phipps Clark Dissertation Award; the Southeast Asia Council of the Association for Asian Studies; the late William S. Wilson Jr. and William S. Wilson III; the David Silk Distinguished Dissertation Award (CUNY); a Nina Fortin Women's Studies Award (CUNY); Mellon Seminar Fellowship (CUNY); a 1998 Elizabeth D. Gee Fund for Research on Women and a 2000–2001 Seed Grant (for research on a different topic), both from The Ohio State University. My ability to write this book owes a great deal to a 1999–2000 Rockefeller Fellowship at the Institute for Research on Women, Rutgers University, and a leave from teaching in the Department of Women's Studies at OSU in the fall of 2002.

Among the many people and institutions shaping the long intellectual and professional path leading to this book are: the Bay Area *Socialist Review* collective of the late 1980s (especially L. A. Kauffman, Michael

Rosenthal, Pam Rosenthal, Steven Epstein, and Donald Low); Dyke TV; the Center for Lesbian and Gay Studies (CLAGS); the Department of Anthropology at Vassar College; the Ph.D. Program in Anthropology at the Graduate School of the City University of New York; (Gerald Creed; Shirley Lindenbaum; Vincent Crapanzano; the late Del Jones; Louise Lennihan; May Ebihara; Jane Schneider; Cristiana Bastos; Arlene Davila; Kate McCaffrey; Yvonne Lasalle; Maureen O'Dougherty; Jonathan Hearn); Penny Van Esterik; Peter Jackson; Lenore Manderson; Marjorie Muecke; Cristina Blanc; Anna Tsing; Aihwa Ong; the late Jan Weisman; Eric Wakin; Kate Wilson; Parissara Liewkeat; Mary Beth Mills; Tani Barlow; Suzanna Walters; Laura Green; Frances Winddance Twine; Jiemin Bao; Janet Baus and Holly Ellison; Sharryn Kasmir; Jenny Terry; Aseel Sawalha; and Eugenia Pisa-Lopez.

Presenting portions of this book at conferences and institutions helped sharpen the argument, particularly from talks given at the Department of Women's Studies at the University of California–Berkeley; Women's Studies and Anthropology at the University of California–Irvine; the Women in Development chapter at OSU; and the Department of Anthropology and the Institute for Research on Women at Rutgers University–New Brunswick.

My millennial year at the Institute for Research on Women at Rutgers University, funded by a Rockefeller Fellowship, was an invaluable source of time for reading, reflection, mistakes, and ultimately for making important headway on this book. I would like to recognize the support there of Bishnupriya Ghosh, Louisa Schein, Beth Hutchison, Marlene Importico, Bonnie Stein, Waranee Pokapanichwong, Charlotte Bunch and the Center for Women's Global Leadership staff, Joanne Regulska, and other Rockefeller seminar participants. At The Ohio State University, where I have found a welcoming home in the Department of Women's Studies since 1997, I have benefited from the presence of a number of colleagues and groups: Jenny Terry, the Department of Women's Studies faculty and staff (especially Ada Draughon), Sally Kitch, Valerie Lee, OSU-WID, Allan Silverman, the citizenship group, the folklore network, David Horn, Cathy Rakowski, Jackie Royster, Amy Shuman, Pamela Fletcher, Judith Mayne, Cindy Burack, Mary Margaret Fonow, and Lu Bailey as well as the enthusiasms and provocations of such students as Jenrose Fitzgerald, Ria Zazicki, Donna DJ Troka, Kate Bedford, Rebecca Dingo, Kathy Sweat, Ela Kakde, Lisa Andaloro, and Amber Griffin, among others. The Department of Women's Studies has been generous in providing research assistants, and these diligent, flexible, and very good-natured graduate students have undertaken various tasks connected with this book: Jelena Batinic, Kate Bedford, Lee Evens, Kazumi Hasegawa, Min Heo, Margaret Hoff, Sangita Koparde, Melanie Maltry, Ieva Zake, and Lu Zhang.

I have to single out a number of people who made specific contributions to this book: Supecha Boughthip, Kanokwan Tharawan, Parissara Liewkeat, Suzanna Walters, Laura Green, Dawn Skorczewski, Sharryn Kasmir, Aihwa Ong, Allan Silverman, and Jiemin Bao as well as several sharp and informed external reviewers. Here I also want to recognize the extensive labor and logic of Sharryn Kasmir, the transformative guidance of Dawn Skorczewski, and the ever-ready eyes and pen of Stephanie Grant: all of them played a crucial role in this book. At University of California Press, I want to thank Naomi Schneider for her long-term interest in this project, her assistant Sierra Filucci for fielding all manner of questions, and Suzanne Knott and Robin Whitaker for rigorous editing. Thanks also to cartographer Rini (Widyarini) Sumartojo who drafted—and redrafted—the maps in this book with very short notice.

My family of origin has always supported my anthropological efforts, and I am grateful to William Wilson, Kate Wilson, and Ann Wilson for that gift. They—my father, sister, mother—as well as my brother, Andrew, and my lover, Stephanie Grant, enrich me with their own vocations and intellects. I appreciate the broader world that Aseel, Mary, Jack and Alex, and Jaime and Reilly create. I also want to recognize the importance of my friends (and their children) in New York and far-flung places for sustaining me and always encouraging my work, even when it takes me away from them.

Finally, turning to my obligations in Thailand, I want to thank: Phramaha Sutep Congprair, then at Wat Mongkolwatanaram in Berkeley; Ajaan Chayachoke and Khun Chiraporn Chulasiriwongs; my official institutional host, the Chulalongkorn University Social Research Institute, particularly Ajaan Napat Sirisambhand; Ajaan Ubonrat Siriyuvasak; Ajaan Kritaya Archavanitkul; Ajaan Peansiri Vongvipanond; Jay Pongsudhirak; Parissara Liewkeat; and the National Research Council of Thailand, especially Khun Tuenchai Niyamangkook. One of the most important parts of my stay in Thailand was my involvement with various women's nongovernmental organizations (NGOs) and activist networks, including the Foundation for Women and Empower, especially Phi Noi, Phi Chum, Surang, Som, Seng, Chompoo, and its students. In the Thai lesbian group, Anjaree and Tang (Anjana Suvarnananda) provided constant challenges and influential lessons, and Tuk, Usa, and other members provided a home of sorts. A special thanks to Eva Kolodner. I am grateful for others who sustained my ordinary life in Bangkok: Pep and his friends, who were my evening escorts to Silom Soi 4; Sandy and Scott Sester and their pal Jeng; Erick White; Sheila Sukonta Thomson of the Gender and Development Research Institute; and Yvonne Shanahan, Nina Schwalbe, and Irene Bosker.

As the book's dedication implies, Nit Kongkam (Nit), Kanokwan Tharawan (Gaye), Anjana Suvarnananda (Tang), and Supecha Boughthip (Chompoo) became important friends to me in Thailand, and they remain so. I am fortunate to have emerged from field research with such generous and genuine intimates. Chompoo, especially, with her critical and compassionate eyes, taught me more than I can say about Thailand, organizing, sex work, and empowerment. I cannot repay the trusting affections of friends like Nit, Gaye, and Chompoo: such is the nature of the important debts we incur in our research and in our lives. And they will also understand and approve when I add an implicit dedication of this book to Stephanie Grant, and of course to Augusta and Josephine Grant Wilson.

NOTES ON TRANSLITERATION
AND DATES

I have transliterated Thai words using modified versions of the Mary Haas system and the "General System" of the Royal Institute of Thailand. This method does not represent the five tones of Central (standard) Thai. For the nonspecialist reader, I have replaced phonetic symbols with more letters more commonly understood in English (e.g., 'j' instead of 'c' for the sounds in *judge*). Where there is already a commonly recognized transliteration, I use that instead of the more accurate formulation: thus I write *tom* instead of *thawm* and *dee* instead of *dii*. For proper Thai names, I have used existing English spellings if known or transliterations according to the principles outlined here.

PRONUNCIATION GUIDE
WITH THAI EXAMPLES
Vowels

a	as in *but* (kathoey)
aa	as in *flan* (ajaan)
ae	as in *deck* (faen, mae, tao kae)
ai, ay	as in *dry* (wai)

ao	as in *now* (sao Mistine, tao kae, khao)
aw	as in *paw* (phaw kha)
i	as in *knee* or *lean* (phi, jin)
oe	as in *her* (kathoey, choey)
u, uu	as in *soon* (bun khun, luuk kha)

Consonants

ch	as in *chip*
j	as in *judge*, often rendered as 'c' (jao, jin, ajaan)
k	as in *skate* (unaspirated 'k', close to 'g' in go) (kathoey)
kh	as in *kite* (khun, kha)
ng	as in *sing* (nangseu, nangsob)
p	as in *spite* (unaspirated 'p', close to 'b')
ph	as in *pin*, not *fin* (phaw kha)
t	as in *stop* (unaspirated 't', close to 'd') (tao kae)
th	as in *tan*, not *than* (Thailand)

A NOTE ON DATES

I have used A.D. years for most dates. Where a citation employs the Buddhist Era (B.E.) year, in accordance with the official system for Thailand, the A.D. year follows in parentheses.

Intimate Economies

Two of Bangkok's well-known tourist attractions offer clues for understanding the powerful effects of the global economy unfolding in Thailand today. The first attraction is the photogenic "floating market," the early-morning market in canals where women sell produce and goods from small canoes. The second is the commercial zone of "Chinatown," specifically Sampeng Lane, a dense street of wholesale shophouses. By evoking colorful markets from Thailand's past, these attractions point to the cultural, even intimate, properties of the economy.

Floating markets feature women in indigo clothes and straw hats selling fruits, vegetables, snacks, and also T-shirts, silk garments, and knick-knacks. On the banks of the canal, warehouse-sized stores are piled high with souvenirs. Organized tours take tourists a few hours outside Bangkok proper to visit "one of the most authentic left in Thailand," where they can purchase items and take photographs of "this millennium old tradition [on the] verge of extinction."[1]

The distinctive picture of the vendors in their small boats, loaded with baskets of produce, offers a recognizable symbol of Thai traditions. Images of the floating market pervade the tourist archive, providing a standard graphic for postcards, coffee-table books, T-shirts, and posters. The familiar boat loaded with produce even appears on an English-language government pamphlet about venereal disease (see figure 1). Cultivated first for the foreign gaze, the image of the floating market has also come to symbolize Thailand and Thainess in materials oriented to Thais. Recently, a photo of women in boats filled with produce was circulated with the phrase "Thais help Thais." The slogan itself was widely employed in a government effort encouraging Thais to buy domestic goods and to rally together following the 1997 economic crisis that began in Bangkok and spread across the Asian region.[2]

Even if most of the examples of floating markets around Bangkok are now choreographed for the tourist economy, this water-borne exchange harks back to a long stretch, if not quite a "millennium old," of Thai history, when canals and rivers provided the major arteries and Westerners called Bangkok the Venice of the East. They illustrate the water-oriented nature of the traditional life of the Thai, whose houses were built on stilts by the rivers that irrigated their rice fields. Perhaps unintentionally, these tourist attractions also highlight a constant observation about Thailand and much of Southeast Asia: that local markets are worlds of women, and that women conduct a good deal of the local trade.[3] By at least the nineteenth century, market women—*mae kha* (mother traders)—exchanged produce, cowries, Mexican coins, Indian rupees, and Thai coinage with traveling male Chinese vendors, acting as the frontier of the market economy in their villages.[4] In any given Bangkok neighborhood and throughout the Southeast Asian region, women vendors still predominate in small markets. Peasant women bring extra produce to nearby market areas or specialize in selling prepared foods, handicrafts, petty commodities, and contraband.

The prevalence of women in markets is virtually a cliché in observations about Thailand, and there are numerous studies of market women. Yet when it comes to discussing the Thai economy, their presence is generally forgotten. Their absence from the discussion results from gendered conceptions of the economy and of Thai identity. In academic, economic, and popular understandings, the "Thai" people and Thai

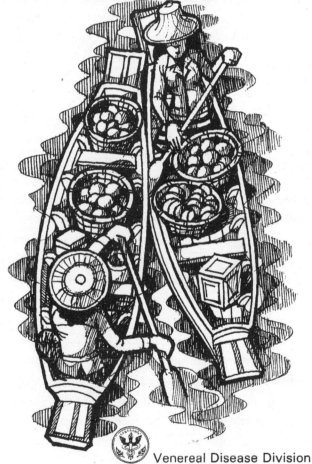

HAVE FUN
WITHOUT VD

Venereal Disease Division

DEPARTMENT OF COMMUNICABLE DISEASES CONTROL
MINISTRY OF PUBLIC HEALTH
BANGKOK THAILAND

Figure 1. An image of the floating market used
on a Thai Ministry of Public Health pamphlet about VD,
targeting English-speaking foreigners. Circa 1988.

culture have been envisioned as separate from the market economy, largely because Theravada Buddhism is central to Thai society (it is the state religion), and Buddhism is often understood as a nonmaterialistic religion. In this way, discourses about Thainess have often erased Thai women's key roles at the economic and cultural crossroads of markets of Thai society. Instead, the emergence of the modern, capitalist economy is typically credited solely to immigrants from China and their Sino-Thai children, an ethnic economy represented in the second tourist site to which I turn.

"Chinatown" is the English name given to a large and variegated market area of old Bangkok. It is known for a patchwork of commerce that includes imported fruit, vegetables, and prepared food; apothecary shops and street stalls peddling sexual aids; bazaars selling secondhand junk and counterfeit goods; and stores specializing in luxury textiles, electronics, coffins, and gold. The best-known market within this area is Sampeng Lane. Sampeng is a tightly packed strip lined by hundreds of small wholesale shops selling imported and domestically made goods: fabric by the yard, paper and plastic goods, novelty items, and bags and hats bearing contemporary logos (often imitations of well-known brands, like Gap or Polo), packaged in dozens.

Despite its claustrophobic feel, Sampeng Lane has been an attraction for visitors at least since the 1960s, when the "News for Nang and Nang Sao" (News for Mrs. and Miss) column in the leading English-language newspaper wrote of its "frequent listing as one of the 'sights to see' in Bangkok." The article explained, "Sampeng Lane is not a tourist trap but is a strictly utilitarian market."[5] Unlike the typical floating market, sightseers come to see utilitarian, business-as-usual operations of merchants, hawkers, deliverymen, and buyers. They also come to savor the area's "local color." Tourist guides encourage trips to Chinatown, providing helpful maps of the many lanes that crisscross Sampeng and sketching the area's "colorful" history of gang fights, prostitution, and opium dens.[6]

ECONOMIC TOURISM

Chinatown and floating markets signal Thai history, tradition, and culture, particularly in contrast with the modern urbanity—the shopping malls, high-rise buildings, go-go bars, or outlying factories—that characterizes more and more of Bangkok. To Thais, they signify different elements of the country's past. To foreign tourists from industrialized countries, they provide the experience of "otherness" that is one of the aims of such travel. Thailand was never colonized by the West. Still, lingering images of ethnic enclaves in port cities from the era of Europe's colonial empires in Asia inform many foreigners' perception of Chinatown and other features of Thailand.

It is noteworthy that particular economic forms serve as symbols of tradition and culture when Thai tradition is typically envisioned apart from the market economy. The historical floating market trade is an example of petty commodity exchange that is based on a surplus of farm products; its traders do not accumulate wealth through this trade. Shophouses typically are small businesses, often owned by a family, of a form called merchant capitalist or comprador capitalist. (See figure 2.) This merchant trade allows businesses to make and reinvest profit (one of the hallmarks of capitalism) and employ wage labor. As examples of Thai history, they reveal traces of modernity within Thai tradition. Well before the massive tourist industry, Chinatown's trade and even peasant markets were integrated into national and international economies. Old-time floating markets, mimicked in tourist versions, were intricately connected to the economic and modernization projects of the kingdom: the canals that women vendors gathered on were designed by the Siamese state to facilitate the export-oriented rice trade, which expanded exponentially from at least the 1850s on, and women's trading was connected to the commercialization of their family farming.

To say that these markets were and are integrated into a larger economic system shaped by international capitalism is not to deny that these

Figure 2. A wholesale shophouse on Sampeng Lane, 1993.
Photo by Eva Kolodner.

trades differ from the economies of global corporations. The older economies of vernacular bazaars and urban merchant trade differ in terms of scale, infrastructure, organization, and values and, significantly, in the ways they are embedded in local communities and culture. The contrast between these traditional markets and modern retail crystallizes the drastic changes that have taken place in marketing, first in the 1950s and 1960s and then dramatically in the 1980s and 1990s. Such broad-sweeping changes to the local flavor of markets make the hawker and merchant compelling tourist attractions. The appeal of such older venues for modern visitors derives less from the nature of their actual economic functions than from their cultural qualities.

The "color" of these antiquated markets derives from their real or suggested connections to older ways of life, indicated by the presence of social worlds, cultural practices, and particular identities. Around Sampeng, numerous Chinese shrines and temples, shark-fin or noodle soup restaurants, and Chinese-language signs lend a distinctly ethnic cast to this commercial space. Most of Sampeng's trade is connected with the Chinese minority of Thailand. This trade involves community, specifically kin and ethnic networks. Shophouse businesses that bundle pocketbooks, sneakers, or keychains for shipment abroad are typically family concerns, drawing on family members' labor and support. The place of families in the public floating markets might be invisible, but the economic roles of women traders—even in the tourist economy—are inseparable from patterns of kinship.

Another way that these premodern market attractions signal cultural tradition is through the people associated with them. In both the floating market and the Sampeng shophouse, the figure of the vendor is key. For the boat seller, the straw hat and indigo peasant clothes or colorful sarong demarcate her role. The Sampeng merchant is less marked by costume than by ethnicity and surroundings. For Thai observers, Chinese male bosses *(tao kae)* form a codified figure, the Sino-Thai commercial family is an established formation, and even their shophouses present a recognizable architectural-economic form. The figures of Thai female dors or of Chinese shopkeepers are marked by gender and national-ethnic identities as well as by class associations of peasant or bourgeoisie; their identities symbolize older economic systems and ways of life.

As even this cursory sketch suggests, in the historical floating market and present-day Sampeng Lane shophouse, social worlds are intertwined with economic systems. Paddling vendors and Chinese shrines are connected to local ways of life. Another example of the overlap of social identities and economies can be seen in the use of kinship terms for the roles involved in commercial exchange: the term for female vendor (mae kha) means "mother trader" or "mother of trade"; *phaw kha* for male vendor means "father of trade"; and *luuk kha* for consumer means "child of trade."[7] This integration of social and economic systems conveys the presence of intimate life, at least in old-fashioned economies. This is how these tourist markets provide clues for understanding the global economy. They invite the question, What is intimate about capitalist modernity?

One of the fundamental questions in current scholarship on the global south in general is how the linked processes of globalization, modernization, and transnational capitalism affect people's everyday lives. Capitalist development in Thailand has changed the stage for citizens' identities, subjectivities, communities, and relationships. It has transformed the ways people support themselves and their families and live day to day, altered the class composition of the country and city, and generated a powerful consumer culture that informs all manner of identities. The effects of capitalist modernity are far reaching, entering the intimate realms of daily life. But the global economy itself is typically seen as lacking the texture of local culture. As the tourist attractions of the floating market and Sampeng Lane illustrate, the effects of global capitalism are often registered as a loss of the social and cultural dimensions of economic realms. The implicit contrast between a multinational chain store and a floating market implies that modern commerce diminishes the intimate texture of public economic realms. *The Intimate Economies of Bangkok* challenges these assumptions by revealing the intimacy within modern global capitalist venues. It might seem paradoxical to look for the intimacy of capitalism, a hegemonic economic system that, almost by definition, is seen as nonintimate and impersonal. To eyes steeped in contemporary urban worlds, modern capitalism lacks the social texture so visible in the floating market or Chinatown. Certainly such signs of social meanings and relationships as ethnicity, gender, and kinship—so visible in antiquated markets—are harder to register amid the shiny surfaces and generic uniforms of modern transnational capitalist institutions. And as I show, the intersection of market economies and intimate life has undeniably been transformed with capitalist development. Yet, as I also show, intimate identities and relationships, specifically gender, ethnicity, and sexuality, have been and continue to be centrally involved in the operations of modernizing markets. Just as floating markets and Chinatown are in their own way modern, newer commercial venues also include social and cultural dimensions, even where these are not easily seen. Understanding the intimate aspects of capitalist markets illuminates the power of and limits on the global economy's ability to remake social worlds.

This book explores the intimate qualities of increasingly global capitalist economies in Bangkok by examining specific commercial sites. Each chapter is grounded in a different kind of market: department stores, the tourist sex trade, a popular downtown mall, a telecommunications marketing office, and Amway and Avon (direct sales). These markets are "modern" in that they are contemporary, shaped by transnational flows, and are associated with and helped to propel modernization in Thailand. Each example captures a moment where commodified exchange is extending its reach into social life—into sexual, domestic, and romantic arenas—and expanding its role in defining public and personal identities. Together, these different venues of the capitalist economy illustrate the "local color" and social and cultural texture of global capitalism in Bangkok.

The term *intimate economies* in the title of this book introduces its rubric for analyzing interactions between economic systems and social life, particularly gender, sexuality, and ethnicity. By intimate, I mean features of

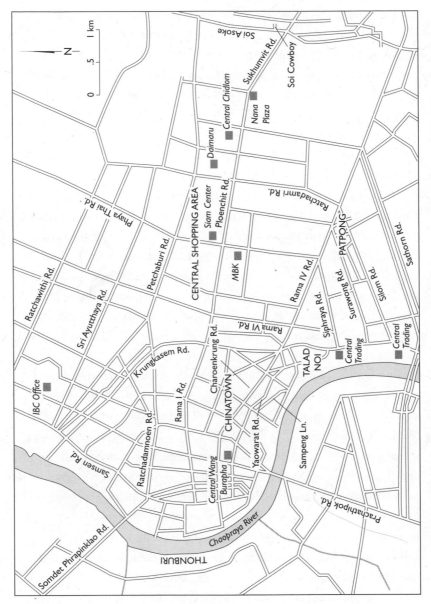

Map 1. Map of Bangkok, showing major market areas of the 1990s. Adapted from draft by Rini Sumartojo.

people's daily lives that have come to seem noneconomic, particularly social identities (e.g., woman) and relationships (e.g., kinship); by calling
these intimate, I mean to capture the deeply felt orientations and entrenched practices that make up what people consider to be their personal or private lives and their individual selves.[8] I take the ethnographic
view of identities as inextricable from, and realized through, social relationships.[9] The use of the plural economies recognizes that there are
different economic systems even within the same society. My approach
is premised on the often-overshadowed notion that economic systems
are not separate from intimate life, as orthodox conceptions of the economy suggest, but are inextricable from social relations and identities. According to cultural anthropology, economic systems incorporate social
and cultural realms that are typically considered "private" and separate
from the formal economy. Inversely, critical social theory suggests that
social life is not separate from, but linked with, economic affairs. Just as
intimate life (e.g., gender identities, sexual relationships, and ethnic ties)
crosses into the public arena of markets and jobs, those public realms
profoundly affect people's private interactions and self-conceptions. The
ways that global capitalist economies involve and shape identities and
relationships differ from earlier modes, as I illustrate in the portraits of
various Bangkok markets. But in this broad anthropological perspective,
economic systems—even corporate capitalism—are composed of social
and cultural processes and are lived in daily life. By intimate economies,
then, I mean the complex interplay between these intimate social dimensions and plural economic systems in a context shaped by transnational
capitalism.

Following canonical anthropology, my approach defines the economy
as systems of production, distribution, and consumption, a definition that
recognizes that societies have been arranged by different economic principles, not all of them governed by a market logic. This view sees economics in kinship and gender systems, in the gendered division of labor,
for example. Kinship and gender systems—or sex/gender systems—
organize work, property, and the distribution of resources: another way

to say this is that sex/gender/kin systems and economic systems shape each other. Kinship is also economic by virtue of its reliance on exchange; families, for example, are constituted by material and symbolic exchanges—including weddings and many sexual relationships.[10] This kin economy or folk economy has also been connected to a "moral economy," an economy that may rely on markets and money but that is governed or at least constrained by local community values and expectations.[11] The logic and values of various kin, folk, or moral economies are generally guided not by extracting and accumulating profit (although families may accumulate great wealth) but by the need to define, maintain, or elaborate relationships to kin, community, patrons, temples, and the spirit world. Considering the interaction of the folk economy with the market economy illuminates the changing configuration of identities and relationships in Bangkok.

BACKGROUND: ECONOMIES AND IDENTITIES IN THAILAND

Before turning to the economic nature of social identities in Thailand's history, it is important to recognize, as many recent scholars of Thailand have, that the terms used to describe Thai life are more complex and contested than they appear, including the term *Thai*. *Thai* properly denotes citizenship in the Kingdom of Thailand, which was called Siam until after World War II. *Tai* refers to the major linguistic and cultural groupings in the country, comprising different ethnicities (Lao, Siamese, Lanna); these categories themselves were formed through historical and political processes. However, the political term *Thai* is often used as shorthand for the various ethnicities considered "Tai." This is problematic because Thai is a national identity forged as a hegemonic umbrella in part to obscure and contain ethnic and regional diversity.[12] Studies of Thailand emphasize that there is significant social variation among different ethnic groups in the country—and also among different classes; among Buddhists, Muslims, animists, and others; between the city and countryside; and among the north, south, northeast, and the central regions (although all have been dominated by the capital city of Bangkok). Ideally, then, simple categories such as "Thai men and women" should be rendered more complex to acknowledge the constructed nature of "Thai" and also to recognize the existence of other sex/gender positions, notably the male-to-female transgender *kathoey* or the masculine female *tom*. Thailand's clearly demarcated gendered positions also intersect with age, status, ethnicity, region, nationality, class, spirituality, and other identity frameworks. Because we have not yet worked out a language to convey these complexities while analyzing broad social trends (that is, when the categories are not themselves the focus of the investigation), I still use the established terms for social identities, like *Thai* or *woman*, as I map intersections between economic and social worlds.

One finds many such intersections in Thai tradition, which has been bound up with diverse economic principles and practices. Until the twentieth century, Thai society as a whole was stratified by a feudalistic ranking system called *sakdina*, using legal and economic measures (typically involving control of people more than land) that were inseparable from social and spiritual characteristics. The centuries-long development of the capitalist market economy in Siam-Thailand influenced and changed this social class system as well as other identities and relationships, including gender.

In village communities, the organization of work, inheritance, and resources, as well as the calculus for evaluating relationships and people, is governed by a folk economy that articulates with, but is separate from, market economies. Exchange is the idiom and mechanism for many, if not most, relationships in Thailand: parent-child, senior-junior, husband-wife, and son-in-law to wife's family, laity-monk, human-spirit, and friend-friend. The interactions between the monastic order and the laity are depicted in terms of transformative exchange: householders (mainly women) provide the daily sustenance to monks, who act as "fields of merit," providing the opportunity to accumulate merit (which is calculated quite materially in terms of a store or amount of substance). Furthermore, at the monk's ordination, the mother's "gift" of her son to the monkhood secures her place in heaven. The enactment and definition of many Thai social identities, such as women's position as "nurturer" or the relations of seniors *(phi)* to juniors *(nawng)*, can also be understood in this light, as an orientation framed in terms of debt and exchange. Anyone incurs debt to a guardian or to one who has offered significant aid and instruction (e.g., teachers), and all children are born indebted, but male and female children have different prospects for repaying that debt.[13] This calculus is part of a folk economy and remains crucial to defining and evaluating gender, sexual, and familial identities in Thailand.

As the example of the floating market vendors shows, the female gender has historically been connected simultaneously to a folk economy and to an evolving market economy, dual investments that are interconnected. The preponderance of Thai women in local markets has implications for understanding the economic dimensions of traditional gender systems. Much commentary about Thailand has remarked on women's visible economic roles, not only in markets, but also in rice farms, all variety of factories, and families, where daughters and mothers bear a responsibility to provide for the unit. While all children are obliged to repay their debts to their parents, daughters' obligations are life-long and are interpreted in quite material terms. Before the late nineteenth century, according to Thai feminist researchers, "economic responsibility was part of a daughter's moral obligation to her parents," and failure to fulfill this duty was considered a serious sin or demerit.[14] As anthropologists note, women's traditional economic practices remain firmly embedded in their social worlds: "Women's economic control [in the family] was managerial, with the household rather than the individual as the basic economic unit."[15] Just as this economic role was not the maximizing individual of economic theory, it derived not from capitalist principles but from the moral, spiritual, and material principles of kin and folk economies. Such cultural principles propelled women to work in agricultural, manufacturing, and commercial economies of all sorts.

While mainstream Western culture views women's obligations to their family—or female qualities of nurturance and femininity—as an *obstacle* to economic participation, the reverse holds true for everyone but the aristocratic elite in Thailand. The significance of market exchange for the female gender is not the by-product of modernity but, in fact, a long-standing feature of Thai gender systems. Thus, Thai women's economic activity can be read as traditional at the same time that traditional femininity for Thai commoners should be understood as deeply economic.[16] Indeed, it was Thai masculinity that was ideally removed from trafficking in market trade, which was historically the low-status province of women and foreign men. Here is another reason that Thai culture is often considered noneconomic and Thais have been declared lacking in entrepreneurial spirit: Thailand's overarching social hierarchy has associated markets and money with foreigners and with women, not with Thai men. At the same time, ethnic, gender, and spiritual identities (to the extent that trafficking in money has been considered problematic for Thai Buddhism) have informed Thai interpretations of the market arena.[17]

Women have remained pivotal in the juncture between local folk economies (which themselves have changed over time) and evolving market economies. The trade of extra produce in floating markets or community bazaars have represented one portion of the web of monetary, barter, and kin exchanges that have characterized many village women's wide-ranging economic practices. Thai women's links to local markets continue into the present.

TRANSNATIONAL IDENTITIES
IN SIAM/THAILAND

Thailand is noteworthy for never having been formally colonized by a European power. The lack of formal colonialism meant that trade provided the major avenue for transnational influence to enter the country. Villagers consumed imported textiles and canned goods well before they encountered European discourses about individualism, hygiene, or race.

For years the global market reached more intimately into local homes than Europeans did. The mediums for this commercial influence were traveling Chinese vendors and Thai market women.

As the capital of Thailand for more than two centuries and a major crossroads for regional trade and travel, Bangkok has historically been a multicultural city. Because Siam/Thailand was never a colony, the tenor of racial, ethnic, and national discourses differs from those of former European and American colonies and territories. The racial prestige of Europeans and whites has not been tied to official political or economic control of the country, as the case has been with colonized countries. The European presence was confined to the capital city, Bangkok, and did not extend into peasant communities.

However, since the mid–nineteenth century, Thailand has been profoundly influenced and constrained by Europe (England and France in particular), Japan (which occupied the country during World War II), and later the United States. These asymmetrical relations can be considered imperialist or neocolonialist, and Thailand shares aspects of the postcolonial condition of the rest of Southeast Asia. Europeans' economic and political power intertwined with national and racial identities and established an enduring high status to whiteness that informs the experience of white tourists and scholars today. In the nineteenth and early twentieth centuries, Europeans used their political clout to force Siam to adopt economic treaties and political arrangements that were favorable to their corporate and colonial enterprises in the region, and they dominated the Thai import-export business. European society influenced Thai laws, public discourse, and elite culture. The modern Thai nation was constructed partly in reaction to European power and Western discourses about progress and civilization, for example, in the imposition of patrilineal surnames and ineffectual laws against polygyny in the 1900s. The legal and economic changes that the Siamese regime adopted, under the threat of European colonization, expanded the scale of the monetary economy in Thailand and ushered in vast changes to the social worlds of the kingdom's diverse subjects.

Apart from migrants from Europe and southeastern China, the foreign residents of Bangkok (mostly male) included Javanese, Burmese, Sri Lankans (Ceylonese), and Vietnamese.[18] Some were war captives, but many came to work at labor or trade. In Siam, organized commerce and long-distance trading was conducted mainly by Chinese, Indian, and Mon men.[19] The national and ethnic identities of these immigrants were inflected with economic roles and meanings, such as class, occupation, and characteristic work styles. Of Bangkok's female residents, most were Siamese women, with a minority of Chinese women.

Precisely because of their collective role in the economy, the Chinese in Thailand have received the most attention. Buying and marketing rice—the engine of the Thai economy until only recently—were the province of traders from China. Chinese residents constituted most of Bangkok's business groups and middle classes. Although subject to special regulations and discrimination during highly nationalist periods of this century, since the 1960s, the Sino-Thai have not been targeted by the state or publicly attacked the way they have been, for example, in Indonesia. A politicized ethnic-national category, the Chinese identity requires further attention.

"Chinese" refers to the migrants who formed part of the worldwide diaspora from the southern coast of China and their descendants, who are also called Sino-Thai. In Thailand, they are separated into first-generation "old Chinese" (*jin kao*) and Chinese offspring (*luuk jin*). The category of Chinese subsumes various language, regional, and ethnic groups: Teochiu (the majority), Hokkien, Hakka, Hainanese (Hailam, in Thai), and Cantonese. In Thailand, as elsewhere in Southeast Asia, the ethnic identity of "Chinese" has been particularly defined in relation to economic practices and meanings and associated with cleverness in money and success in trade or, at the lower end, with "coolie" wage labor, forming long-lasting images of anonymous laborers or clever traders. But this economic-ethnic group is also defined by well-known cultural traits and practices, such as ancestor worship and a detailed ritual calendar, effective ethnic groups and networks, and strong kinship relations. All of these can also be understood as part of a folk or kin economy but are inseparable from participation in the formal capitalist economy. With the increasing power and legitimacy of business in Thailand, Chineseness has also transformed into an ethnically inflected and often positively valued identity, at least for successful businessmen.

"Chinese" is also a gendered identity. In discourses about Thailand, the Chinese ethnicity is often represented in terms of masculine roles. The prevailing figures are the tao kae merchant, *jao sua* tycoon, and patriarch, but also the laboring "coolie" and characters from well-known Chinese court sagas. Before the 1920s, most but not all of these migrants were men. Many had children with or traded with Siamese women, so that a good number of those who count as "Chinese" in Thailand have Siamese female ancestors. But some immigrants from China were women, especially after World War I, and their labor was key to Sino-Thai commerce. Discussions of the Chinese role in the Thai market economy tend to erase the active participation of women, both Chinese and Thai, including traders, wives, and daughters.[20]

CAPITALIST DEVELOPMENT IN THAILAND

As this introduction shows, Siam/Thailand has long been shaped by transnational flows of people, goods, and money and by international political contexts of colonialism and its aftermath. Markets, operated by "aliens" and Thai women, were a key medium for local communities' relations to broader worlds. From the 1950s, the government and local businesses undertook to revamp Thailand's economy, to spur industrialization, install more capitalist organization, and articulate more with the global economy. International economic trends toward greater transnational investments in emerging markets and political arrangements of the Cold War and post-Cold War periods (including U.S. involvement in Indochina wars, which injected millions of dollars into the Thai economy) fashioned Thailand's economic directions as well.

The chapters in this book illustrate aspects of Thailand's capitalist de-

velopment in the post–World War II period, using specific market forms
as windows into the changing intimate economies of Bangkok society.
Surrounded on the mainland by communist countries, Thailand pursued
a laissez-faire capitalist path to economic growth that encouraged foreign investment, industrialization, and tourism, with relatively few regulations (including little protection for peasants, workers, or the environment). From the 1960s until 1997, economic measures grew at rates
among the highest in the world. These developments resulted from increasingly corporate and industrial systems of farming (e.g., commercial
shrimp farms), manufacturing, and finance. Scholarship on Thailand has
been grappling with the wide-ranging uneven effects of global capitalism on social structure, cultural values, and daily life. To address this impact, it is important to pay attention to the specific characteristics of capitalism and to investigate how a capitalist economy interacts with and
changes existing economic and social systems.

Capitalism is an economic system oriented to "the market" (ultimately
a global market) that uses money to measure value, pay people for work
or debts, and conduct exchange. The exchange system of capitalism is
commodified exchange in which goods, services, labor, and even money
itself derive their meaning and value from the market. Capitalist enterprises are oriented to making profit and accumulating capital to reinvest.
In capitalist logic, the market drives the overall economy, yet market exchange itself depends on production. For example, in Thailand, the economics of retail and trade, real estate, and consumption depend on commercial agriculture, more recently on manufacturing, and on the readiness
of large numbers of people to work for wages. Capitalist development
spreads an economic system that is profoundly different in organization
and logic from folk, kin, and small-scale market economies.

On the ground, however, there is no one single capitalist economy.
As capitalist market economies expand and become more global, they interact with other economic systems. For example, a local manufacturer
uses kinship and village networks to coordinate putting-out piecework
systems. The floating market (both the tourist and historical versions)

and Sampeng shophouses suggest that a variety of market forms can be integrated within an overall economy structured along capitalist lines. Likewise, kin and folk economies continue to exist and interact with market economies; for example, the marriage gift the groom's family gives to the bride's family has been inflated and now includes consumer items and cash as well as gold and sometimes livestock. Offerings to ancestors and spirits include imported whiskey, and among the votive offerings burned for recently deceased relatives are paper versions of such goods as cars and televisions.

The nature of the overlap and interaction between capitalist economies and long-standing social institutions, such as community standards for prices or the gendered division of labor, varies considerably in place, time, and setting and is itself the subject of much theoretical and political debate.[21] Compared with kin-based farms, feudal societies, or markets governed by community-bound moral economies, modern capitalist systems of production and marketing are considered less embedded in social life and less inflected with local cultural meanings and identities. Yet capitalist economies are predicated on, and continue to interact with, these local social realms. The nature of capitalism's engagement with social life, and with the folk and moral economies so central to it, remains an open question, one I study empirically, by examining the changing mix of capitalist and other economies in particular ethnographic and historical sites.

Undeniably, the separation between capitalist and noncapitalist arenas, between market and nonmarket exchanges, is important in local worldviews and value systems. In Thailand, the shifting borders between capitalist and noncapitalist economies cause palpable public and individual anxiety. As with the tourist appreciation of old market forms in contrast with modern retail, Thais' experience of significant differences between economic modes depend not merely on actual systemic differences (and may ignore this level) but also on cultural values and modern ideologies. Tellingly, these borders are often symbolized through gender and sexuality, as is evident in the public judgment of sex workers, whose work blurs the divide between market and personal exchanges, a point I take up in chapter 2. The example of sex work conveys the importance of the intimate dimensions of people's navigation of capitalist development interacting with local economic systems.

In this book, I address pressing questions about the impact of the global economy on Thai sex/gender systems by following directions suggested by recent transnational and Western feminist theory. Fulfilling Gayle Rubin's call for "a political economy of sex,"[22] scholars in feminist anthropology, geography, and other fields combine historical or material approaches with a committed attention to the symbolic dimensions of representation, discourse, and meaning. Accordingly, they situate the construction of gender and sexual identities in relation to systems of power that govern work, resources, mobility, authority, and so forth. This synthetic approach is well represented in work on island Southeast Asia (Indonesia, Malaysia, and the Philippines) that studies contested gender meanings in factories, markets, households, and plantations.[23] Recent work on women or gender systems in Thailand (located on mainland Southeast Asia) complements this approach.

Many authors have pointed out that capitalist development in Asia has relied heavily on women's work, for example, in offshore manufacturing industries (or "global factories").[24] Thailand's economic growth has been underwritten by women's labor in raising rice and food, caring for families at home, selling goods in markets, and providing services for the tourist economy in restaurants, shops, and go-go bars.[25] Women migrate to Bangkok and other urban centers to work in light manufacturing and in commerce and services, often in greater numbers than male migrants. In addition, in the 1960s to 1970s, U.S. military installations drew large numbers of village women into service work on bases and in rest and recuperation (R&R) areas, a practice that led to an enormous foreign sex trade.

Contemporary research on Thai gender systems investigates how state modernization projects and this economic development are transforming elite, peasant, and urban gender arrangements. Besides chronicling women's significant, but often officially neglected, labor in economic development, a number of studies have asked how industrialization, capital flows, and export economies in Thailand have specifically affected Thai gender systems, understanding gender as intersecting with class, ethnicity, and region. Ethnographers such as Andrea Whittaker show complex shifts underway in the provinces as women's material obligations as daughters, nurturing wives, and mothers push them into the market economy. Mary Beth Mills shows how young migrant factory workers from rural areas have experienced conflict between the demands of their villages and those of the city as they try to reconcile their roles as daughters and new cosmopolitans in navigating new work regimes and consumer possibilities. Other authors describe the ways Thai categories of sexuality and gender (e.g., male-to-female, third-gender kathoey) are transforming in relation to diffuse social and cultural transformations. Perhaps most discussed is the sex trade, particularly the trade for foreigners that expanded when the tourist industry burgeoned after the Vietnam War. I build on these studies in my investigation of the intimate economies of five market forms in Bangkok.[26]

THE INTIMATE ECONOMIES
OF CAPITALIST MARKETS

The chapters of this book cover the rise of capitalist retail in the middle of the twentieth century to the expanse of the consumer economy during the economic boom of the 1980s and 1990s. Their juxtaposition captures the range and variation in the commercial and public life of Bangkok. In the hodgepodge of Bangkok, in the course of a routine day, people crisscross diverse commercial spaces and employ plural economic systems, ranging from spiritual offerings, to gifts, to commercial exchanges—sometimes in the very same site. Viewing multiple market venues provides a cumulative perspective of the intimate effects of global capitalism in the city.

Chapter 1 illustrates the growth of modern corporate markets in the postwar period through the example of the department store, showing how gendered ethnicity was involved in these transformations. The chapter uses a portrait of the Chirathivat family (nee Jeng until 1950), immigrants from Hainan who ran a small shophouse in Bangkok that paved the way for Central Department Store, which opened in 1957. I focus on the father and son who formed this company (with important family labor and resources), men who encapsulate the changing nature of the ethnic masculine role of Chinese businessmen, from the Chinese tao kae merchant to the "flexible" corporate executive.

From the late 1970s until 1997, the rapid growth in the economy was accompanied by a burgeoning tourist trade and a proliferation of shopping complexes so dramatic it was dubbed a retail revolution. These two developments in tourist and retail markets have centrally involved young women's identities in particular, as workers and consumers. In chapters 2 and 3 I investigate how the infrastructure of commodified exchange impacts their gender and sexual identities. The prostitution industry clearly combines market exchange with gender identities and sexual relationships. Chapter 2 centers on the small but well-known portion of the trade focused on foreign customers represented by the go-go bar. This discussion concentrates on the diverse exchanges that make up the trade and considers how these are implicated in sex workers' public and personal identities. In chapter 3, I consider the rapid proliferation of shopping malls in the 1980s. Malls provide infrastructure for a new cross-class consumer culture that facilitates different sexual and gender positions, including the role of tomboy, or tom. Both examples show how consumers' and workers' intimate relations are conducted through and shaped by modern markets and how this engagement is producing expressions of the female gender that contradict dominant norms.

As markets have changed with capitalist development, so has the occupation of selling. The work of marketing has become a modern and professional position, one contrasted with the old-fashioned market vendor or shophouse merchant. In chapters 4 and 5, I consider the class, gender, and sexual dimensions of the professional identities being ushered in by transnational corporations. In chapter 4, I discuss a marketing office in a successful Thai (or Sino-Thai) information technology company. Tele-communication represents a combination of local Thai companies, in this case Shinawatra, and transnational corporations, and this sort of modern market requires educated, cosmopolitan workers who can flexibly meld global and local culture and affiliations. In chapter 5, I look at the import of an American reinterpretation of old-time door-to-door selling in direct sales companies like Avon and Amway. While Avon, Amway, and their Thai versions promote professional images of their distributors, notably in the figure of the Avon Lady, Thai sellers' participation in these corporate institutions involves their own configurations of locally meaningful identifications and relationships that in some cases depart from the sleek commercial figures. These two chapters show how Thais' affiliations with transnational corporations involve gender and class identifications.

These five markets chart contradictory symbolic and social identities at play as capitalist market economies become the stage for more and more of daily life in Bangkok. They chronicle the ways that ethnic, gender, and sexual identities (composed through relationships) cross and separate multiple economies. Together, they provide a partial portrait of the ways that global capitalism is refashioning intimate life in Bangkok.

METHODS

The research for this book centers on two years of fieldwork in Bangkok from December 1992 to January 1994 and observations made on visits ranging from 1988 to 2000. During my two years in residence, I lived in a neighborhood at the edge of Chinatown, the observations of which inform my historical discussion of Sino-Thai business families in chapter 1. Working part-time at a marketing office of the leading cable TV company provided a modern opportunity for "participant observation" in the classic sense. I also was fortunate to participate in several non-governmental organizations (NGOs), including the lesbian group Anja-ree and a multi-issue feminist organization, the Foundation for Women. I undertook most of this investigative fieldwork alone, without employing a research assistant, although I was aided greatly by friends and colleagues.

I began this project by observing the major market areas of the city. This provided a sense of how selling and shopping work and a "map" of consumption in the city. On the basis of this survey and with questions concerning gender identity in mind, I selected some of the markets for study, although only later did it occur to me to include others, notably the go-go bars and the marketing office where I worked.

For a given market venue, I gathered background information about the history and infrastructure of the market, observed the site or practices involved, and conducted interviews (usually informal). Because this investigation is concerned with the form of markets, I spent some time identifying the infrastructure of a given venue, using an array of information sources including informal interviews, observations of behavior and architecture, material objects, and primary texts and secondary literature, especially the business press. Through these observations (filtered through my analytic questions about identity), over time I identified key intersections between the market's economics and features of social identity and relationships. My understanding of broader cultural discourses about market economies, folk economies, and identities in Thailand derives from synthesizing observations of public life with analyses of textual sources, including government media and popular culture.

Most of the people I interacted with were twenty to forty-five years old, reflecting both Bangkok's demographics and the nature of the markets I emphasize. Many of these subjects were of Chinese descent, as at least a third of Bangkok residents are, although they did not necessarily identify themselves as such. People's economic backgrounds varied, ranging from minor royalty to peasants, with residences ranging from old family estates to condos to slums. With the exception of sex workers, most of the people I discuss here were not poor, being involved in trade, office work, or professional employment.

I formally interviewed students, teachers, and advertising professionals, among others, about their consumption practices and use of markets.

However, I did not find formal interviews with women very productive, especially for in-depth elaboration of experiences. I also shied away from formal interviews because of a sense of the hierarchical meaning of interviews in Thailand.[27] For the most part, I relied on informal interviews and day-to-day conversations, in which I noted women's frequent and repetitive references to shopping and physical appearance and observed various vendors' sales pitches. Regarding language, I used both Thai and English with informants and associates and often a combination of the two, depending on the wishes and capacities of my interlocutors. The book rests on the understanding that people's practices create meanings, and so some of my material comes from observing such things as what women wear, how they move through commercial space, their interactions, and the like. This approach allowed me to gauge priorities, emphases, and values involved in social identities and relationships and to situate them in relation to various market venues.

The structure of this research differs from canonical ethnography in that it does not focus on one group of people in one locale but shifts across places and groups, a methodology known as multisited research.[28] The different market sites required separate, if overlapping, research strategies tailored for each case, including library and archival research and participant observation. For example, chapter 1, as a historical discussion of the shift from the shophouse to the department store, relies primarily on archival and textual sources. Because the subject of prostitution has received an inordinate, and often unwelcome, amount of international attention, it presents one of the most fraught topics in commentary on Thailand. Studies of sex work risk reinforcing the stigma associated with workers in the trade, raising challenges that I address in my discussions in chapter 2.

RACE, ECONOMICS, AND SITUATED ETHNOGRAPHY

For some time now, anthropologists and feminist ethnographers have grappled with the question of how the investigator's own identity is implicated in her research. In this book, I attempt to acknowledge my presence where it is relevant to the material at hand. Yet the power relationship between researcher and subject, while undeniably significant for feminist scholars, is not in itself the subject of this book. Given that this book concerns transnational flows of capital and culture, however, it makes sense to consider how the national discipline of American anthropology and my presence as a white American anthropologist take part in these broader processes of globalization. There is the bare fact that the United States' great financial and political power underwrites U.S. citizens' ability to conduct research in less wealthy nations such as Thailand. Relatedly, my white identity situated me in a privileged position: white people receive favored treatment both subtle and obvious, a condition that benefits the tourist, businessman, and anthropologist.

International knowledge about Thailand, including ethnography, is produced in this asymmetrical transnational context. The often close links between studies of Southeast Asia and global geopolitics have been noted, especially in relation to U.S.-funded counterinsurgency research during the era of the Vietnam War.[29] Anthropology's relation to capitalism has been less examined than its relation to state interests and racial or colonial dynamics. It seems possible that anthropological and business forms of knowledge overlap and interconnect. In Thailand, Western commercial writings are coterminous with the onset of major anthropological studies. Cornell University's pathbreaking anthropological studies of Thailand, for example, coexisted with other texts produced for Western consumption in the 1960s: travel books, U.S. military research, World Bank studies, and intelligence prepared for Western businesses.[30] The cultural interpretations of anthropologists have informed the depictions presented in tourist guidebooks and business etiquette guides. Thus, my own production enters a populated field of English-language knowledge about Thailand, not only operating within but also partaking of the context of global capital.

In my research, I tried to avoid reproducing racial and national power relations by being aware of U.S. and first-world power and by participating in Thai NGOs, in some cases an ongoing participation that has lasted for years. I have attempted to resist reproducing colonialist or Orientalist approaches to knowledge in a number of ways: first, by beginning my early studies with a critical evaluation of Orientalist categories in Western discourse. Second, from my first trip to Thailand, I attended to, and was influenced by, Thai observers' research and analyses, both academic and activist. Third, I have tried to take account of the problems in representing less powerful "others." To this end, I embed discussions of potentially exoticized figures, such as butch tom or sex workers, within a spectrum of gender and economic configurations in an attempt not to sensationalize these marginalized identities. Finally, my choice to study the effects of global capitalism in Thailand is motivated by the recognition of similar processes underway around the world that incorporate the anthropologist herself, as much as any citizen of Bangkok, in their complex fold.

Following anthropological convention, I have used pseudonyms for individuals discussed, except for well-known public figures.

CHAPTER ONE

From Shophouse
to Department Store

THE DEPARTMENT STORE

Thailand's first full-fledged department store is said to be Central Department Store, which opened in an area of Chinatown in the mid-1950s and remains one of Thailand's leading companies.[1] It was founded by, and is still operated by, the Chirathivat family (who were known by the name "Jeng" until that decade), an immigrant family of humble Chinese origins.

The department store is a specific form of selling, a highly centralized institution offering a wide range of goods and services organized into discrete departments. This mode of retail originated in Europe in the mid–nineteenth century, one of the earliest examples being the French Printemps store.[2] It represented a revolutionary way of marketing goods for urban industrializing Europe and the United States (and later Asia), a simultaneous transformation to modes of consumption and modes of retail operations. The operations of the department store radically differ from the small shophouses and local markets that preceded it. The department store employs a large staff of formally educated sales clerks, accountants, managers, and buyers and uses sophisticated marketing techniques within a modern infrastructure dedicated to consumption and with a centralized organization oriented to accumulating profits on a grand scale. The department store concocts a theater of consumption in ways that minimize the signs of its history or its workings. To understand the emergence of a capitalist consumer economy in Bangkok, I look behind the scenes at the local social worlds that produced this modern market form.

However European the origins of the department store, it would be a mistake to see the installation of this retail form in Bangkok as a Western affair. Thailand's department stores developed within Asia, products of the Chinese diasporic community in Bangkok and, after the 1960s, of Japanese corporate expansion overseas. This chapter traces the roots of modern retail to the Sino-Thai shophouse economy that characterized most of twentieth-century Bangkok. It shows how kinship, ethnicity, gender, and class were integrally involved in transforming the small family shop into this cosmopolitan version of retail and illustrates the intimate economies that produced the "modern" capitalist economy in Thailand.

The story of Central Department Store is well known in Thailand, often recounted in the business press as an exemplary "rags-to-riches" immigrant tale. The standard version of the story focuses on the Jeng patriarch, Tiang (?–1968), and his eldest son, Samrit (1925–1992) (nee Hokseng). As with other classic rags-to-riches stories, when the broader context and a greater cast of characters, particularly women, are included in the narrative, the picture becomes more complex. For example, that Tiang had twenty-six children is well known, a celebrated feature of this successful enterprise; that he had three wives is usually politely glossed over. The Jengs/Chirathivats have remained rooted in kin and ethnic networks at the same time as they have choreographed transnational corporate retail and consumer culture in Bangkok. Their history illustrates the ways that capitalist development in Thailand was a social affair, deliberately created in ways that involved and affected identities and networks.

During fieldwork, I observed Sino-Thai shophouses and countless branches of Bangkok's several department store chains. The chief sources for my historical discussion here, however, are commemorative texts from the funerals of two key members of the Jeng/Chirathivat family: Samrit, Tiang's eldest son, and Tiang's second (or minor) wife, Bunsri (nee Buneng until sometime during 1930–1950).[3] The texts are called cremation volumes or funeral remembrance books *(nangseu thi raleuk ngan-sob)*, issued at the mourning ceremonies before the cremation. These two examples are an amalgam of testimonial letters, recollections, photographs, and, in the case of Samrit, hundreds of pages of history of marketing, retail, and Central Department Store in Thailand. Because these texts are commemorations of notables, written or commissioned by intimates, they are partisan representations of the people and of the larger story and, hence, quite selective. (One indication of this selectivity is the virtual lack of discussion of Tiang's third wife, Wipha [or Vipha], in the memoirs of his first-born son and his second wife.) The identities and economies of the diasporic Chinese in Southeast Asia have long been a politically weighted subject,[4] and this context of public discourses about "alien" Chinese economies shapes these funeral commemorations. Overall, they present cumulative narratives structured by salient themes (e.g., success and education) and by telling silences (e.g., about the third wife and the broader political context, particularly anti-Chinese policies). Using these texts and secondary materials, I composed a history of the Chirathivat family business, situating this history within the broader social, cultural, and representational contexts of Sino-Thai communities, Thai nationalism, urban growth, and economic development in Bangkok particularly between the 1920s and the 1960s.

DIASPORIC MERCHANTS

For the better part of the twentieth century, Bangkok residents bought goods from small shops, generally run by Chinese or other immigrants, or from local markets, typically staffed by Thai women—local forms that were surpassed by department stores and modern retail outlets only by the 1990s. Indeed, such modern retail forms as the department store chain evolved from the businesses and social worlds of the Chinese community in Thailand.[5]

Immigrants from China and their descendants were key to developing the market economy of Thailand. The 1920s launched a massive wave of emigration from the southern coast of China to ports worldwide. At this time, far more women began to leave China and join expatriate Chinese communities in foreign cities such as Bangkok;[6] among these were Tiang's first wife, Waan, Waan's mother, and later his second wife, Buneng/Bunsri. Tiang and Waan began as the Jeng family on the Chinese island of Hainan. Their homeland was impoverished, a bleak landscape that taught them hard work and thrift, according to the funeral texts.

Tiang and his first wife traveled to Siam after her parents had settled in Bangkok. Hearing reports of piracy around Hainan, they returned to China to look after Tiang's father. In 1925, they had a son they named Hokseng (later adopting the name "Samrit"). Tiang and Waan waited until Tiang's father had passed away and his funeral ceremonies were concluded before leaving Hainan, notes Samrit's funeral book (thereby establishing the couple's filial piety and ritual observance). Samrit's memorial text repeatedly stresses examples of strategy, training, and preparation in the family history. For example, the memorial reports that his parents systematically rocked his cradle to ready him for the two-month boat trip. In 1927, when Samrit was two, the Jeng family took a *sampao*, or Chinese junk, to Bangkok. They represented first-generation migrants, referred to as *khon jin* (Chinese) or jin kao (old Chinese) in Thai.

The long history of the Chinese diaspora in Southeast Asia, a mostly male diaspora, includes a pattern of return migration known as sojourning:[7] even if migrants stayed abroad for years, many eventually returned to China (or intended to), often to marry and have children. The increase in women migrants after World War I (encouraged by the British) produced the new flow of heterosexual couples emigrating together from China and led to more permanent settlements in Southeast Asian cities, which changed the prevailing pattern of male sojourning. By 1949, the revolution in China ended emigration and return migration. Tiang and

Waan and Waan's parents were part of this new phase of family, rather than male sojourner, migration.

According to Samrit's funeral texts, Tiang and Waan decided to settle in Siam because of its economic opportunities and its sizable Chinese population, which included Waan's parents. Relocating to new lands involved networks based on ethnic, language, and kin affiliations, often through formal groups organized under the banner of family name (*sae*, e.g., sae Jeng) or of language-region (e.g., Hakka, Hokkien, or the majority Teochiu). For migrants, Chinese identity was organized by these geographical-language-ethnic groupings and was also demarcated by migrant generation (e.g., jin kao). The Chinese identity also bore different connotations depending on social class and gender: the Chineseness of the female brothel worker (many were from China), her working-class client, the well-to-do male merchant, and his Chinese bride for whom he paid a handsome marriage gift, all carried different meanings. Migrants' affiliations complicated the simple category of "Chinese." Together, the Chinese populations in Siam formed a mestizo or creole community and a hybrid identity conveyed by the English term *Sino-Thai*.[8]

The Jeng family settled into this Sino-Thai world; this rich community, however, is not described in these texts. Business and funeral accounts of the Jeng/Chirathivat family portray Tiang as the autonomous head of his family and describe the family in isolation rather than existing within a creole Sino-Thai community. Yet it is not difficult to embed their story in a broader social context. Clearly the Jengs drew on a network of in-laws, Hainanese, and other members of Bangkok's sizable Sino-Thai community. Connected to groups based on surname and Hainanese identity, they also became ensconced in cross-ethnic Chinese networks that extended into other countries such as Singapore.

The description provided in the funeral book of Samrit relies on a narrative of patriarchal agency and authority: "Tiang brought his family to live with his father-in-law, Naay Mr. Tonghua."[9] A husband living with the wife's family after marriage was utterly typical for rural Thais, but it contradicted the pronounced patrilocal (virilocal) practices of Chinese kinship systems. Yet Tiang, Waan, and Samrit lived with Waan's parents in a Chinese area by the Tha Chang pier. They worked in her parents' store, called An Fong Lao, which sold unhusked rice *(khao san)*.[10] Bangkok's businesses were in one way or another tied to the rice trade, which was the fundamental industry for the country as a whole. Plantations and family farms sold their rice to Chinese merchants, who floated the harvests down the canals and the Chaopraya River. Rice traders such as Waan's family clustered by piers or along Bangkok's numerous waterways. In the 1920s, when Tiang and Waan arrived, the rice trade was booming.[11]

After working with Waan's parents for two years, the funeral texts report, Tiang borrowed 300 baht (then approximately U.S.$130) from his father-in-law, Tonghua, to start a business.[12] (Or, one could say that the couple borrowed the money from Waan's parents.) The Jeng family moved to Thonburi, an area of orchards and houses across the river from Bangkok. Their first store was a coffee shop that also sold odds and ends, apparently "in the manner of Chinese Hailam [Hainanese] everywhere."[13]

The family soon moved again, to a new wooden two-floor shophouse by the Jomthong train station in Bangkhuntien, also across the river from Bangkok. The funeral text explains, "They opened the house as a store," which referred to the common form of the shophouse; again on the first floor, they sold coffee, some short-order food, and odds and ends. On the second floor, Waan worked as a tailor, making clothes to order. This type of general store was the all-in-one shop of its day. The store's odds and ends came from Sampeng, the crowded lane of shophouses that was the major wholesale market for textiles and consumer goods in the country. Father and son regularly traveled across the river to buy the bulk goods on Sampeng Lane for resale in their dry goods store, locally known as Saam Liam, or "Three Corners."[14]

In turn-of-the-century Bangkok, ethnic groups tended to be slotted into different jobs. As a group, the Hainanese were characterized as the poorest of migrants from China, associated with lower-class labor. Hainanese men (Hailam) worked as gardeners, waiters, stable grooms, porters, peddlers, or fishermen (positions considered coolie work), although Hainanese were also associated with small coffee shops, the hotel business, and sex-trade businesses; it was said that men from Hainan also made up much of the clientele of brothels.[15] Hence, linguistic-ethnic groups like the Hainanese were inflected with class and occupational associations: Hainanese identity was linked with coolie work and coffee shops. The Ngaans, Waan's family, were unusual in being immersed in rice trading, which was not typically a field Hainan migrants entered. Aside from Europeans involved in large-scale rice export, the commercial families and leaders of business and industry came, by and large, from the major Chinese ethnic group, the Teochiu, or the Hokkien. It is unclear how Waan's parents came into the resources to be involved in Siam's leading economic sector, but these ethnic-occupational links were trends rather than firm castes.

The Jeng family's shift from the An Fong Lao unhusked rice shop to the Three Corners general store represents a shift between the primary and secondary sectors of Bangkok's market economy: from the rice trade to businesses servicing the city's growing population. Small shops, opium parlors, brothels, saloons, and other services, mainly run by Sino-Thais, catered to populations earning wages, generally migrants.[16] Retail was limited. Shophouses like Three Corners sold small amounts of imported canned milk, kerosene, or novelty items as well as local manufactures such as cigarettes, matches, and soap.[17] The intertwined rice-export and urban-consumer trades shaped the expanding capital city and drove the market economy. During the 1920s through the 1950s, significant Sino-Thai companies got their start in agricultural businesses (like Mah Boonkrong, discussed in chapter 3) or consumer goods (like the Jengs/Chirathivats), with a few involved in manufacturing.

Most of this business was conducted from small wooden shops, typically joined in rowhouses. As city life relocated from canals to new roads, these two- and three-story buildings came to define the urban landscape in the Chinese quarter surrounding Sampeng Lane and beyond.[18] (See figure 3.) On the one hand, the shophouse represented the frontier of the market economy, bringing global imports to local com-

Figure 3. Bangkok shophouses in Chinatown, 1993.
The corner building has an optical shop on the ground floor
and residences above. Photo by Eva Kolodner.

munities; on the other hand, the shophouse represented an old-fashioned economic form. It combined production, distribution, and consumption—economic functions that were ideally to be separated in a "modernizing" economy.[19] Whether in small-scale manufacturing or wholesale or retail businesses, families and hired hands typically lived and worked together in the shop. The intimate economies of the shophouse provided the prevailing business form in Bangkok from the 1920s until the 1980s and was the precursor to the radically different economic form of the department store, which supplanted it.

THREE CORNERS

Three Corners was a successful shop. Although the details of the business are not spelled out in the funeral texts, over a decade and a half, the store clearly produced enough income to support a growing family of two wives and ten children as well as to accumulate capital for later investment. The Jeng family prospered and entered the middle class.

The Three Corners store was a family business, and its shophouse served as the Jeng family home from the 1930s until 1947. Shophouses' mixture of production and consumption, family and work, in a single building involved the identities and relationships associated with the sex/gender and kinship systems of creole Sino-Thai communities. Here I turn to the intersection of the family life, ethnicity, and economics for the Jengs.

Countless observers have noted that Chinese identity in Thailand is linked to economics. "Chineseness in Thailand is linked to economic capital," anthropologist Jiemin Bao explains, and "commercial orientation and business success are taken as a major criteria of Chineseness by both ethnic Chinese and Thai."[20] One of the key figures capturing these associations is that of the tao kae, the male Chinese boss. Gender, class, and ethnic associations consolidated into a stock figure marked by language, clothing, and style and portrayed in comic books and movies as a short-tempered, plump, recognizable character. *Tao kae* is also a term applied to, and used by, actual merchants like Tiang.

Chinese men were associated with polygyny and prostitution. Their sexual license drew on elite and common Thai conceptions of male sexual privilege (e.g., to be *jao-chu*, or to philander). But their sexuality was underwritten by what they considered their economic responsibility for their families. More so than ethnic Thai men, who were mainly farmers, nobility, or civil servants, Chinese men earned wages or accumulated wealth. Economic responsibility granted them sexual privilege, and jin kao fuse the "Thai jao-chu [philandering] masculinity with their own money-oriented brand of masculinity."[21] Thus, first-generation Chinese-Thai men's economic role was linked with an ethnic model of gender and sexuality.

Not surprisingly, there is no discussion of philandering or brothels in these commemorative texts. The funeral accounts reveal that Tiang conducted himself as the patriarch of a large family. At the Three Corners store, he took a second wife (a minor wife), and while head of Central, he married again. In 1938, Tiang returned to Hainan and courted a young village girl, Buneng Han (in Thai, Bunsri), who lived in a poor village ten kilometers from his old home. He brought her back to Bangkok when she was eighteen.[22] At first, Bunsri lived with relatives not far from Sampeng Lane while Tiang "paved the way" for her to come join the family in Three Corners, although it is not clear what these preparations entailed. Bunsri reports that they married when he brought her over to Bangkok.[23]

Bao explains that in the southern areas that Chinese emigrated from, "a minor wife was accepted as a family member, and lived in the same house with the major wife."[24] Polygyny was common among both the Thai aristocracy and the well-to-do Chinese men in Bangkok. Yet despite the commonality of the practice, three years before Bunsri arrived, a new Thai law officially outlawed bigamy and required men to register their marriages with government offices. The law's codification of monogamous heterosexual relations was a response to the judging gaze of would-be European colonizers, who frowned upon the polygyny of the court. But in practice, the law was widely ignored, and multiple marriages were unregulated. The minor wives of Tiang and Samrit are all recognized in family trees and in these texts.

Tiang ultimately fathered twenty-six children: eight with Waan, thirteen with Bunsri, and five with his third wife, Wipha. In 1940, when Bunsri was twenty, she had her first child. Her funeral commemoration includes a photograph of her surrounded by seven of her children, the oldest a teenager, the youngest a baby in her lap. She breast-fed all of her thirteen children, according to what she told a women's magazine that interviewed her when she won a national award for being an exemplary mother in 1988.[25] The desire for large families derived from Hainanese norms, but it also fit with the vision the Thai government and development experts had for Thai citizens. Although Thailand later became famous for a successful population-control program, the Thai government adopted a pro-natalist position from the 1940s through the mid-1960s. It criminalized abortion, formed the Wedding Promotion Committee, and awarded bonuses to large families (probably aimed at ethnic Thais; it is doubtful the Jengs/Chirathivats received one).[26] Birth rates increased and the population of Bangkok and the country grew. Even in this fecund time, Tiang's twenty-six children stand out as an exceptionally large family.

Business and popular accounts of Central Department Store follow the rags-to-riches formula of individual masculine energy, inspiration, and agency creating achievement. They do not dwell on the women in the family. Yet women's labor was crucial to the business. Sino-Thai family firms typically relied on the work and management skills of wives and daughters.[27] The early years of Three Corners and Central Department Store show this to be the case; Waan's tailoring, for example, was important to their early trade. Bunsri describes her work as confined to the home, but she performed store-related work in the house, which, after all, was in the same building as the shop. She also performed significant household labor, which involved doing the housework, looking after children, and cooking, including elaborate preparations for festivals. She was a clever shopper and effective household manager.

Bunsri also worked in other, subtler ways, including critical emotional or relationship labor. She worked to maintain good relations with Tiang's other wives, for example, and, again and again, is described as promoting feelings of warmth and togetherness in the large and potentially divided family. She oversaw family meals and kept the peace among the many siblings, nieces, and nephews (she says Tiang was away all the time, and so she disciplined the children). Her children describe her as a significant motor of the family; with all this work, she says, she was "too busy to fuss with the store." Bunsri also maintained important ties to the broader Chinese community and regularly contributed to Buddhist temples, often as a lay follower at the ancient Wat Saket. Her funeral commemorations include an enthusiastic tribute from the Han family name group (the Hantrakul Foundation) to which she belonged. The letter notes her generous giving of time and resources to this foundation. The funeral texts include four photos of Bunsri at various merit-making activities, and she says that her merit will pass on to the next generations.[28]

Labor in the household and business and the meanings of that work are gendered. The Jengs/Chirathivats' tight-knit family feeling is often noted in accounts of the family's success. This kind of incorporation does not automatically result from being part of the same family but is achieved by emotional and household labor. Bunsri's keeping the peace and emphasizing collaboration among family members helped inculcate the orientation necessary for competitive work in a large dynamic corporation. While Bunsri was recognized as hard-working (a trait attributed to the harshness of her childhood), much of her family efforts were not considered "work" but were ascribed to her personality or character. But her domestic, charitable, and spiritual activities can be interpreted as kinship labor: the seemingly noneconomic work to maintain the relationships that are crucial to both family and business.[29] Such behind-the-scenes kinship labor was critical to the growth and operations of the store.

In her research among jin kao (old Chinese) families, Bao demonstrates how Chinese women's household labor was integral to the family's economy, ethnic identity, and kinship relations.[30] According to Bao, "'Chinese femininity' is often tied to being 'mother of the house' (mae-ban) and working both inside and outside the family, while 'Chinese masculinity' is associated with a man's earning power."[31] Throughout these funeral texts, the work of kinship mingles with the work of business, but in a gendered way. Samrit's role of looking after his younger siblings is represented as inseparable from his economic roles; Bunsri's similar efforts, on the other hand, are viewed as a separate "housewife" role and attributed to her temperament. The relationship of Tiang's wives' and daughters' family roles to the business is not emphasized the way it is for the roles of Tiang or Samrit (although the gendered nature of the family-business mix shifts from the first to the second and third generations, as I show below). However gendered, the Jengs' domestic life intimately overlapped with its business operations and prepared the next generation of family members and workers, who became key in launching their department store.

EDUCATION

Both funeral books stress the training, education, and socialization of children in the context of a family business. Three Corners provided a crucial business education for Samrit and his siblings. Bunsri took the children shopping and says that she and Tiang taught the children about the value of money and goods, even the candy allowance they took to school.[32] From first to ninth grade *(maw saam)*, Samrit worked in the store, buying bulk items on Sampeng Lane, unpacking and shelving goods, and using his fluency in Thai to navigate Thai society (presumably his parents would not have been as fluent as their children). Samrit's commemoration reads: "Mr. Samrit grew up in this house, with his father as an example of earnest hard work. Thrift and love for his siblings were the principle things Mr. Tiang continuously taught Mr. Samrit."

Education has been an important part of Chinese or Sino-Thai efforts to reproduce or improve their financial (class) position, and formal education was stressed in the Jeng house. After attending the temple school across the street, Samrit and two brothers, Vanchai and Suthipol, went to a well-known academic school in Bangkok. All of Samrit's classmates went on to study at universities (until the 1960s, work in government or professions held more prestige than work in business). Samrit wanted to pursue medical studies. His father, however, took a different view of further education, insisting that Samrit study business and English, and Samrit enrolled at the English-language Assumption Commercial College. This anecdote establishes the path that led Samrit to run Central Department Store, but it also sets up a contrast in paternal styles and the evolution from the first-generation patriarch, Tiang, to the second-generation Samrit, simultaneously eldest son, family caretaker, and coworker.

After the eldest three brothers studied in Bangkok, Tiang's other children and his grandchildren went abroad for their college education. Sending children to study in Europe, Australia, or the United States has been a typical strategy of Thai aristocratic and business families, one that has spread to the middle class.[33] Bunsri proudly noted that all of her children studied abroad. When asked which of her children's many accomplishments made her particularly proud, she pointed to the son who earned a Ph.D. (in economics, at the University of California–San Diego); he was the only one of Tiang's twenty-six children to earn a doctorate degree. These costly degrees reveal the family's increasing financial wealth. International education has been an investment that produces status (or cultural capital) and fruitful international connections (or social capital).

The commemorations of Samrit cohere into a narrative about education and training: practical training in the store, emotional training in the family, formal academic learning, foreign language acquisition, and absorbing technical and factual knowledge. His funeral text includes the section "Life of Knowledge" and repeatedly notes his respect for knowledge and education in work and in daily life, highlighting his capacity to learn from texts and experience, particularly from foreign (Western) sources. Samrit's eldest daughter writes (in English): "He greatly valued knowledge. He saw accurate, timely, broadly based understanding of the world situation as essential to a full life and successful business. . . . In consequence, his knowledge and ideas influenced all aspects of business and family life."[34] Although he did not study abroad, Samrit received a rigorous education and could read and write English (better than many who do study abroad, notes the funeral text), using this skill to draft contracts and correspond with foreign businesses. He maintained ongoing interests in architecture and engineering and applied his amateur knowledge of these fields to his businesses. As his daughter notes, knowledge was relevant to business and to family life as well, a blending of the public and the private being typical in his story.

Such education involved class and gender dimensions. In valuing education for class mobility or cultural capital, Sino-Thai families transformed conventional Chinese gender practices. Numerous Sino-Thai families educated their daughters, nieces, and granddaughters, often further, in fact, than Thai families did (largely because they could afford to). Once women began entering the university in sizable numbers in the 1960s, middle- and upper-class Sino-Thai women became well represented among college students, academics, and professionals.[35] This education has allowed them to play vital public roles in Bangkok society. They have entered family businesses and other corporations (Sino-Thai women entrepreneurs are considered especially powerful in real estate). Others fill the ranks of urban activists, NGO workers, and feminist activists and have been a significant force in democratizing the Thai government.

While Bunsri had limited formal schooling on Hainan, the Jeng/Chirathivat family educated its daughters. Under Samrit's watch, they all went to the Mater Dei school. Over time, expectations for daughters' education and work life transformed markedly. Most of Tiang's daughters became "housewives," according to the descriptions in the funeral commemorations, which provide no information on these women's work history. Yet many of the second- and third-generation Jeng/Chirathivat women—the daughters of Samrit and his siblings—studied abroad and joined the family business. In a clear index of generational and gender transformations, Tiang's first grandchild, Samrit's eldest daughter, became a doctor, realizing her father's own youthful desire. As I show later, the transformations to the family business, from shophouse to modern retail, involved changes—and continuities—in the economic, gender, and ethnic identities of the men of the Jeng/Chirathivat family as well.

POSTWAR ECONOMY

From the end of 1941 until 1945, Japan occupied Siam. The occupation and war caused considerable hardship for the residents of Bangkok. Samrit had to cease studies when his commercial college was shut down. Waan was ill at the time. With scarcities and speculative hoarding, obtaining medicine for her was difficult, and, in this way, Samrit's funeral memoir hints, the occupation hastened her death. After Waan passed away in

1945, Samrit, then twenty years old, and Tiang's minor wife Bunsri, twenty-five, began to share the responsibilities of caring for the children of both mothers. After Samrit married, he and his first wife, Wanida, raised their children alongside Tiang and Bunsri's offspring.

The popular accounts of Central attribute its success to the innovation of the immigrant patriarch, Tiang, who was the formal head of the business until 1965. In the postwar period, however, the story of Central becomes the story of his son Samrit. In the 1940s, Samrit worked for a variety of establishments: Paramount Pictures, Borneo Thailand, and a Chinese school (where he taught the required Thai curriculum). Through this work, Samrit added to networks from school and family circles, forging connections that extended into the diaspora communities in Singapore and elsewhere. This work experience also provided important business training, and that is why it is included in the commemoration: it shows how Samrit learned about work with foreigners, unethical practices, and various business techniques and systems (especially methods of distribution). All of these developed Samrit's style of business—his character, even—and paved the way for his success in modern retail.

Even as the occupation by Japan and the war brought undeniable suffering, the retreat of European enterprises during the war provided openings for local Sino-Thai entrepreneurs.[36] A friend of Samrit's was importing English-language books and invited Samrit to sell the books to stores in Bangkok on a percentage system; after the friend pulled out, Samrit decided to pursue the business himself. He approached his father to invest, but Tiang "worried that such a large new business would not be successful and would cause hardship for the family, especially Samrit's 10 younger siblings."[37] Father consented to lend son a few thousand baht (suggesting that he had accumulated capital from Three Corners).[38] Samrit's collateral for the loan was his wife's gold necklace—her marriage gift (bridewealth) from him and hence a form of collateral that remained within the family. With this capital from his father and some from two friends, Samrit leased a rowhouse in Bangkok and opened the first Central Trading store in 1947.[39] Central Trading sold American and other foreign magazines, often back issues from the war years. Because the main capital investment came from Tiang, he has been considered the founder of this store.

Central Trading, however oriented to imported culture and new technologies of retail, emerged from, and to a large extent remained within, the Sino-Thai family shophouse economy. Tiang, his second wife, Bunsri, Samrit, and the other children moved from Thonburi back to Bangkok. The family lived in the same building that housed the store, in shophouse style, similar to the buildings in figure 3.

Central Trading occupied a new rowhouse on Charoen Krung Road in the quarter called Talad Noi (minor market). (See map 1, in introduction.) During my fieldwork in the 1990s, I lived in this area. By then, the land where Central Trading had stood was taken over by a new multinational hotel and tourist shops, but just beyond, the mundane neighborhood of Talad Noi shophouses remained. Talad Noi, called "the automobile graveyard" in Teochui, was full of workshops that salvaged automobile and metal parts and also odds-and-ends shops and a small market square of wooden stalls, from which vendors sold meats, produce, and prepared food. At times, this market space was used for productions of Chinese opera, in a typical integration of markets and community. As it did during the time of Central Trading, Talad Noi today juxtaposes dry goods shops, small workshops, and modern shops, but most of its residents no longer work in the shophouses. Many of them commute to job in factories, businesses, or government offices elsewhere. Samrit's new magazine store, the first "Central," presents a transitional moment in the transformation from the local shophouse community to the modern geography of home and work.

Hang Central Trading, as it was called in Thai (*hang* means "venue" or "store"), was a small shop of fifty square meters, selling local and international newspapers and magazines, as well as the odds and ends from Sampeng Lane and various salvaged items (such as paper used in shipping). Samrit's siblings helped stock the shelves and worked around the store, with explicit training from him. The funeral commemoration notes that he refused to spend money other than buying some drinking water from a woman vendor. Samrit saw the need for modern goods that suited the growing cosmopolitanism of the postwar Bangkok bureaucratic and business classes, in particular their orientation toward Western styles, goods, and knowledge. Inspired by advertisements in the foreign publications he was selling, Samrit began to import cosmetics and off-the-rack clothes, merchandise new to the Thai market.

In 1950, Samrit opened another store near the first, not far from the famous Oriental Hotel. (Today, a KFC franchise, a chain operated by the Central Group of Companies, occupies the spot.) This newer branch of Central emphasized modern marketing techniques, introducing a showcase to display goods—a first in Thailand—and advertising the store extensively. At the general post office nearby, Samrit mailed hand-addressed postcards announcing the arrival of imported *pocketbooks* and *magazines*, transliterating (instead of translating) the English terms. A 1952 advertisement for this Central branch beckons:

New Merchandise in

"SummerLand" *sweater* (women's and children's), "Manhattan" *shirt*, "Wings" *sport* shirt, Central and Bayford socks, "Hit" underwear and *petticoat*, "Botany" *necktie* and *bowtie*, French stationery, English toys, American S.K.S. Cards, and new and novel items for winter.[40]

A classic entrepreneur, Samrit parlayed postwar opportunities, state policies, social networks, and family capital—including his wedding present to his wife—into a profitable enterprise. He applied the lessons of Three Corners and early work experience and read the spirit of the times. Having learned about the significance of distribution channels, Samrit used connections to establish himself as the sole agent for numerous Western brands in Thailand, adopting a role formerly occupied by Europeans. During this period, Sino-Thai businesses supplanted European ones as the brokers for Thailand's intersection with the global economy, serving as polyglot agents crossing national and cultural borders. Families like the Jengs were particularly well placed to translate the nationalist and class aspirations of Bangkok's elite into businesses with transnational ties. The traffic in transnational texts and culture has remained the heart of Central's business.

CENTRAL AND MODERNITY

The modernization of retail was embedded in kinship relations, ethnic and national ties, and the cosmopolitan culture of the Bangkok elite. Even as it developed out of the mix of small shops and local markets, the modernity of Central represented a departure from the crammed odds-and-ends shophouses of Three Corners, the Talad Noi workshops, and Sampeng Lane—and from outdoor markets staffed by Thai market women. Central still operated as a family business, but its appearance differed more and more from the ethnically inflected, small-scale (and traditional) Chinese family store or workshop. These distinctions were not an accident. Samrit's interpretations of "modern" retail lay not just in the goods sold but also in the style of selling and the operations of the store.

The store's name reveals the ways that conceptions of modern economic forms were woven from different strands. According to store history, Samrit derived the name "Central" from an idea of his father's. Tiang admired an administrative organization of the Chinese government called Tong Iang, or "Central" ("Klang" in Thai), which managed conflict among political factions.[41] According to the account of the origins of the store's name: "Tiang wanted to use the Thai word 'Klang,' to mean a center for trade. Samrit saw that 'Klang' did not sound nice and chose the word that had the same meaning in English, 'Central,' meaning 'the heart or the center,' to indicate the center of goods and service that best met the wishes of customers."[42]

Central's corporate history and the funeral texts typically suppress political commentary, particularly the Thai nationalist and anti-Chinese regimes. In 1950, the unfolding Chinese communist revolution concerned the Thai government and its allies. For these reasons, calling attention to the Chinese political organization seems a risky choice. However, their choice focused on form, rather than political ideology, illustrating the pragmatic approach to politics taken by many Sino-Thai business families.

Names were by necessity instrumental and flexible for the Sino-Thai, who had changed their first names, nicknames, and surnames as they settled in Thailand. The Jeng family accepted the local nickname "Three Corners" over the Chinese name they had chosen for their Thonburi store. The name "Central" also reflects this strategic approach. The preference for English points to its hegemonic role in signifying modernity—necktie, magazine—in Thailand and worldwide. English reflects the orientation of elites in the multicultural city of Bangkok. Thais often convey this appeal by saying the English term sounds "nice," as illustrated by Samrit's evaluation of *central* as inherently more melodious than the Thai *klang*, and by the explanation given for Thai companies selecting other "nice" English names, such as Robinson's Department Store. But the linguistic hegemony was incomplete. The choice of "Central" synthesizes Western and Chinese influences; although an English term, "Central" represents an enduring orientation to China. Early stores were marked by signs in Thai, Chinese, and English.

Conceptually, Samrit saw a fit between the centralizing political function admired by his father and his own visions for a new mode of retail. The spiral logo of the store offered a visual rendition of these themes (see figure 4). Centralization represented the economic ideals of the day, which was large-scale, vertically hierarchical, and separated into clear functions—like Ford's factories (as compared with later corporate emphases on decentralization, niche marketing, and plurality). This rationalized organization was explicitly and implicitly contrasted with the prevailing market forms of the shophouse and the local bazaar. The Jengs' inclination to differentiate from these vernacular forms, and from the class and ethnic connotations associated with them, became more pronounced with the inauguration of the department store form. Yet the shophouse form of Three Corners continued at Central Trading, behind the scenes

Figure 4. Central Department Store logo from the 1960s.

and under a more modern guise, helping the family to rise in class status and to accumulate the capital necessary to launch a new mode of retail. And, as I show next, the place of ethnicity was significant for the family business, because the Jengs' "Chinese" identity was located within the broader context of nationalism and modernization.

THE JENG FAMILY AND THAI NATIONALISM

During the years that the Jeng family was operating the Three Corners and Central Trading stores and launching the Central Department Store, "Chinese" identity was a complicated political issue in Thailand. From the late 1930s through the 1950s, the Thai state, under dictatorial rule, centralized and expanded its power over the country. These efforts explicitly codified the meaning of "Thai" citizenship, culture, and economy[43] and subsumed marked regional variations in religion, language, culture, and identities under a new Thai identity. Between 1939 and 1942, the government issued a series of national conventions, Rattha Niyom,[44] which established the nation's name, flag, language, religion, anthem, and character traits: the apparatus that defined Thailand as a nation of "Thais," centered on the Tai ethnic group. State efforts such as the Rattha Niyom were also directed at regulating or assimilating "alien" groups, mainly the Chinese. The Alien Registration Act required nonnationals to carry photo identification cards. Resident Chinese were compelled to adopt a Thai surname, to follow the Thai version of Buddhism, and to place their children in Thai-language schools.

The prominent role of the Chinese in the nation's economy was considered particularly problematic by Europeans and Thai elites during the first half of the twentieth century. The government extracted revenue from Chinese subjects by charging residence fees, fining disfavored ethnic practices (such as posting Chinese-language signs), and taxing establishments that catered mainly to their own communities, steps that at times led to active protest from the Chinese community.[45] The government also promoted economic nationalism for Thais. Slogans broadcast over the radio urged Thais to buy Thai products and wear Thai clothes. Economic policies like the Alien Business Law privileged Thai nationals and Thai businesses; to increase the presence of displaced Thai peasants in small businesses, nine occupations were officially reserved for Thai nationals, among them female hairdressing and, in 1952, dressmaking.[46] The Chinese were prohibited from holding licenses for coffee shops and market stalls, and the position of shop attendant became reserved for Thais (a stipulation that remained for decades). These promotions represented an explicit effort to help Thais—particularly ethnic Tai men—become more integrated into the monetary economy, in a vision of nationalist development that attempted to change the gender and ethnic nature of economic activity. Given that the Jengs ran a coffee shop and Waan had made clothes in their first store, it is not clear whether or how they managed these restrictions.

The combination of economics and nationalism, however, was itself contradictory. On the one hand, official "traditionalists" promoted "Thai" culture and the purchase of Thai-made goods, for example, the sarong (although the prestigious style of women's sarongs had been adopted from Lao styles, which were closer to Western skirt styles). On the other hand, various regimes also encouraged "modern" consumption, for example, exhorting Thai women to wear (and therefore buy) Western-style hats and skirts in order to present Thai subjects as cosmopolitan. The orientation to modern consumption in the postwar period increased the strength of retail shops operated by "aliens," the imported-goods shops run by European or Chinese proprietors, and the Chinese laundry shops required to care for these fragile foreign textiles. Thus, modernization efforts that regulated Sino-Thai commerce often ended up promoting it.

The Thai government also applied its economic nationalism efforts unevenly. In order to exert more control over (or at least benefit from) Chinese commerce, Thai politicians entered into partnerships with key Sino-Thai businesses, such as the growing Bangkok Bank. These relationships meant that the businesses "secured licenses, promotional privileges, government contracts, and other crucial favors."[47] Many of today's well-known dynasties like Central got their start during this period, using friendly relations with the state to expand during the military dictatorship of the 1950s.

What did it mean for the Jengs to be "Chinese," "Hainanese," or "aliens" in the context of anti-Chinese Thai nationalism? Of necessity, the family navigated this nationalist context in their domestic and work life in the Three Corners and later Central Trading store. Indeed, they succeeded in part because they complied with expectations for Chinese in Thailand, blending Thai and Chinese practices in a hybrid fashion typical for many immigrant Chinese families and Sino-Thai descendants. Samrit studied at the local temple school with Buddhist Thais, taught the Thai language, and mastered English. (There is no note of him learning Chinese.) The Jeng family's Chinese names were traded for Thai names with similar sounds or meanings.[48] Hokseng (meaning "successful fortune") became Samrit (meaning "achieved, succeeded"); Tiang's first wife became Waan (sweet); and his second wife, Buneng, became Bunsri, nicknamed Nin. The family kept the Jeng surname until 1950, a time when they were dramatically expanding their business. They adopted the name Chirathivat (also spelled Jirathiwat), meaning "long-standing grand culture." (Patrilineal surnames, so core to Anglo and Chinese kinship systems, had not been introduced in Siam until 1913, as one effort to modernize in relation to European ideals.)[49] Sino-Thai (and Thai) family identities were forged not only in relation to custom but also in relation to the Thai state and social climate.

In the funeral commemorations, the space given to ethnic identity or

Hainanese or kinship networks is minimal, yet by most accounts, Chinese ethnic-language groups and the creole Sino-Thai communities were (and are) central to Chinese social and business communities in Bangkok and were pivotal to the Jeng/Chirathivat business. Hainanese youth in Bangkok had links to those in provincial cities such as Phitsanuloke, for example.[50] The Chinese Chamber of Commerce was important in the formation of a strong business community. Details in the funeral texts point to the presence of these networks, for example, in naming the sources of capital for business start-ups. Bunsri, an active member of her Han family group, also sent money to Hainan. The flow of remittances to China caused official alarm about a drain of capital but also helped enrich the Sino-Thai banks that coordinated them.[51]

The Chirathivat funeral texts relay other signs of ethnic practices and relationships. One photo, which appears to be from the 1960s, shows Bunsri posed with Tiang. He is seated, wearing a Chinese robe, with tusks behind him, the figure of the Chinese patriarch; she is in a shiny, sleeveless dress of contemporary cut, with styled hair, standing beside his chair in bare feet. For many Sino-Thai business families, Chinese practices and symbols—such as rites for the ancestors, distinct funeral customs, and a complex calendar of holidays and rituals, including Chinese New Year celebrations and moon-cake festivities—reproduced their Chinese ethnicity. Such visually codified practices presented the signs of Chineseness to the Thai public as well.

In later years, corporate retail like Central Department Store and supermarkets competed with old shops in Chinatown in selling the paraphernalia associated with many of these ethnic practices: the votive papers, black and red Chinese calendars, and moon cakes (which Central advertised extensively). The department store came to link the reproduction of Chinese ethnic identity with consumer culture. Modern retail thus emerged from, and in turn helped to shape, modes of ethnicity and kinship that shifted with capitalist development and transformations to Thai nationality.

CENTRAL DEPARTMENT STORE

In the official Thai calendar, A.D. 1956–1957 was the turn of the Buddhist Era century, from 2499 to 2500 B.E. Ushering in this new Thai century, Central opened its first major department store. The new Central was a five hundred-square-foot store located in Wang Burapha in "Chinatown." This was the largest and most comprehensive store in Thailand, carrying a greater diversity of imported merchandise than Central Trading had, and it represented an enormous investment of ten million baht. It is considered the first true department store in Thailand.

In the 1950s, the area known to foreigners as Chinatown was the prevailing shopping district of Bangkok. People who grew up in Bangkok from the 1950s through the 1970s remember it as the heart of consumption in the city. Families would come from across the river in Thonburi or from outlying areas to shop at shops such as Tai Fah or Nightingale Olympic (which advertised Vassarette bras). Yet for the middle class and upper classes of Bangkok's million residents,[52] Central Wang Burapha was *the* department store. Central provisioned Bangkok's bourgeoisie and elites with the changing mix of fashions, housewares, and services they required, as well as supplying goods needed for ongoing practices such as a new set of clothes for the Chinese New Year celebrations. The department store profited from the growing disposable incomes of government bureaucrats and business families as well as from the wealth of Thai aristocracy and upscale foreign visitors. Out of this middle-class and elite consumption, Central generated capital to reinvest in expanding the business and in other projects.

One of the Chirathivats' projects, given the success of the Central Wang Burapha store, was to open another branch of the store in the area, on Yaowarat Road, the main artery of Chinatown, a street lit with gold shops, restaurants, and apothecary shops. But this branch of Central quickly failed. Its failure points to important variations in class and consumer orientations. Of Yaowarat, Central's corporate accounts explain, "Chinese residents in this area were very economical by nature and preferred to buy from the market and small shops rather than from big stores."[53] The class and habits of this local community differed from much of the upwardly mobile commercial Sino-Thai world of Bangkok: Wang Burapha's consumers, also largely "Chinese," were eager and able to participate in the department store's mode of consumption. This difference is an indication that Bangkok's Chinese belonged to different classes.

The refusal of locals to patronize Central Yaowarat also demonstrated the persistence of older habits of consumption. Most of Bangkok's Thai and Sino-Thai consumers continued to buy from neighborhood shophouses, specialty markets, and bazaars until at least the 1980s. Among those so oriented, in fact, was Tiang's second wife, Bunsri, a first-generation immigrant who was not unlike Yaowarat's frugal residents. Her funeral commemoration notes her love of shopping, not in department stores, but in fresh markets: "My mother loved shopping at the market a lot," says her daughter; "in terms of seafood, Mother was an expert, and wanted to purchase it herself." She was also a keen bargainer. The failure of the Yaowarat store and Tiang's wife's shopping habits testify to the endurance of shophouse and market forms, entrenched in class-based and long-standing patterns of consumption.

MODERN INNOVATIONS

Samrit Chirathivat writes, "Our success grew out of our determination to bring Thailand into the modern world."[54] The all-in-one shopping center far surpassed the offerings of a general store with a range of goods (e.g., furniture) and services (e.g., shoe repair) that provided for workaday and home life. True, small shops (like the Jengs' first store in Thonburi) also provided meals and tailoring, but the consolidation of all of these in a spacious, stylish interior pointed to the 1950s and 1960s conception of urban modernity as grand, concentrated, and highly attentive to appearance. The economic form of the department store—its infrastructure, organization, marketing techniques, and scale—had social and cultural implications that quietly paralleled profound changes underway in consumer society. Central Wang Burapha, for example, was the first store in Thailand to feature fixed prices for products, with price tags on its imported stock, a new concept in selling goods in Thailand. Ever the keen student, Samrit came up with the idea of price tags by observing practices in stores abroad. This innovation in merchandising illustrates how a range of changes can result from a transformation in basic economic practices.

The entrenched marketing mode had been bargaining (or haggling), a form in which customer and vendor interact dialogically.[55] Fixing the prices of goods radically changes the interactions between sellers and buyers and requires less market "intelligence" from each. The shopper need not be familiar with current prices and reputations or be skilled at negotiations—traits Bunsri transmitted to the Chirathivat children. (Thais I knew who felt inadequate at bargaining preferred this form.) Such skill was particularly associated with women and with the Chinese (and other ethnic groups, such as the Mon). This shift reduced the skill required of the female consumer, or "housewife," and changed the aesthetics and experience of shopping. It also changed the work of selling, because the salesperson need not continually calculate profit margins. Fixing prices differentiated department stores from shophouses and market stalls (although produce markets often set prices as well). It required the storeowners' cultivating customers' trust in Central and its brands rather than the customers' relying on a direct relation with the storeowners as merchants. For foreign visitors or Thais who traveled abroad, price tags made the codified value of goods easily commensurable with international systems of value. The practice of fixed prices spread across much of Bangkok retail, becoming a hallmark of "modern" trade.

The department store depended on technologies of display, architecture, and engineering. Samrit took a strong interest in these fields. In travels and readings, he looked for ways to improve his stores, for example, by calculating a way to add an elevator in the store parking lot. In 1964, the Daimaru Department Store, a subsidiary of a two-centuries-old Japanese firm, opened a branch in an emerging shopping and business district. Daimaru was the first serious competitor to Central, and it raised the standard for modern consumption, with novel imports from Japan and an even more stylish design. Daimaru introduced the enthralling innovations of escalators and air-conditioning. The technology of escalators offered not only excitement and a cutting-edge infrastructure but also served to clearly distinguish the seasoned from the novice shopper: stories about watching the grandfather's or the peasant's fearful approach of the moving stairs continued for decades. The Japan-styled department store thus fashioned an interior realm of avant-garde comfort. Later retail entrepreneurs in Thailand borrowed from Japanese and American styles of retail.[56]

DEPARTMENT STORE LABOR

The department store articulated with changing class arrangements that accompanied the rapid development of Bangkok. Notably, it provided the ideal vehicle for the changing identities of middle-class consumers (which it helped to shape). The department store also articulated with the changing face of labor. From the 1950s on, the rise of wage work, the decline of small family farms, and the onset of rural to urban migration created a growing population of male and female wage laborers, altering the class composition of country and city. Central famously employed the Chirathivat children but also hired salespeople and other staff and, by law, employed Thais as store attendants. (By 1987, Central employed seven thousand people in five stores.)

By employing this new Thai wage labor force as well as members of the family and the Sino-Thai community in a new market economy, Central altered the identities and relationships involved in selling. This department store form specifically changed the role of the seller from the Chinese tao kae merchant and the Thai market woman to the uniformed sales clerk. The position of salesperson no longer required market knowledge or bargaining skills (let alone the skills required for negotiating with police, local patrons, and government officials). However, department store selling requires other kinds of knowledge: literacy, for one, and familiarity with the consumption world of the store. In fact, to qualify as a sales attendant, a candidate has to have completed at least the official minimum elementary school education (currently sixth grade) and sometimes secondary school (as high as tenth grade)—levels that a fair number of rural migrants or urban poor have been unable to reach. In 1960, a quarter of the women in Thailand and a tenth of the men were considered unable to read and write.[57] While the literacy rates are much higher today, many of Bangkok's factory laborers, sex workers, and domestic workers do not have the educational qualification for being a department store clerk.

These transformations represented changes and continuities in gender. Sales counters in Thailand are disproportionately staffed by women, although men are placed in such departments as electronics or men's wear. In the late 1960s, according to one report, sales work accounted for 40 percent of women workers.[58] According to Thomas Kirsch, this tendency reflects a general division of labor in Thailand that assigns men to positions of political and religious authority and women to work connected with the market economy.[59] Even as marketing work changed and local markets lost their preeminence in everyday consumption in Bangkok, marketing work and the sphere of consumer markets have remained associated with the female gender and the Chinese ethnicity in Thailand.

Service work involves workers' identities in material ways, as it highlights their appearance and self-presentation. Department stores, banks, and the like put workers in uniforms (paid for by the workers). Banks and hotels train workers in applying cosmetics. Accordingly, customer-oriented service work increasingly relies on the workers' own consumption of consumer goods such as pantyhose and makeup (often purchased in modern retail outlets like Central).

Lower-class Thais and students working part-time have been trained to suit the middle-class theater of the upscale department stores (described as a process in the United States by Benson).[60] Modern retail stresses the attitudes and behaviors (rather than the skills) of its sales staff. Retail management books list such relevant character traits as friendliness, cheerfulness, courtesy, tact, moral attitudes, dependability, enthusiasm, initiative, alertness, poise, and mannerism. Sales work has represented professionalized, respectable work in the "formal sector," bearing different class, ethnic, and status associations from vending in markets.

Samrit himself was "a man traditionally proud of his appearance." He was also famous for promoting correct values and attitudes for the workers in his store as well as for executives and family members. His funeral commemoration lists his "Principles and Philosophy" concerning work, business, and family, culled from years of letters, exhortations, and notes. These include:

> Don't be extravagant . . . ;
>
> Dedicate your time to working for the company more than for yourself;
>
> Always treat everyone with fairness . . . ;
>
> Business expansion should not make professional friends suffer;
>
> Have the bravery to punish those who have done wrong. . . .

The tenth principle instructs followers to "avoid 10 disagreeable things" including smoking, talking too much, not being on time, showing off, slothfulness, and being unwilling to listen to others.[61] His sense that work involved ideas about character and performance and overlapped with kinship and community has a modern ring and reflects the changing symbols and operations of business during Thailand's decades of economic growth.

SINO-THAI FAMILY CORPORATION

The innovation of the department store form, introduced by Samrit Chirathivat and his family, involved gendered family relations and ethnically based business practices grounded in a shophouse economy. In turn, the expansion of this version of retail affected kinship, gender, and ethnic identities as well. Here I focus on the identities of the owners, members of the family business, suggesting continuities and ruptures in the kin-based economies of modern commerce.

The Chirathivats mixed Chinese, Thai, Western, and transnational practices in family life as in business. In the 1950s, Tiang's family transformed itself, following the example of other burgeoning Sino-Thai merchant families. First, it adopted the Thai surname Chirathivat. Second, it separated home from business, moving to a compound house in a historically Thai area of Bangkok.

In 1956, the growing family moved to a residence near Silom Road, a developing business district. The household included thirty people: Tiang, his second and third wives, Bunsri and Wipha (Waan had died); Samrit and his wife, Wanida; and the collective of Chirathivat children. (Samrit eventually fathered ten children by first wife, Wanida, and his second wife, Kanika.) The family's move away from the shophouse to a compound marked a shift from an old style of combined business and residence to a modern style that spatially separated home and work. The Chirathivats' daily home life no longer took place amid the objects and activities of work. According to her memorial, Bunsri continued to do much of the cooking and housework, but now it was formally separated from the family business.

The historian Judith Walkowitz describes the radical impact of the department store on 1880s London, including "the radical division of production and consumption; the prominence of standardized merchandise with fixed, marked pricing; ceaseless introduction of new products; the extension of credit; and ubiquitous publicity."[62] Credit took a while longer to arrive in Bangkok, but the other features Walkowitz lists were core parts of the department store form. In particular, disaggregating business and home, as the Chirathivats did, perfectly complemented the department store, which was predicated on its distance from the mixed shophouse economy and on the radical division of production and consumption. As William Leach writes of American department stores such as Macy's, "The point was to give shopping space its own unique identity as a place for consumption and nothing else."[63] The replacement of kin with paid sales workers in department store operations also delinked family from work.

Department stores' new modes of life inserted themselves into existing cultural practices, often redefining them, for example, marking holidays and intensifying and recasting the gift giving associated with them as well as codifying the elements of Chinese rituals like moon-cake offerings. (Modern retail also introduced the widespread recognition of Christmas as part of the Thai winter holiday season.) These new cultural modes were predicated on an economic schema that separated home and work, thereby redefining family, gender, and sexual identities. With cosmopolitan home furnishings and up-to-date clothes, the department store form fostered consumption for home and family, a sphere that was otherwise ideally separate from the formal economy. Especially for women, the department store in Thailand, as elsewhere, symbolized a separation of the productive economy from the consumption connected to the home, family, and self, a separation that was in imagery (if not in fact) gendered to equate production with men and domestic consumption with women. Thus Bunsri's skill at shopping, cooking, and managing a home represents the older model of the housewife that the department store, at least symbolically, transformed to one predicated on consumption. The formation of the modern market economy expelled much of women's household, family, and productive labors from what is viewed as the "economy."[64] The modernization process that intensified in Thailand in the 1950s and 1960s reduced the place of kin (or moral) economies in farms and trade. Spatially, symbolically, and economically, the department store crystallized these transformations.

Many of these shifts were incomplete, however, often more fully realized in representations than in actual practice. Thai women have one of the highest rates of labor-force participation in the world, for example, and numerous married women work for pay. Moreover, kinship continued to play a significant role in even the most modern manifestations of Bangkok's economy. As a corporation, Central remained by and large a family affair, in a hybrid mode of family business that combined kinship and corporate relations. The entire family appeared for the opening ceremonies for new branches. Tiang Chirathivat held formal control of the Central Group until 1965, when Samrit took over until his own death in 1992. At various times, Samrit's brothers were leading executives in portions of the diversifying empire;[65] they also sat on the boards of other companies and organizations. Central employed Tiang's and Samrit's children, at times their sons-in-law or daughters-in-law, and the children of Samrit's younger siblings as well. Currently, Samrit's third daughter, Yuwadee Pijarnjitr, is the president of the Central Department Store company, having been the president of the chain's flagship store. Busaba Chirathivat, a daughter of Tiang and his third wife, Wipha, is an executive at the chic Zen branch of Central. Other daughters of this generation work in the family's retail and hotel development concerns. Their labor represents continuities with Sino-Thai and Thai women's work in marketing and in family firms but also represents Sino-Thai women's increased economic power and prominence in these businesses.

Marital and sexual relations continue to be the backdrop to Central's business operations. The Chirathivats have been one of the elite intermarrying and joint-venturing families that form Thailand's capitalist class.[66] One of the Chirathivat sons dated the daughter of the founder of competing department store;[67] another married a member of the queen's family.

Samrit's brother Suthikiati married the first Thai Miss Universe (1965), Apasara Hongsakula, whose sister is active in national and city politics. Of course, such intimate relationships at times strain, rather than consolidate, social networks. In the early 1990s, rumors and photographs circulated across Bangkok insinuating a relationship between Apasara and General Suchinda Krapayoon, the leader behind the 1991 coup and subsequent crackdowns on democracy protests. This gossip compounded rumors that a series of fires in Central stores in 1995 were arson, the implication being that they were connected with this affair. For the Chirathivats, known for a relatively low profile and modest lifestyle, such public drama was uncharacteristic and unwelcome. Yet given the volatile mix of military, government, beauty queens, and capitalists that make up Bangkok's power elite and the overlap of private and public interests, such eruptions are not surprising.

THE CENTRAL EMPIRE

Over a few decades, Central grew into the largest department store chain in Southeast Asia and reported "a sales-per-square-foot figure equal to Macy's."[68] In the 1960s, Central opened two branches: one branch near Daimaru Department Store, which did not fare well and closed soon after, and an ambitious successful branch in the burgeoning business strip of Silom Road. In 1973, not far from Daimaru, it opened a cutting-edge new branch, Chidlom, which became its flagship store and has remained popular for its cosmopolitan styles. By 1993, Central had ten branches in Bangkok and was key to the proliferation of shopping malls during the height of economic boom of the 1980s. Central's success helped spark the rapid growth of the consumer economy as investment in department stores increased, leading to a range of class-stratified stores, including those more oriented to working- or lower-middle-class customers. Over the next decade, Central expanded this retail boom to the provinces, opening branches in the north and south.

As Central Department Store grew, the Chirathivat family looked for other investments for their profits. Samrit and other Chirathivat family members transformed Central into a conglomerate of thirty interrelated companies involved in retail, hotels, property development, import and manufacturing, and fast foods, with interests in publishing and other ventures as well. The retailing portion includes three department store companies (Central, Robinson's Department Store, and Zen Central Department Store); discount stores or "hypermarkets"; supermarkets (real profit-makers); fast-food chains (Mister Donut, Burger King, KFC, Baskin Robbins); "category killers" (Office Depot); and franchises of specialty shops (Marks & Spencer, Body Shop, and Watson's Drug Store). These projects involve collaboration with corporations from Hong Kong, the United States, England, Australia, France, the Netherlands, and Thailand and with governments such as the SLORC (State Law and Order Restoration Council) regime in Myanmar, where Central operates a floating hotel.

Central's businesses span retail and manufacturing, which are interconnected. Sino-Thai businesses installed forms of retail to match an industrializing economy even before industrial factories were developed on a large scale in the 1960s. These retail forms were predicated on importing goods, yet their growth was inextricably linked with the local manufacturing boom of the 1960s to the 1980s. In the 1960s, the Thai government promoted industrial manufacturing of goods for sale in Thailand, or import substitution manufacturing. At the behest of Sino-Thai manufacturers, the government eventually promoted production for export, which took off in the 1980s. With the rise of Sino-Thai banks, local wealth became transformed into larger sums of capital, whose investments often involved ethnic, kin, and social networks. Taking advantage of capital and government support, Central's Garment Factory makes licensed goods for Wrangler, Lee, Maidenform, Jockey, Perry Ellis, and Jantzen as well as Adidas and New Balance. It also manufactures and exports toiletries, candy, TV, and audio equipment to Japan, Hong Kong, Australia, Southeast Asia, the Middle East, and the United States.[69] However much Central has engaged in manufacturing, the public face of the department store obscures any links to factory production, instead presenting a seamless environment oriented to consumption and service.

By the 1990s, the retail business became fiercely competitive. The Central Group was compelled to place some of its businesses on the stock exchange, reducing the family control over them. Central has also hired more nonkin and foreign management, including at least thirty overseas executives and managers, particularly to draw on transnational expertise in restructuring and new distribution technologies, but also "to upgrade its image away from that of a family-run business."[70] When the Thai economy entered a serious currency crisis in 1997, the centrality of kin-ship and ethnic networks to Sino-Thai businesses such as Central, CP, and Shinawatra (discussed in chapter 4) was labeled "crony capitalism," their hybrid form identified as a problem for the Thai economy, espe-cially in the eyes of foreign investors. The close relation between the Chi-rathivat family's Central conglomerate and the Sophonpanich family's Bangkok Bank, for example, was criticized but also strained when the bank sued the retail empire over nonperforming loans. Central, like other firms, moved to minimize this crony image by hiring more outsiders, gen-erally foreigners, for management and executive positions. (Shop atten-dant remained an exclusively Thai position.)

ETHNICITY AND MASCULINITY IN RETAIL

The meaning and value of Chineseness changed over the many decades that the Jeng/Chirathivats cultivated their business, becoming more a hy-phenated Chinese-Thai identity, positively rather than negatively valued for its strong associations with the market economy. Bunsri's 1998 fu-neral commemoration mentions "Thais of Hainanese descent," a phras-ing that marks an ethnic national identity: Chinese changed from alien to ethnic Thai in Bunsri's lifetime. The Chirathivat family, like other Sino-Thai business empires, is now considered a successful "Thai" fam-ily dynasty, and its business is represented as Thai in contrast with for-eign capital from Japan, the United States, and Europe.[71]

This hyphenated Sino-Thai identity results from the convergence of changing interpretations of Thai citizenship, of Chineseness, and of the market economy itself. As the prestige and power of the capitalist economy has risen over the past few decades, the status of those asso-ciated with its upper ends—the entrepreneurs, professionals, tycoons, and bourgeoisie—has risen accordingly. These shifts and Thailand's changing relations with China since the mid-1970s have changed the place of Chinese-identified culture for the Thai public. Chinese dynasty folktales have become popular models for business or political success.

Craig J. Reynolds writes, "The commodification of Chinese identity signifies the triumph of the Sino-Thai bourgeoisie as the national bourgeoisie," although lingering prejudice remains.[72]

So complete is the shift from "alien" to "Thai" that, in the 1980s, Samrit attempted to have the government deploy the Alien Business Law—which had been developed to regulate the Chinese in Siam—against an influx of foreign retail investments.[73] The Jeng/Chirathivat family's national orientation had changed from Chinese to ethnic Thai in relation to their class interests as domestic capitalists. The shifts in Chinese identity also reflect the Chirathivats' strategic and flexible relation to national and international politics. They, like other Sino-Thai business dynasties, have close connections to political families. Longtime politician and former prime minister Anand Panyacharun writes a tribute to Samrit in his funeral commemoration, noting that they met in 1973 in Washington, D.C. Samrit's strategic relationship to political conflict is conveyed in an anecdote about convincing nervous investors to risk their money on an enormous shopping mall project he proposed for a relatively undeveloped suburb of Bangkok. Investors worried about a variety of threats, especially communist organizing. Samrit argued that communism grows when there is deprivation and no avenue for change, so that the communist system appears as the best option (at least it offers rations!). If capitalists do not invest in Thailand, he reasoned, communism will only come about more quickly. As a solution, Samrit proposed that they invest six hundred million baht in Central's suburban Lardprao shopping complex in order to develop Thailand, prevent communism, and, not incidentally, turn a good profit (which they did).[74]

These shifts in economic and ethnic identity are inflected with gender and sexuality as well. As I have mentioned, while the cultural mode of the department store refashioned women as housewives and consumers, women also occupied economic roles in the new retail form, including Thai shop attendants and Sino-Thai managers. The operations of the department store have also been accompanied by changing versions of ethnic masculinities in Thailand. In some ways, Samrit continued the jin kao immigrant generation's practices and identifications of his father: he embraced the provider role, which is central to the gender, ethnic, and economic status for Sino-Thai men;[75] and he married twice (although details of the marriages are unclear). His brother, Suthikiati echoes Samrit's dedication to work: "I still enjoy working. It is my life."[76] But after Tiang, most Chirathivat men adopted a different masculine code, at least concerning the public display of virile polygyny. (Even the scandal involving the younger Chirathivat and the former Thai Miss Universe represented the wife's promiscuity, not the husband's, and hence realigned the conventional associations of sexual promiscuity, class, and gender in the Sino-Thai world.)

The figure of Samrit represents a change in the linked identities of Sino-Thai businessman and patriarchal head of the family. The commemorations of him suggest that, in his mind, business and family were one. His daughter writes, "Business was at the center of my father's life but he was also a man concerned with family; indeed to him business and family were inseparable." Such a figure is continuous with earlier jin kao men, but with differences: Tiang, the patriarch, decided on Samrit's course of study; Samrit allowed children to pursue their own studies and choose their own spouses. His principles and philosophy for the family included nurturance and a democratic approach. "My earliest recollections as a child," notes his daughter, "are of the family business meetings at which he allowed me and the other children to voice our opinions."[77] According to the testimonies in his funeral commemoration, Samrit raised his father's twenty-five other children (by three wives) and his own ten children (by two wives) more or less together, as one brood: his children, growing up alongside his siblings, called him Go, Hainanese for "elder sibling" (in Thai, Phi). (Tiang, according to Bunsri, was rarely home when the children were up.)

Samrit evolved from a boss merchant (tao kae) to a new kind of tycoon (*jao sua*), characterized by flexibility, diverse education, and emotional orientations. He adopted an affectionate, rather than authoritative, family leadership style, which carried into or overlapped with his commercial leadership at Central. Samrit's melding of kinship and business reflected a change from earlier generations and constructed a different mode of ethnic masculinity, one that was far less patriarchal and far more flexible—more suited, in fact, to the demands of business under the conditions of globalization and consumer capitalism.[78]

The shift from the shophouse to the department store did not completely divide home and work for the Chirathivat family or for their consumers. But the department store changed the meaning and configuration of kinship, gender, and work. Until it was displaced by the shopping mall, the department store presided as the major consumer institution of Bangkok and thus provided the infrastructure for the unfolding intimate economies of the developing capital. In the next chapters, I explore how the expanse of transnational capitalist markets in tourism and retail affects the identities and relationships of women workers and consumers.

CHAPTER TWO

The Economies
of Intimacy in the
Go-Go Bar

When outsiders comment about gender in relation to Thailand's economic development, what they most often note is the sex industry, a trade that has historical roots but has grown and transformed as a result of Thailand's modernization projects and transnational forces. This chapter investigates Bangkok's prostitution industry for foreigners, *farang* (Westerners) in particular, which is only a small corner of the large "market" for sexual services in Thailand but has attracted the most attention.[1]

The use of *market* for the sex trade is often a metaphor, invoking a large (even global) trade in women. By juxtaposing this trade with department stores, shopping malls, marketing offices, and direct selling, I mean to view the trade ethnographically as a set of sites and practices that expand commodity exchange, incompletely and contradictorily, into further reaches of social life. In the discussion here, I follow a number of writers who stress the economic dimensions of sex businesses that developed following the 1960s,[2] turning my focus to the exchanges that are involved in the trade. As with the other markets discussed in these pages, I explore the interplay between market exchange and other kinds of exchange present in the sex trade, showing how interacting economies affect gender and sexual identities. Because this market presents a more controversial form of trade than Central Department Store, Avon catalogs, or cable television do, I begin by describing my own awkward en-trée into this complex commercial and cultural milieu.

On my first trip to Bangkok, I met with Arlene, an American who was then engaged in research on sex work in Bangkok. Arlene and I wanted to visit a particular disco but decided that first we would briefly visit Soi Cowboy (Cowboy Lane), a lesser-known strip of go-go bars oriented to farang men (that is, men from Europe, the United States, Canada, Austra-lia, and New Zealand), which was established during the Vietnam War era. Soi Cowboy is a small alley of first-floor bars in the eastern sprawl of Bangkok. We entered a club called Darlings, sat at the bar, and began to talk in Thai with the bartender, a young short-haired woman named Mot.

After we had finished our drinks, we were ready to continue to the disco located several kilometers away, in Patpong, the most famous of the red-light areas catering to foreign men. When we told the bartender that we were leaving, she seemed quite disappointed and asked us to stay. We wrote a note on a napkin inviting her to join us. "I can't," she wrote back, "I'm working." Arlene knew something about the operations of the bars from her research in Patpong. She asked the barkeep if it were not true that if we paid a fee—what is known as the bar fine, or the "off"—she could go. How much was it? We paid the 200 baht (U.S.$8) and hailed a *tuk-tuk*, one of the noisy three-wheeled taxis pervading Bangkok.

Arlene wanted to go back to her apartment, so we stopped there first. As we waited, Mot told me she was the eldest child of a family in Khon Khaen, which is in Isan, the poor, northeast region from which most of the female workers in Soi Cowboy, and many in Patpong and other for-eigner red-light areas, originate. Many of those working at Soi Cowboy have migrated from the same villages, following kin and friend networks. Mot had followed friends. She had not been in Bangkok even three months. In fact, she and I had been in the capital about the same length of time; yet I had freely traveled all over the city, whereas she had re-mained on the short lane of Soi Cowboy, working in the bar and living in the small dorm room above it. She said she had never been taken "off" by a customer. She had never been to Patpong or to a disco.

The disco that was our destination, Rome Club, still stands in a short trendy alley of bars just a stone's throw away from Patpong's three lanes catering to Western or East Asian men. From its founding until 1994, Rome Club was known for its gay clientele. It was also rather loud with pulsating lights and ubiquitous monitors projecting music videos. The crowd was mostly male, both foreign and Thai. When we arrived, Mot appeared stunned by the size and mass of the place. While a disco might seem much more commonplace than a go-go bar to us, to Mot, Rome Club was far more overwhelming than the smaller one-room outfit Darlings, where she worked. I asked her what she wanted to drink. She said milk.

As we sipped our drinks on the balcony overlooking the dance space, I explained the gay nature of the place. Far from recoiling, she was intrigued and asked questions, for example, wondering whether there were gay women there. She took my hand to navigate through the crowd. We went to dance on the packed dance floor, but she wanted to quit before one three-minute song was completed. She grew increasingly unhappy. Finally, she said she wanted to return to her bar: there were too many men in the disco. Arlene saw her to a tuk-tuk and gave her money to return to Soi Cowboy. I never saw her again.

CONTRACTUAL CONFUSION

After Mot left, Arlene and I felt uncomfortable about this encounter, and I mulled it over for a long time after. We wondered if we had acted improperly. Did we do the right thing? Our understanding had been that this engagement was neither a commercial transaction nor a sexual transaction—we paid fees on Mot's behalf but not *for* her services—and we reckoned that she understood our view. Clearly we had underestimated the discomfort she would feel in a flashy, predominantly male venue. Who knew that a friendly gay disco could be more shocking than what she was already used to? But her discomfort raised more troublesome questions about our behavior and role in the evening. Were we customers, or should we have behaved as if we were? We took her out of the bar; should we have paid her for her time? Our confusion about what kind of relation the night entailed—whether or not it was sexual and whether or not it was commercial—involved interpretations of the codes of the trade, about which we realized we were unsteady. The communication and contracts of the nightlife involve an admixture of gender, sexual, racial, and economic dimensions.

Thinking over the night, my colleague and I of course also wondered what the bartender must have thought, having two women invite her out to a disco only to head directly for an apartment. We did allow for the possibility that Mot might have viewed us as customers, that she could have conceived of women as customers—that is, that commercial sex could run along homosexual or bisexual lines. In later years during fieldwork, I learned of a range of workers' relations with other women, yet being taken "off" by a female customer was relatively rare among them. (A female customer typically was part of a heterosexual couple contracting a worker, an encounter that workers said was almost always initiated by the man.) So it is unlikely that Mot had had any experience with female customers.

Underpinning our view of the evening was the assumption or belief that we were different from male customers, a gender distinction it seemed the bartender did indeed share, given her response to Rome Club as well as the tenor of our earlier conversations. But whether or not our interaction with Mot was commercial is not simply one of our gender identity or our sexual intent: in fact, other dimensions may matter more than these. Simply being a farang can be enough to establish the position of customer. National, racial, and regional identities (which are also economic identities) can override the entrenched heterosexuality and prevailing gender schemes of the trade. However, given that Thailand (Siam) was never colonized by European powers, these encounters should not be read as automatically reflecting enduring colonial dynamics, in the way that they might in postcolonial settings.

As we discovered, our companion knew as little as we did about relevant protocol. It turned out that all three of us were awkwardly inexperienced at intimacy in a commercial context. Just as Mot was new to urban life, she was new to the particular logic and practices of the sex trade. In the apprentice-like position of bartender, she was learning the workings of the bar, but she had yet to put these observations into practice.

The uncertainty exhibited by the three of us had as much to do with our lack of familiarity around commercial intimacy as with nervousness around sexual possibilities. It had to do with the contractual codes of the trade, which are linked but not reducible to gender and sexuality, race and nationality. It appears that the ability to apply commodity exchange to intimacy is something one learns.

Our uncertainty in this encounter, which ultimately concerned the economics of our brief interaction, illuminates some of the effects of capitalism on intimate life more generally in Thailand, which is the subject of this book. The uncertainty about whether our engagement was commercial or not points to the existence of other, noncommercial modes of interpersonal exchanges. I consider these alternative modes of exchange to loosely make up an economic system, defining economy broadly, as anthropologists and social historians do. This economy differs from, but overlaps with or even competes with, capitalist economies. I speak of this economic system as a folk economy or moral economy, meaning that it is a system governed by and oriented to kinship and community relations,[3] rather than by capitalist accumulation. The rapid growth of the Thai economy from the 1960s until 1997 has intensified the influence of capitalist economic modes in all areas of Thai life—farming, craft making, leisure, sexuality, even Buddhism, the state religion. As the market economy has extended its reach into new social realms, it has not entered an economic vacuum but has interacted with these other systems governing production and exchange, even as it supersedes or subsumes them.

This chapter builds on these observations in exploring the economics of intimacy in the sex trade. I discuss the sex trade in relation to various dimensions of the economic: the settings that structure, shape, and drive the industry; the microeconomics of the bar; the different kinds of exchange transactions women engage in; and the different kinds of economic logic or knowledge these transactions are based on. In learning the commodity exchange of the job, women are simultaneously learning about class, but also gender, sexuality, nationality, and race, in the transnational sites of bars, restaurants, and hotels. The chapter considers the ways economies and social identities encode each other in the sex industry: how commodified and moral economic systems are part of constituting or signaling those identities, but also how the identities associated with women workers code economic questions and concerns. Through working and by drawing on the heterosexual orientations of their social backgrounds, the women learn how to contract intimate relations for money.

The reflective anecdote above points to the problematic nature of representing women working in the sex industry. Of all the venues I discuss in this book, the sex trade presents the most controversial and over-represented case. Because the international sex trade is predicated on its sensational and spectacular qualities, it is fueled by texts. Hyperrepresentations of well-known sites reinforce the links connecting racialized and gendered sexual services with particular developing nations (or specific cities or beaches) such as Thailand, Bangkok, and Pattaya. These associations help re-create the trade in its problematic forms. Disturbed by the fame of the industry abroad, many Thais (especially nationalists, and the middle and upper classes) are hostile toward the women who work in the industry or toward writers and NGO workers calling attention to the issue. Thus, more representation can actually impede, rather than help, local efforts to improve or change conditions of the industry. My approach to writing about this topic addresses the political context of representation. First, I do not isolate the sex trade and subject it to separate (positive or negative) scrutiny, but instead juxtapose it with other markets where market exchange intersects intimately with gender and sexual systems. Accordingly, my analysis emphasizes economic over other equally salient dimensions of sex work. Like the shopping mall or Avon and Amway, the go-go bars represent one venue where commodified exchange is expanding its reach into domains conventionally governed by other kinds of social and economic logic and where capitalist markets are embedding themselves in the intimate realms of social relations and identities. In this way, commercial sex work condenses key features of the place of gender and sexuality in the expanse of the capitalist market economy in Thailand.

My discussions in this chapter derive from more than ten years of studying the sex industry in Thailand, including wide-ranging informal conversations and ongoing observation as well as textual sources, rather than from formal and scheduled interviews. I visited bars on six trips to Thailand spanning 1988 to 2000. During fieldwork, two of my neighbors in my flat near Chinatown were women living with white boyfriends they had met in go-go bars, and we had many casual discussions sitting in the floor's common area. For a year and a half from 1993 to 1994, I participated in a sex worker advocacy organization unique in Thailand for its secular approach, which does not involve "reforming" or "reeducating" workers. There I helped teach English, translated letters to and from customers who were abroad, and took part in street theater that distributed condoms inside and outside the bars. Given the spirit of this organization and of my volunteer work there, in this chapter, I draw most of my illustrations from observations I made separately, outside this group (as with the anecdote above), although it is impossible to bracket the many lessons I learned there. At times I also draw on published accounts of the trade, work of admittedly uneven merit, when they succinctly represent features I observed in general.

ECONOMIC FRAMES

The go-go bar is a particular recent business form shaped by—in fact, produced by—larger local, national, and international forces. These interlocking realms have created the supply of workers, the demand of foreign (and local) customers, and the infrastructure necessary for migration, tourism, and related services. The sex trade for foreigners is distinct from the much larger sex trade oriented to Thai and Malaysian men, yet it partakes of the same contexts and conditions.

Southeast Asian feminist analysts such as Than-Dam Troung, Pasuk Phongsapich, Siriporn Skrobanek,[4] and others situate the overall sex industry—of which the foreigner service sector is only one small part—within a broader historical and social context.[5] They credit the supply of workers available for this trade to the nation's regional and class inequalities created by government and business focus on exports, tourism, and big businesses (strategies forged in relation to the International Monetary Fund, the World Bank, and local and foreign investors). Economic and political policies have long privileged the capital and "underdeveloped" the countryside, making it necessary for the younger generation to migrate to cities, especially Bangkok, to earn wages.[6] The particular infrastructure for the foreigner-oriented trade has roots in the era of the Vietnam War, when U.S. and Thai governments militarized areas of Thailand and centralized Bangkok rule. U.S. military bases in Thailand established key features of the subsequent tourist industry: the go-go bar form, strips of R&R bars (including Soi Cowboy), and a population of former entertainers, girlfriends, and wives who needed work after the GIs left. Although men's demand is the motor driving this industry, customers remain virtually undiscussed in writing on the trade.[7] Male customers' own reports and the few writings on them suggest that intersecting conceptions of race, nationality, gender, age, and presumed cultural behavior—conceptions that both reflect contemporary global inequalities and resonate with colonial discourses about colonized populations—are integral to their desire for these erotic services. While foreigner demand is not the focus of this chapter, my approach assumes that it, too, like the supply, is created out of a combination of economic, gender, class, race, and sexual systems.

The relatively small sex industry oriented to foreigners is staffed with young men and women and the third-gender, or transgender, male-to-female kathoey, most of whom are migrants from the countryside, especially from the northeast, Isan. Isan workers such as Mot take part in a

large and established flow of male and female migrants from the countryside to Bangkok, which re-creates a mobile labor force available to
work in factories, to clean homes and businesses, to drive taxis, and to
guard buildings.[8] Some bar workers come from landless or urban families. One worker in a beer bar came to work, she said, after her brother
sold the family farm (which traditionally often passes down to the
youngest daughter, who inherits it by staying home to care for her aging
parents) in order to finance the bridewealth for his marriage. A majority of Thais still belong to farm families, and many of the workers in Patpong and Soi Cowboy belong to families that own and run small farms.
But with prices for selling rice low and the need for cash and demand for
consumer goods increasing, families cannot support themselves through
farming alone. Since at least the 1970s, they have relied on the younger
generation of sons and daughters both to support themselves and to con-
tribute more or less to the household through wage work.[9]

Factory jobs, domestic work, pink-collar work, retail, and service work
are interrelated, having developed in conjunction over the last few
decades.[10] Before working in bars, many a teenager began with more commonplace and much lower-paid work. Many have worked around the
clock as domestics for negligible salaries for Bangkok families before moving to the bars. Others have worked in manufacturing. A woman I met
at a newer go-go bar development, Nana Plaza, had worked as a seamstress in the Kader Doll Factory (which produced Cabbage Patch dolls)
until a fire razed it in 1993, the world's worst factory fire to date. Unable
to find other work, she then came to work in a bar.

One of the workers I knew best was Ploi. We met at a panel on women's
rights in Thailand, where she had come with her boyfriend. They had
met in a go-go bar, and he now supported her. Ploi grew up in a remote
village in Isan, whose district town was relatively small and sleepy. The
youngest child, she had helped farm and raise buffaloes as a child. Then,
like most of her older siblings, she had had to leave her hometown to
find wage work. First she worked in two small factories outside Bangkok
and later did housecleaning in Bangkok, before going to work in Pat-

pong. (Interestingly, I only learned of her housecleaning a long time after knowing her, then only from an interview she gave to a Thai journalist. Ploi was more ashamed of that work than the bar work.) Two other women I knew from my neighborhood first worked as domestic workers, both for Sino-Thai families. Wanpen came to Bangkok at ten years of age, having completed fourth grade, after her widowed mother remarried and "forgot us," she said. Her pay was 200 baht (U.S.$8) a month, which after four years increased to 300 baht (U.S.$12) a month.

When women come to a particular foreigner bar, as with Mot, Ploi, and Wanpen, it is usually through a female network of peers, friends, or relatives—not agents, traffickers, or recruiters. Ploi, for example, had a Bangkok neighbor who worked at Patpong and later joined a bar where she knew the mamasan (female manager, from the Japanese term). Wanpen, too, had a friend who told her she could make 500 baht (U.S.$20) a day. Chain migration from the countryside to the city, or from less to more industrialized countries, is a typical feature of capitalist development in the third world. What this means is that bars often hire women who know each other. Unlike Patpong, many of the workers in the bars of Soi Cowboy are "kin," in that they come from a particular area in the northeast. Workers in one bar may come from one small cluster of villages. In this case, whether a woman lands in a particular go-go bar or a factory or household depends a great deal on these personal chains and on where she is from. Beginning this work was frightening to most women I knew, but having friends and kin there helped ease the way. While generally women do not discuss their experiences with customers in great detail with one another (as far as I could see), the familiarity with coworkers also affects their experience at work. It can create camaraderie on the job—seen, for example, in the playful group dancing to Isan music after the bar has closed. This solidarity also helps when returning to the home region. When women bar workers return home during the Thai New Year celebration in April, for a significant event at a temple *(wat)*, or to help with harvest, they often make the trip with other women who are in similar situations, which can diffuse speculation or commentary. The world these women live in now is not isolated from, but exists in a web of relations extending to, the home village and, to different degrees, across Bangkok. And their social connectedness illustrates one of the ways that this market, the sex trade, intimately involves local relations and identities in Thailand. As I show below, this background, which includes economic orientations, enters into and shapes their practices in this work as well.

THE GO-GO BAR ECONOMY

Framing the activities and interactions in these bars are the encompassing economies of tourism, real estate, and bar operations. Since 1980, at the advice of the World Bank, the Thai government has spent money and designed policies to promote tourism as a major avenue for economic development. Tourism is one of the largest industries in Thailand and has brought in more foreign currency than any other business. It has also underwritten the three brassy strips for Western customers (Patpong, Soi Cowboy, and Nana Plaza) as well as the private clubs on Thaniya Lane that are dedicated to Japanese and Korean men. The intersection of tourism and sex work is captured by Patpong's nightmarket, a dense cluster of street vendors selling knockoff clothes and souvenirs, which lies between Patpong's visible go-go bars. Underlying the various venues oriented to foreigners is Bangkok real estate, itself a highly lucrative field. The owner of the most famous lanes on which the go-go bars developed in the 1970s and 1980s is a specific person, Mr. Udom Patpong.

Lining the lanes of Patpong are shophouses that stack a second-floor layer of bars on top of the ground-floor bars, which open onto the street. The largest conglomerate is the Thai-owned "King's Group" of bars, including King's Corner and King's Castle (as well as the beauty shop to which women go before work); these are interspersed with bars like Pussy Galore, Safari, and Supergirl. There are open-air drinking bars called beer bars, small stalls without dancing or shows but with cable television and some women to sit with (and take out). The organization of these clusters of go-go bars in Patpong, Soi Cowboy, and Nana Plaza is like a mall: the spectacle draws consumers, from whom shop owners profit, while the owner of the land profits from rents. Also profiting from the trade in the Patpong area is a range of establishments such as pharmacies, medical clinics, a supermarket offering Western products, ATM machines, beauty salons, and a slew of Western restaurants: Brown Derby, McDonald's, Pizza Hut.

The sex industry is oriented to the customers, an orientation that is inscribed into the architecture and space of the go-go bar. Banks of seats form a darkened perimeter around the room. From here, or from bar stools, customers can view the narrow stage by the drinks bar. This infrastructure of seating and lighting maximizes the customers' view of an array of women and directs the gaze away from customers as a whole. A worker can watch a customer enter and can scan a room or meet the eyes of one customer, but she cannot take them all in at once.

Bars sell spectacle and fantasy, affection and flattery, and access to an array of available young women. They do not "sell" the sexual services of women in the way a massage parlor or brothel does. They sell drinks and access to women who are available to sell their time and services. If workers engage in sexual acts, they do so most often outside the bar (although some establishments have upstairs rooms for this). Taking a woman out of the bar during bar hours requires paying the "off," approximately U.S.$8 in the late 1980s and U.S.$14 by the mid-1990s. Workers are expected to encourage the customer to buy drinks for himself (costing U.S.$2 to $4) and a specially designated "ladies drink" for them (often orange soda, roughly U.S.$3), on which they receive a commission. A 1968 pulp paperback guide called this commission arrangement "the Tokyo–Hong Kong system,"[11] flagging Asian transnational influences on the forms of the Thai sex industry. (The massage parlor is also associated with Japanese origins as well.) Most bar profit comes from selling drinks, which in turn relies on the provision of erotic entertainment, companionship, and a number of women to choose from. It is the women workers—the spectacle—who attract spectators and transform them into consumers. Their work is to be available and to attract, entertain, and please the customers. Their presence and efforts produce income for the bar owners, taxi drivers, nightmarket vendors, police precincts (Bangrak, the Patpong precinct is the wealthiest precinct and most coveted assignment in Bangkok), local businesses, and, by extension, the government and economy of Thailand.

The cornerstone of the bar economy is provided by female labor: female hostesses or waitstaff, bartenders (barmaids) like Mot, dancers, and sex-show performers. However, in order to run, bars require a number of different kinds of workers filling distinct roles, as a help wanted sign from Nana Plaza indicates (figure 5), including positions other than those serving or going off with customers. The sign in the figure reads: "WANTED IMMEDIATELY! / Dancer Female / Bartender Male / Server Male Female / Hostess Female / DOORMAN / Good Salary / Contact Here 7:00 P.M.–2:00 A.M." There are DJs, virtually always men, and the touts or bouncers, who can be male or tom, or female or kathoey service workers. To manage the staff, particularly the service workers, the bars hire a mamasan to oversee the establishment and informally act as go-between for customers and workers. She is often recruited from among the workers for the one position available to slightly older women (say, twenty-six and up). Bartenders are male and female. Being a bartender offers women one position where they are not required to go out with customers or necessarily pressed into sexual relations for money. All of these workers wear uniforms (which they pay for) and a numbered badge.

Women who do not go out with customers find that their salary leaves little left over after rent (which may be paid to the bar owner for a bed in a dormitory above the bar), city living, and the requirements of the job (clothes, makeup), let alone fulfilling family obligations or their own goals. To earn more money, a barkeep might accept the occasional offer of a customer to go "off." So for Mot, leaving with us could have served as part of the education of the sex trade, a training for going out with

Figure 5. Go-go bar help wanted sign posted in Nana Plaza, 2000.

"real" customers. Generally women graduate to the positions of server and dancer, which are oriented toward being taken off by customers and are paid a bit more salary each month. This is the site where women learn to apply monetary exchange to intimate interactions.

Ploi, who had worked as a factory worker and domestic worker, began in the go-go business by working in a Patpong bar for two months without going off with customers. Then life in Bangkok was interrupted by dramatic political upheaval. In May 1992, military crackdowns on democracy protests transformed the city: "bang bang" was the way Ploi illustrated the state of violence. She returned briefly to her home in Isan, but her elder brother advised her to return to Bangkok, pointing out that there was no work for her at home. Since she knew the mamasan at the Patpong bar Supergirl, she went to work there. She worked ten days as a bartender. Then, after an unrewarding drunken sexual experience with a Thai neighbor, she explained, she concluded that she might as well earn money sleeping with foreigners. With some trepidation, she took up a position as a dancer. Her decisions to enter bar work and to change jobs inside it were not unusual.

In order to receive the base salary (the equivalent of about U.S.$200 a month in the early 1990s), a service worker must punch in on time prepared to work (that is, made up) and must generate income for the bar through specified sales goals: a number of "ladies drinks" (of which women receive a share) and bar fines ("off" payments) (of which they do not). Ploi and other workers are not forced to take specific clients; however, they are compelled by this salary arrangement to be taken off with customers six or so times a month in order to receive their base pay. In this system, the workers pay for themselves, generating their $200 salaries through the combined intake of bar fines and ladies drinks. The labor regime for women workers underwrites the go-go bar and beer bar businesses and are, by extension, a significant feature of the tourist economy. At the same time, the job engages the women in a range of market exchanges: with their employer, with related services and shops (such as company-store beauty parlors), and with customers.

JOB DESCRIPTIONS

The women who engage with customers the most are the servers and the dancers. Uniformed servers seat the customers, take their drink orders, bring their drinks, and often sit with them as well. The uniforms vary from bar to bar; in a number of establishments, they simulate schoolgirl uniforms, although with shorter skirts. Many women work as servers because they do not want to dance. Onstage, a dancer wears a bathing suit (bikini or one-piece) or bra and panties (or in some bars, goes topless or uses pasties) and pulls her robe around her after her set is done. Despite the prominence of such shows, bodily modesty in Thailand remains a virtue. Modesty is culturally and situationally defined and subject to change: for example, Thai attitudes toward women's exposed breasts has become more modest, although elder women in the countryside may still tie their sarongs below their chests. Women do not regularly appear nude in front of one another. Locker rooms typically provide private stalls. At the beach, many women still swim in clothing—jeans and T-shirts—rather than a bathing suit or underwear. Western customers have reported surprise at the modesty of male and female go-go dancers in private rooms. Many workers were reluctant to identify themselves as dancers to me. Ploi remembers feeling incredibly shy at wearing so few clothes, shy to the point of fainting, she said.

The order of the dancers is marked on a blackboard or sign posted by the mamasan. At her turn, a dancer steps up to the stage (sometimes after first making an offering to a spirit shrine), where two to four dancers already are moving through their routine. Each dancer performs what is generally a three-song set. She dances at the first pole and, at the change of song, moves to the next pole. How a woman dances and with what degree of commitment or energy varies from dancer to dancer, and this does not appear to be a place where owners or mamasan exert much control over the women's labor. Some shuffle, holding on to the pole; others shimmy up and down it. Some look away, some look and smile at customers, and sometimes the women engage each other while dancing. After the last song in her set, a woman steps down from the stage, wraps her robe around her, and is expected to mingle with customers who beckon her or whom she approaches on her own.

The sex shows use a distinct category of dancers from the bar or contracted from outside to perform specific shows. In Patpong these shows are confined to the second-floor bars. They include exotic dancing (e.g., dripping wax from a candle onto your body), heterosexual copulation (on a motorcycle or some other unusual prop), female-to-female sex (e.g., a shower scene in a glassed-in room), and vaginal stunts (e.g., pulling out a string of razor blades). Bar workers are paid a bit extra each month if they perform in these shows. (The performers of heterosexual coitus are contracted from outside and perform at several different bars.) According to Ploi, the sex-show performance is not a desirable position from the point of view of workers. Even dancing, with its revealing clothing, can be a source of embarrassment; the sex shows push this immodesty much further. In her mind, taking this job was an act of desperation for a meager amount of extra income.[12] Ploi held that the customers disdain the performers, but the widespread existence of these shows suggests they hold some draw.

Working conditions within the bar are hardly ideal. As laborers in an informal industry, workers enjoy little to no protection in terms of hours, holidays, or pay. Selling sexual services has been criminalized since 1960 (although a 1996 law relaxed the penalization of women workers). While arrests of women working in Patpong were unlikely during my fieldwork, the women remained vulnerable in the eyes of the law, and, particularly in Soi Cowboy, they could be fined for not following regulations about nudity (for example, having uncovered nipples). Bars make regular payments and gifts to police and may, in fact, be owned by active or retired police and military. This situation makes appeal to police for protection from abusive owners or customers or for assistance in the case of violation of their rights rather an unlikely scenario for workers. (Hence, public calls for greater state involvement, such as those often proposed in elite Thai or foreign discussions of the sex trade, are misplaced.)

The space and labor of the bars present an arena in which customary lines between intimate and public, commercial and noncommercial, and labor and play can be blurred; this blurring occurs in ways that can make the work itself complicated and problematic. In some bars, the women must use the one available bathroom for their restroom and dressing room, sharing the space with customers. Some men extend the transactions of the bar into that space, engaging the workers in banter and play as they use the room. The structure of this industry, which is oriented to customers, does not eliminate women's own agencies and strategies, yet it does frame and constrain working women's negotiations of these sometimes clear, sometimes blurred interactions.

THE "OFF"

Ploi met her long-term Dutch boyfriend in the bar. He contracted with her for a short-term encounter. Some bars feature upstairs rooms where workers provide "short-time" sexual services. These are technically illegal, because an establishment is forbidden to sell or host sexual services. Women usually return to working in the bar after their engagements upstairs. Sometime later, Ploi saw him in the bar and approached him. He did not remember her, but they struck up a conversation, and he was impressed with her English-speaking abilities; later, he brought her some English-language books. They began to go off from the bar. Because workers typically provide sexual services *outside* the bar, they must negotiate several transactions with customers rather quickly in the din of the room: that they will leave the bar; that he will pay the "off"; and how much money he will give her for her time. After going off, worker and customer negotiate more specifically what they do and for how long. It is typical, women said, to go first to a European or American restaurant and then perhaps to a disco (before going to a hotel). There are a number of hotels available near Patpong that the customer might use if his regular hotel does not allow guests to enter rooms (meaning sex workers, often interpreted as any young Thai woman). Sometimes, a woman stays with the customer until around five o'clock the next afternoon, when it is time to go the beauty parlor to get made up and return to work. When a woman begins to see a customer regularly, she may invite him to pick her up after work, thereby saving him the cost of the off (and costing her one of her required times). Ploi and her customer had this arrangement after a short while.

My focus here is not the sexual services these women provide. Their exchanges around sex and around other dimensions of interacting is my focus. Workers do not generally rationalize their services on the basis of particular acts, body parts, or even the amount of sexual relations, as Western workers do (who, for example, charge more for particular acts or refuse to kiss customers at all). It is not that anything goes—such acts as sodomy or fellatio are considered undesirable, and many workers will not perform them or will try to avoid them. Thai workers effectively sell their attention and services to a customer for a period of time, which represents a nonrationalized mode of labor and contract. That this system is less compartmentalized, less commodified, is one of the reasons for its appeal to consumers from the industrialized countries of the global North, who express frustration with the mechanized and, indeed, hypercommodified nature of prostitution or other heterosexual relations in their societies.

Although perhaps most episodes are one-time encounters (either "short time" hour or so or "long time" overnight), all the women have occasional connections that last longer. Under this circumstance, the economic logic of the encounters shift. Workers might see a customer several nights in a row, or, if he is living in Bangkok, regularly over time. Many go on trips with customers to beaches or tourist resorts: these trips are calculated according to a single price for the whole time, factoring in the men's expenditures on travel, room, and board. Sometimes the customers want a tour guide, sometimes romance, sometimes a wife. Each of these involves transactions, virtually always in English, about duration, money, activities, scheduling, and preferences.

In the apartment building I lived in Talad Noi, Chinatown, two of my neighbors had met their boyfriends (*faen*, "sweethearts") while working in bars. Ben lived with an Israeli man who had invited her to live with him, although the terms of their relationship were unclear to me. Wanpen was older and more seasoned and had (I eventually learned) two children. Her long-time faen worked in construction some of the year in Australia but paid for her apartment and support while he was gone. Both had time to themselves, and we would sit in a communal rest area drinking and talking some afternoons and evenings. Wanpen would also take herself out to the Patpong disco where she used to work; her faen did not like discos, she explained, and she drank free of charge because they still knew her there. They did not speak of their faen in romantic or sentimental terms:

Ben confessed that she did not like Israeli nationals (this was after some of her faen's friends had visited), and Wanpen said she did not understand Australian English. But clearly, both women preferred these relationships to working in a bar, even if they provided no security. Both took up studies at the NGO school where I volunteered, Ben with particular enthusiasm. After four or five months of living together, Ben's patron dismissed her, giving her a small amount of cash. (Another woman replaced her immediately.) She returned home to her village but only briefly: she had to earn money and so had to return to work (in the bars), she told me when I next saw her. Ben was visibly wearied by this experience and said she was now too tired to continue her studies. Wanpen, on the other hand, moved with her faen to a house in Lardprao, near the Central Department Store complex there, and was bringing her five-year-old son and a sister to come live with them. The trajectories of these relationships vary widely, as the economic interpretations within them do. (I have known of sex workers supporting their farang boyfriends, for example.)

When the customers leave Thailand, as most of them do, many conduct a correspondence with a bar worker. I served as one of the "scribes" translating these communications. The women often ask the men for money, and sometimes the two make an arrangement in which he wires money regularly to the woman's bank account. The workers therefore need to open bank accounts and provide the number and address to customers, which is an impressive accomplishment for those who were not taught to read or write Thai. Workers often did not relish articulating with middle-class Thai institutions such as banks. They reported being the target of knowing scorn from bank tellers when they deposited sums that were larger than the presumed earnings of the average rural migrant worker.

The structures of the nightclub, go-go bar, and their ilk produce a working situation with more flexible transactions and ongoing negotiations than those found in, for example, the massage parlor or brothel or, for that matter, the factory or private home. In terms of their engagements with clients, women negotiate with whom and for how much they will go and do what for how long—a brief interlude, an hour, a night, a week, or longer. As so much pro-sex-work writing has pointed out, it is important to emphasize workers' capacity for strategies and choice, or what's called agency. For my purposes here, the *relative* latitude around the quality and nature of commodified sex makes it all the more critical to understand how women see and use material exchange in their intimate relations and self-understandings. The contract between women and customers is diffuse, and over the course of a long-term encounter, their interactions shade into, or overlap with, noncommercial relations. The work requires women to shift among these registers with fluency. Their ability to do this involves not only calibrations about amounts of payment and kinds of services but also the kinds of economic and social logic underpinning different moments for both participants. This ability to navigate the mixture of intimate economies is one of the key dimensions of the job.

WHAT WOMEN LEARN

Dancing, selling "ladies drinks," contracting for time and erotic services, and navigating commercial sexuality is learned. Labor is a form of knowledge creation, offering a socialization that can be seen as an education. The acquisition of the modes and manners of the work in a go-go bar involves explicit and implicit instructions, rewards, decisions, and discipline, which unfold in a complex business structure and which are shaped and circumscribed by national and global contexts.

The trade teaches women how to become sex workers. In the bar, women need to sell so many ladies drinks to earn their salary and commissions, and so they learn to ask men to buy them drinks. In taking care of "guests," women draw on entrenched lessons about tending to others, lessons that are imparted particularly to young women. According to one anthropologist, "Thai girls, not boys, are taught to anticipate and be aware of others' needs constantly."[13] Yet this preparation is modified and transformed in the commercial and sexualized context of the bar, where women learn how to engage in flattering and cajoling interactions, to caress thighs and lie about looks. These also constitute their earliest lessons in speaking English on the job. Workers learn to discuss whether they will go off with the customer and for how long. At some time they learn to negotiate payments and sexual practices. Such skills by no means come automatically.

Many customers report that novice workers, as well as women occupying a gray area of freelancers, will not set a fixed fee but will rely on the customer to give a gift of money at the end of their engagement;[14] this is one reason that novice workers are often preferred. The women may ask the more experienced mamasan for advice in setting fees or for help in negotiating with a customer in the bar. They also learn from other women, but this seems to take place indirectly and informally rather than through overt instruction. For the most part, women do not explicitly recount the details of a particular encounter, which are considered private matters, although they will describe cheapness or generosity and display any gifts. Certainly, new workers watch economically successful workers, who provide role models in their demeanor and allow the possibility of asking for what, at first, sounds like a large sum of money. Hence, how much a woman commands then depends on how experienced she is and also on her temperament for these negotiations, perhaps as much as it depends on her desirability to customers.

The work develops the emotional and practical knowledge and practices necessary to function in a variety of settings in a foreign language with foreign customers of higher status. They learn English, maybe some German, or Japanese if they work in Thaniya Plaza. A number of them visit Europe, America, Hong Kong, Singapore, and Japan to work or to accompany a customer (or both). They learn about how customers see women, for example, how white or Western women are perceived as unappealing (large vaginas, large bodies, large voices) and how Thai women are perceived in relation. Bar workers are able to participate in Bangkok's consumer culture to a greater degree and at much more upscale levels than other migrants. In general, by accompanying foreign tourists, the sex worker sees a wider array of middle-class venues and tourist sites and partakes more often in leisure and consumption practices of the relatively well-to-do than do middle-class Thai women, let alone fellow villagers working in factories or private homes. Bar workers are exposed to cosmopolitan consumption and come closer than other migrants to realizing the aspirations for urban modernity that color the migration experience.[15]

Women learn how to embody in their appearance and manner the racial, gender, and sexual ideologies held by customers. Their dancing style on the poles bears no relation to Thai dancing in villages or in local discos, but instead replicates a by-now-transnational go-go-bar bump-and-grind form. Women also develop modes of challenging or manipulating these constructions of their personae. Ploi lied about her age and pretended her English was not as good as it was. Some hid sarcasm in their praise. In dictating letters, the women often called attention to customers' assumptions that they were less intelligent, resourceful, or moral than the men and countered these judgments by explaining their pragmatic strategies given the hard conditions of their lives.

The aim of this work is to earn an income and better pay than that available at other "low-skilled" wage work. The job's particular operations and disciplines provide lessons in its own economic logic. Women learn to see the attentions, flattery, and services they provide men in terms of the money it can produce. While virginity and monogamy are prized, the women learn to brave judgments about promiscuity and to calculate their bodies, services, and attentions in terms of cash. In these ways, the workers absorb the lessons that their racial, economic, and gender subordination (or their performance as subordinates) can provide a source of income and also that they can contract their erotic and affectional intimacy according to specific amounts of time and money.

A crucial part of the training is the calculation of interpersonal relations in terms of commodity logic. Sex work thus trains women in the particular economic intimacy that characterizes the industry. It also provides a crash course in cosmopolitan commodity exchange. Necessarily, and also by choice, women become more thoroughly urban consumers as they dress for the job and dates and consume for their own pleasure or compensation. Some of these lessons differ from those of working in factories, cleaning houses, or growing rice. Nonetheless, as with all such practical education, these lessons about commodified labor occur not in the go-go bar or on the shop floor alone but in relation to knowledge and values from the workers' broader social worlds.

THE MATERIALITY OF THE MORAL ECONOMY

Working women, in their approach to and accommodation of sex work—in learning to become sex workers—bring with them relevant practical knowledge and cultural values concerning money, relationships, identity, and so forth, orientations that they share with fellow workers from the region. In order to consider women's interpretations of their transactions in the bar, I consider a common set of orientations deriving from local communities in villages or provincial towns. The complex economies of their villages, which I sketch briefly here, have long been characterized by the coexistence and interaction of market and nonmarket economic principles. These are landscapes pervaded by capitalism, markets, and consumerism. But they are also pervaded by nonmarket economies, which I refer to as a moral economy, kin economy, or gift economy—the diffuse practices and principles typically organized around general reciprocity or formalistic exchanges according to a logic governed by social relations and social position. This view suggests that, rather than a complete rupture, there are continuities between the mixed village economies and the work in the bars.

Most of the women workers I met during my fieldwork had been born into rural farming families in the late 1960s and into the late 1970s. They represent a generation that has grown up during intensely rapid social change, nationalist projects emanating from the capital, and a reverberating international economy. These workers grew up oriented to Bangkok, wage labor, and urban-style consumption.[16] As children, even poor girls would have been exposed to popular music and movies; before radios and tape players became common in villages, traveling merchants brought record players and movie projectors to provide entertainment and promote sales. Now, television is found in many a poor household, and at least some shop or home in the village plays videos to an audience for a small fee. Ploi's family had had a black-and-white television nearly a decade before they had running water.

Women's material calculations with customers draw on their practical knowledge of markets, money, wages, and consumption. These women share a subtle but cumulative familiarity with vernacular marketing because it remains the province of women in local bazaars. They are also building on a history of consuming imported goods and urban styles that have characterized "traditional" Thailand for sometime, because the market economy has long connected the countryside to the capital and to transnational flows. What I explore in more depth here are continuities between the explicit materiality of intimacy of the bars and local moral economies.

Among the local types of knowledge that women bring to work in the bars are ideas about the codes of relationships and the measure of identities, which are in part based on economic logic and which include their own materialist dimensions. Moral economies are hardly removed from the calculus of material measures, and this includes the operations of Theravada Buddhism. By considering the materiality of the moral economy—the ways that kinship and community centrally involve exchange economies—we can see possible continuities between the go-go bars and the village.

Part of women's orientation to material exchange with foreign customers derives from a traditional economy of intimacy, or a folk economy. Local codes for social relations and identities, notably those structured by heterosexual kinship systems, involve the idiom and practice of exchange. Relationships in Thai society are inflected with defined patterns of exchange obligations, typically hierarchically so, and often bear gender and sexual implications. There are those of elder-junior or patron-client, those of caretakers and children (with greater obligations for daughters), those between human beings and the spirit world, and those surrounding romance, courtship, and marriage.

For example, what is glossed as filial duty is interpreted by parents and children, especially daughters, as a quite real debt. This indebtedness toward parents, as well as toward guardians, teachers, and caretakers, is called *bun khun*. *Bun khun* describes the feelings and practices involved in certain relationships organized around generalized reciprocity, the slow-acting accounting of an exchange calculated according to locally interpreted scales and measures. Sons and daughters face different options for making good on their filial obligations to their parents. Conventionally, young men are ordained as monks for a brief period in their adolescence, a prestigious act that guarantees their parents (mothers in particular) will go to heaven. Women repay their filial debt by taking care of their parents or guardians, a duty that is reinforced by the tendency for youngest daughters to look after their parents at home (in turn, inheriting the house). A daughter's care-taking obligation increasingly is measured in terms of material support: cash, television sets, a home.[17] Thus, as many have pointed out, this active sense of filial obligation, bun khun, contributes to some young women's decisions to earn more money by working in a go-go bar than by factory or house work: it is the desire to be appropriate daughters that makes them inappropriate women. Their material support often enables the families to live beyond their (eroding) means and maintain their status in the communities—to have a new television or VCR, or ordain a son, but generally not to buy more land. The women also serve as brokers of modernity for their village, introducing current elements of global style and the world economy. Ploi bought her Isan family a new television set and helped pay for a new foundation for the house. Interestingly, she was not expected to provide significant support for her family; this is probably the major reason she was able to leave Thailand and managed to study for a high school equivalence and then a professional degree in Australia.

As in most kinship systems, in traditional Thai society, courtship is not mutually exclusive from material exchange, as such intimacy already includes material transactions, albeit according to a different logic from the commodified versions of the sex trade. Women's expectation of material exchange in social relations, including sex and "romantic love," resonates with broader patterns of kinship and community. In courtship or marriage, men and women are not supposed to touch in public, and youth are not encouraged to "date" alone. (This is changing, at least in Bangkok.) Publicly, virginity is expected of women at marriage. In the not-too-distant past in Isan, if the community discovered that a male and female youth had touched each other, the young man would be compelled to pay a fine to placate offended village spirits and also the girl's family. The amount depended on the part of the girl's body touched.[18] Bridewealth provides a clear example of the place of material exchange in folk economies. The practice of bridewealth continues today, with high rates of inflation. It is a precisely worked out amount of cash, gold, and gifts, all of which are proudly displayed, enumerated, and photographed or videotaped at the wedding. Thus sexual exchanges between men and women have long been accompanied by material, even cash, exchange; this kinship economy links heterosexual relations with material exchange.

I am suggesting that some of the conventional materiality of heterosexual relations form a backdrop for women's participation in, and interpretation of, their transactions with customers. Particularly in longer boyfriend relations, women draw on established orientations to romantic or patronage relationships. To describe the obligation she felt to her Dutch sugar daddy, Ploi conveyed her indebtedness for his support and teaching with the term *bun khun*. The evaluation of men in terms of generosity and the extraction of more gifts can be read not only as a symptom of financial need but also as a manifestation of this other economy. Thus, women arrive in the bars familiar with some form of material calculation of sexual intimacy or male-female relations.

THE BORDERS OF THE GIFT ECONOMY

The continuum of economic intimacy I am proposing should not be over-stated. The cultural logic of the sex trade market is different from the moral economy of authorized heterosexual relations. Unlike the cus-tomer's payment, marriage payment represents a groom's obligations to the bride's family, which ideally include his agricultural labors on the wife's family lands: thus this calculation is embedded within ongoing kin ties. Even where the local economic practices of the temple or community are saturated with monetary values and consumer goods, the Thai folk economy insists on its own borders and separations between market and intimate relations, borders that sex work of necessity blurs. Melding com-mercial and folk economies in the arena of commercial intimacies remains a contradictory and ambivalent affair. While short-term commercial ex-changes with customers may provide more money, longer-term interac-tions predicated on this moral economy are experienced as more au-thentic, intimate, esteemed, and more critical to women's sense of their own identity. We can see the presence of this moral economic logic in a range of exchanges practiced in the communities of Soi Cowboy, Nana Plaza, and Patpong.

One example of the folk economy is the spiritual offerings that are a routine part of life in Thailand. On a birthday or an occasion for atone-ment, women place gifts of food in the bowls of monks during their early-morning rounds. Many make contributions to a Buddhist wat (temple), particularly in their home village. A group of bar workers connected with the advocacy organization made a donation of large ceremonial candles to a Thai temple during the season for this sort of offering *(thod kathin)*, stopping by a bar to show off the gifts on their way to the wat. When she was my neighbor, Ben showed me a statue of King Rama V she had pur-chased. This king is venerated as a quasi-deity, and his image often graces shrines in shops and stores or is sometimes placed on the top of cabinets, such as in the flat Ben lived in. I later ran into her at a noodle stall after she had been on a pilgrimage to a wat. Workers also leave offerings at outdoor shrines that register the powers of territorial spirits. There is a large shrine at the mouth of Patpong major's lane, which overflows with offerings of garlands, incense, and wooden elephants, placed there by day-time office workers, bar workers, and owners of stalls in the nightmar-ket. This appeal to spirit worlds occurs inside the bars as well. Each bar features its own small shrine elevated on a wall or post, and some work-ers make offerings at the start of an evening or before they first begin a round of dancing, as we saw earlier. At Nana Plaza and Soi Cowboy, par-ticularly during a low period such as the rainy season, workers conduct a playful customer ritual. They take a wooden phallus, dunk it in water, and beat it around the doorframe, chanting (or yelling), "Come, cus-tomers!" While this last ritual may involve a burlesque performance, over-all these spirit offerings testify to a relationship of obligation that is expressed through gifts and is understood through an idiom of exchange (often using purchased commodities) and yet, no matter how instrumental the motivations of the supplicant, follows a separate logic from that of the market.

Even within the transactions of sex work itself, workers often shift relations from a monetary logic to other forms of material exchange. According to the author of an idiosyncratic memoir titled *My Wife in Bangkok*, "Many girls made it clear that you were helping them out finan-cially, and it was not a straight cash-for-sex deal. They felt better and so did you. If the woman went butterfly [took up with other men], well, you didn't donate enough to the family and she had to make ends meet."[19] These more diffuse calculations of exchange particularly characterized longer-standing interactions. At some time, most workers have an ex-tended connection to one customer, whether for a few days, a trip away, or even months or years. Once engaged in one of these longer connec-tions, women will very quickly cease to calculate the price for each evening or may cease to name fixed prices at all. The women I talked with called these clients boyfriends (faen) earlier than I would have guessed and bought them little gifts or romantic cards. One twenty-five-year-old and remarkably confident woman asked me for help picking out a knickknack for Bob, the American she had been seeing for two weeks who worked on equipment maintenance. (I vetoed the doll and suggested snacks.) More routinely, workers practice generalized reciprocity in their relationships. They are often generous with their families, friends, and intimates, including those longer-term customers. When there was a gathering at the advocacy group I participated in, the tables overflowed with the fruit, sweets, and food they had brought. They offered to pick up my tab or give me gifts or prepare a plate of food for me as a teacher, friend, or guest at the center. These other types of economic logic occur within the places and orbit of the sex trade.

Work in the go-go bar thus combines commodified exchange with other principles of exchange within "personal" relationships. If we take these forms seriously as exchanges, we can see that there are a variety of economic principles at play even in this highly commodified world. It is possible to read these nonmarket behaviors as manifestations of the moral and kin economies. This local folk economic system has continuities with sex work and is intertwined with market economies, yet it is also distinguished from market exchange logic and capitalist logic. This distinction in behavior and especially values is critical in the arena of intimacy.

Foreign customers also distinguish between different economic rationalities for intimacy. While they are drawn to the convenience and erotics of commodified and racialized sexual services, traits they in fact celebrate in writing, talk, and behavior, Western customers also recognize clear borders between market and moral economies. As the customers become boyfriends, the contractual nature of the relationship shifts, and in general the expectation is that the orientation to the material dimensions of intimacy will shift as well. Often the onset of this shift is when the man reports feeling jealous about the women's sex with other customers, and he is moved to provide more long-term support rather than take her off night to night. Wanpen recounted the transition in her relationship with her Australian *faen* in this way, as Ploi did. In their telling, they implied that they anticipated the man getting jealous and told him about other encounters to elicit those feelings and a greater com-

mitment. Other women also reported making remarks designed to in-
stigate sexual jealousy.

At times the customers' distinctions between the different kinds of economic logic differ from the women's distinctions, a rupture often attributed to a quality of the woman, sex workers, or Thais. To some men, the
women's intimate rationality, which derives from both folk economies and
on-the-job training in the bars, appears to deny or contradict romantic
relations that are understood in the West as noneconomic. Letters from
these men often express an anxiety about whether the bar worker's interest in them is primarily monetary: they have become nervous about the
commodified nature of the relationship. For Western customers, service
workers' economic calculations make them seem acquisitive, materialistic, or even "mercenary." Some "customer advocate" literature casts the
women as innately greedy and immoral.

The irony here is that, as the women become more and more experienced and effective at commodified exchange, as they embody the work,
they are considered less and less desirable by customers, who do not want
workers to betray the impact of this trade or its raison d'être. Part of the
attraction of Thai women as opposed to Western sex workers is that their
labor is not as rationalized or commodified. It is the same contradiction
that generates the Western ideal of the "hooker with the heart of gold":
the woman treated as a commodity and steeped in commodification,
whose own behavior and giving nonetheless still reproduce a different,
nonmarket economic logic.

THE ECONOMICS OF STIGMA

Working women address similar judgments every day, whether in stores,
banks, embassies, from passersby, or in the pervasive discussions and imagery in Bangkok mass media and public culture. The local ethical, economic, and social questions adhere to the bodies and souls of the women
involved, who act as the metonyms for the trade as a whole. These women
are entering a notorious industry and shouldering a serious stigma that

is directed only at them, rarely at the customers (who as men are expected to frequent prostitutes), and only rarely at owners or traffickers. (Recently there has been more criticism launched at male consumers in response to the HIV/AIDS epidemic and Thailand's modern image: internationally at pederasts and locally at working-class Thai and Malaysian men.) The prostitute stigma derives from promiscuity (which can simply mean a woman with more than one sex partner) and, moreover, from money. To the public eye, these workers dramatically embody materialism and market exchange, a position that energizes the widespread disdain for them. It seems also that the public concern with sex workers as a blight on the nation's image, or as social disorder, codes a more inchoate criticism of the rapid commodification of their own economies and lives. The boundaries, overlap, and distinctions between commodified exchange and other forms of material exchange are strongly felt, even, or perhaps especially, when they are unclear or changing. Thus, public and personal anxieties are often coded through gender and sexual subjects. For instance, tom (tomboys) in the mall (discussed in chapter 3) signify the excesses of capitalist development, as gays and lesbians do. Prostitution offers a cardinal example, positioned as it is at this exact frontier of intimate exchanges, an intimate site where market and folk economies meet.

Reading stigma economically helps explain its public force and misunderstandings between customers and workers. It also illuminates features of work in the go-go bar. Even with the status that money and clothes bring or the pride derived from doing right by their families, workers must struggle with public stigma. While many women flout conventional opprobrium to some degree, they are still affected profoundly by Thai and foreign judgments of them. Women regularly disagree with the view of them as greedy, materialistic, or even promiscuous. Yet some told me they felt grateful that their "boyfriends," former customers, did not despise them for being sex workers; in writing letters to their customers, a number said, "Please do not hate me for what I do."

What my approach suggests is that one way workers navigate this stigma is to attempt to redress the problematic associations of com-

modified exchange—that is, through the mode and form of exchange itself. Women revise and reinterpret the brashest forms of commodified
exchange by interpolating market calculations with their own folk exchange conventions. The workers' swift reciprocity in the form of gifts
to customers or the embrace of a more diffuse relationship can be seen
as a shift in economic modes. The preference of many women for
longer-term relations, even where they provide less income and offer no
security, might be seen as a preference for the principles of the gift economy over the pure monetary logic of commercial sex: bride-price over
price, as it were. Distinctions between being good and bad in this world
are distinctions about economic orientations and practices—whether you
are greedy or generous, materialistic or moral, or applying the principles of capitalism or kinship. These subtle shifts are reactions to or com-
pensations for the condemnation of their work in intimate commercial
exchange. Since the women are stigmatized as the embodiments of commodified exchange, they demonstrate their commitments to other exchange modes in intimate relations and in their identities. The presence
of a moral economy in the sex trade not only continues the village gift
economy but also, at the same time, results from the work of commercial intimacy. In this way, nonmarket exchanges are an inextricable part
of, and are even generated by, capitalist market exchange.

NAVIGATING COMMERCIAL INTIMACY

The Thai women who work in the safer, more flexible parts of the sex
industry, namely, these go-go bars, learn to use and manipulate their
image as commodities as well as commercial forms of exchange itself,
particularly in the zone where different forms of intimate exchanges co-
exist. The bars offer incomes and their own forms of leverage, mobility,
and status. Even those steeped in commodified intimacy, the sex workers and their clients, try to reconcile their commercial transactions with
their visions of intimate reciprocity and the borders between different
modes of intimate exchange. But this exchange takes place within a larger

stage of first-world power, government control, and many-layered economic arrangements.

This chapter has situated young Thai women's sexual "deviance" in relation to overlapping and changing intimate economies in Bangkok. In the next chapter, I explore a different juxtaposition of female sexual transgression and capitalist markets, by exploring the expressions of new modes of sexual and gender identities in the shopping mall, particularly the role of the tomboy. While malls and go-go bars offer fundamentally different settings, they both represent the commodification of leisure and the increasing role of market exchange in social relations. Together, the two examples show how configurations of sexual relations and practice are emerging at the juncture of enduring folk economies and global capitalism.

CHAPTER THREE

MBK: The Retail Revolution
and the Infrastructure of Romance

On my first visit to Thailand, I was struck by the frequent sight of boyish or mannish women. I wrote in my notes, "What are all these Thai
women with short hair, cigarettes, and men's shirts?" The term for these
women, I learned, is tom. The word *tom* commonly conveys the English
meaning of tomboy, although it has a wider meaning than the English,
including adult women and also more explicitly lesbians. *Tom* refers to a
girl or woman who adopts male clothing, demeanor, or appearance—
females who enact a female masculinity and at times a transgender female-
to-male identity.[1] (Not all smoke cigarettes.) I saw these boyish or mannish women everywhere: as guests at weddings, participants in temple
events, workers at go-go bars, and vendors and consumers in markets and
shopping malls. Especially at the Mah Boonkrong mall, I noticed a disproportionate number of tom as workers selling lingerie or luggage from
small stalls and especially as consumers, strolling arm and arm with friends
and *dee*, the tom's feminine companion, or femme.[2] Here were female
modes of identity and relationship that had not at that time been mentioned in the scholarship on gender in Thailand. The lack of attention
to tom-dee in the literature was striking, given how prevalent they were
and how little they accorded with prominent images of Thai femininity.
Since that time, a number of Thai and foreign writers have studied or

written about tom.[3] Their work has explained how tom identity accords
with, or challenges, cultural configurations of gender and sexuality.[4] Authors have also pointed out that the categories of tom and dee are closely
associated with modernity, an association flagged by the English origin
of the terms: *tom*, from "tomboy"; and *dee*, from "lady."

In this chapter, I pursue this association between tom-dee and modernity by elaborating on the prevalence of tom and dee in shopping malls.
Shopping complexes allow a venue away from home or school that provides a space of freedom for youth with disposable income and, in this
way, hosts a variety of expressions of identity. The connection of tom-
dee to malls is more than a reflection of the latitude found in commercial venues for people to be their (preexisting) selves. The connection
between tom-dee and malls illustrates ways that expanding capitalist markets are affecting intimate life in Bangkok. Tom are exemplars of these
processes. While the categories of tom and dee predate the mid-1980s
growth of shopping malls (the genealogy of these terms has yet to be written), the figures of tom and dee became prominent during the pronounced
economic development of the 1980s and 1990s, particularly in the consumer culture that was a central part of the boom. Taking the Mah
Boonkrong Center as my chief example, I use the prevalence of tom in
shopping malls as a window onto the interactions between evolving market economies and changing Thai sex/gender systems. My research draws
on extensive observations and a few informal interviews during 1993 and
1994 fieldwork and from visits ranging from 1988 to 2000, supplemented
by wide-ranging experiences with Thai tom and dee outside the mall.

The Mah Boonkrong shopping complex, which is often referred to
by its English initials "MBK," is possibly the best-known shopping mall
in Bangkok. MBK emerged amid a proliferation of shopping complexes
in Bangkok of such scope and newness it prompted business commen-
tators to declare a "retail revolution" underway.[5] To provide a context
for this discussion, I first trace the infrastructure of this cross-class
consumer economy before considering the economic dimensions of the
tom identity. The chapter demonstrates the ways that the speculative

commercial economy of shopping malls indirectly—and at times unintentionally—serves as an influential stage for configurations of gender and sexual relations that are emerging among Bangkok youth, including tom and dee.

THE ECONOMY OF THE RETAIL REVOLUTION

The growth of shopping malls represents a relatively recent development in Bangkok. From the 1960s to the early 1980s, Bangkok's consumer culture was clearly stratified by class and comprised a mixture of local markets, shophouses, department stores, and upscale retail. Most Bangkok residents shopped at local markets, shophouses, and bazaars, such as a popular weekend market on the Pramane Grounds by the palace. Middle- and upper-class residents bought clothing and furnishings at such downtown department stores as Central or Daimaru and at Bangkok's few elite shopping complexes. The three-story Siam Center, for example, founded in 1972, was the preeminent venue for well-to-do stylish young Thais and foreign residents. Its modernity was signaled by the English word *center* and its English marquee reading "House of Boutiques." Western students at the American School in Bangkok (many the children of American military and intelligence attachés involved in the Vietnam War) were chauffeured from school to this chic mall. The extent of transnational consumer culture in Bangkok remained confined to a well-to-do minority, and department stores, especially Central, reigned as the pinnacle of modern shopping.

The rise of the industrialized manufacturing of exports such as processed food, electronics, shoes, and clothes from the mid-1980s through the 1990s caused a sea change in the consumer economy in Bangkok. Manufacturing, retail, tourism, and real estate propelled the Thai economy to grow at among the fastest rates in the world. The 1980s "retail revolution," financed by wealthy Sino-Thai families, foreign investors, and joint investments between Thai and international companies, spread a transnational consumer economy to a wider swath of Bangkok's population. The development of the malls involved the combined efforts of corporations, investors, and the Thai government in a conducive climate of available capital and ready consumers. The economics behind gleaming new shopping complexes and fashionable consumption were typically rooted in older ethnic and kin economies of Sino-Thai firms that were adapting to and profiting from changing economic and political contexts. This was the case with MBK. As with Central Department Store and Shinawatra, the MBK company emerged out of an interplay of ethnic, kin, commercial, and state institutions and combined Asian and Western investments and influences.

Gracing the entrance to MBK are two bronze busts of the firm's founding couple, Mah Bulakul (1897–1964) and Boonkrong Bulakul (1906–1979), which are usually adorned with garlands. (See figure 6.) They represent the Sino-Thai founders of the Mah Boonkrong Drying and Silo Company, which in the 1930s was one of the powerful family companies dominating the rice trade. Collaborating with the government allowed them to profit from otherwise anti-Chinese state policies of economic nationalism.[6] Later, the family expanded from milling and trading rice into a cleaning service, real estate, and hotels and was renamed Mah Boonkrong (MBK) Properties and Development PCL. In the 1980s, MBK—at times led by a powerful Hainanese-Thai businesswoman, who was not part of the Bulakul family—participated in the speculative finance and real estate investment boom with the MBK Center project. Its business history illustrates the development of contemporary consumer economy of Bangkok from regional and local social worlds.

MBK and the shopping mall economy in general were encouraged by the Thai state, which fostered the development of Bangkok as a commercial city. In the 1980s, the Thai government aided retail and real estate investments with business-friendly policies that offered minimal regulation and promoted international trade (to the dismay of local companies like Central Department Store, which protested the competition from transnational franchises). Policies promoted joint investments between foreign and Thai companies. MBK had a number of such arrangements

Figure 6. Busts of founders of the Mah Boonkrong Drying
and Silo Company in the entrance of the MBK shopping complex:
Mah Bulakul and Boonkrong Bulakul. Photo by author.

with foreign concerns, such as Tokyu Department Store. Many of the
"made in Thailand" products sold in MBK's shops were produced by
jointly owned manufacturing companies. The state was also involved in
the spaces of consumer culture. Privatization of government ground generated valuable lands available for commercial use: Central Department
Store has built an enormous complex on land leased from the state rail-
way, for example, while MBK leases its land from the flagship public university, Chulalongkorn University. Indirectly, the Bangkok government's
choice not to create public parks and other spaces for recreation and
leisure apace with the growth of the city only enhanced the significance
and power of commercial venues like malls as the predominant spaces
available for leisure and recreation in the city.[7]

Aihwa Ong suggests that we understand the increasing role of corporations in social and cultural life in relation to the ways that globalization and privatization have changed governments. She suggests that Asian governments are letting the market economy take over more of the "cultural regulation of society—especially of the middle classes," a point I explore in chapter 4. One of the ways that corporations are taking over the regulation of much of the urban population is through the increasing importance of transnational consumer culture, which operates through censorship and self-censorship to limit explicitly political content.[8]

The state is not incidental to creating the consumers for modern retail, either. In ambitious tourist promotions in 1987 and 1998, the government helped bring foreign customers to Bangkok's retail venues with campaigns that highlighted shopping opportunities for handicraft goods, gems, and inexpensive brand-name goods. Department stores and shopping malls followed suit with targeted promotions that increased tourist consumption in their stores. But the retail boom depended mainly on the consumption of Thais, which was facilitated by the state. MBK's location by the state university, which includes a model secondary school, professional schools, and numerous institutes, supplies it with a steady stream of well-off young consumers. Although the purchase of imports drains Thailand's overall foreign currency holdings, and thus can be a national liability, the Thai government fostered modern consumption because corporate retail signaled Thailand's progress (particularly in contrast to disorderly street markets or old-fashioned shophouses). As with the department store in its day, the shopping mall crystallized the city's and nation's modernity. According to a major business magazine, MBK "sheds new light on the further growth and expansion of Bangkok as a truly modern Asian city."[9] With the proliferation of shopping malls, Bangkok's downtown areas were compared with those of Singapore, Hong Kong, and Kuala Lumpur.

Unfolding developments in state policies, urban space, capital, and consumer culture created a fertile climate for Bangkok's retail industry. Profits from manufacturing, tourism, and established enterprises fueled real estate investments. Downtown rents escalated. For property investors, the inflation of the value of real estate made the rents derived from retail more profitable than the rent or sale of housing or factories.[10] Bangkok appeared under construction, as office buildings and commercial venues sprouted across the expanding city. By the mid-1980s, Bangkok had thirty-nine branches of department stores, seven shopping centers, and seventeen more complexes underway, increasing the floor space dedicated to retail over two hundred times.[11] The authorized sprawl of shopping complexes based on speculative investments sculpted a new geography of the city oriented around commercial venues and brought a shopping complex within reach of all Bangkok residents with some cash to spend.

Such was the context for MBK. Mah Boonkrong Properties invested U.S.$120 million in the MBK "trade center," which opened during 1984 and 1985. At the time, it was the biggest shopping complex project ever seen in Bangkok. It included the MBK mall, the Tokyu Department Store, a hotel (which took more than a decade to complete), an office building, and a car park. Connected by a pedestrian overpass to a smaller mall named Bonanza (a reference to the old U.S. television series, popular in Thailand), the MBK mall partakes of and helps define a zone of consumption larger than itself. (See map 2.) MBK forms one side of a central area of stores, shops, and restaurants known as Siam Square (which is different from, but bracketed by, the older Siam Center building). Siam Square is uniquely appealing because of restricted automobile traffic, small navigable lanes (unlike the congested eight- to ten-lane roads that crisscross the city), and pedestrian overpasses that allow shoppers to stroll outdoors—an activity virtually impossible anywhere outside Chinatown. Siam Square is accessible by many bus routes (and now from a elevated sky train). Indeed, the pedestrian nature of MBK and Siam Square makes the area exceptional among the crop of modern shopping complexes, which are organized around car access, and makes it particularly accessible to young people.[12]

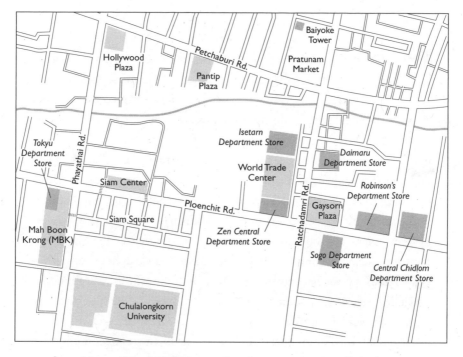

Map 2. Map of MBK area, showing concentration of retail.
Adapted from draft by Rini Sumartojo.

MBK, Siam Square, and their ilk have made transnational consumption accessible and attractive to a good number, although not all, of Bangkok's many worlds. During boom years, Thais were spending more and more, even faster than their incomes increased and even when the government adopted austerity measures.[13] Thais spent more on "recreation and entertainment" than they did on clothes and rent.[14] This statistic reflects the importance of commercial sites for social life as well as the high value placed on leisure as its medium. By the 1990s, half of the purchases of everyday household goods in Bangkok were made in department stores and shopping malls.[15] Such consumption became an important practice across most classes in Bangkok and set the stage for much of daily life in the city.

SPECTACULAR DIVERSITY

After a slow start (coinciding with a recession), MBK leased most of its space and became successful as a mall.[16] By the time I first visited in the late 1980s, it was famous in Bangkok for offering a cornucopia of goods, sights, and sounds on its multiple floors. The diverse spectacular quality found in MBK became the hallmark of the retail revolution in general. It symbolized a frontier of youth consumer culture in Bangkok, the emblem of cutting-edge consumerism of the time. A decade after MBK's opening, the mall still provided the reference point for a hyperstimulating shopping experience. When describing a new megasized complex, Seacon Square, one journalist noted that it "revolutionized the Mah Boon Krong concept," adding, "at least there are no claustrophobic crowds—yet."[17] This spectacular extreme of claustrophobic crowds, vibrant noise, and a diversity of goods and consumers is produced by the rent structure and a commercial economy oriented to diverse niche markets.[18]

The retail revolution intensified the department store economy with a new scale and a new form: the mall, the enclosed all-in-one shopping centers combining department stores (typically including supermarkets in Thailand), scores of shops and stalls, food, and cinemas or other entertainment, a configuration inspired by similar venues in Hong Kong and Singapore.[19] This economic infrastructure, in conjunction with broader social transformations underway in Thailand, has generated important cultural effects that bear upon sex/gender identities in direct but also in subtle and unintended ways.

The proliferation of such sites has created new settings for much of the city's social life. One scholar describes such shopping venues as "the parks of Bangkok,"[20] and indeed, they provide arguably the major quasi-public spaces of the city: the spaces for social life, social reproduction, and public engagements increasingly are commercial ones like MBK. Department stores and shopping centers mark major public holidays and the changing of seasons with elaborate displays for the king's or queen's birthday and announcements of "summertime" specials. As modern commercial venues have become indispensable in the work, leisure, and day-to-day life of most of Bangkok's residents, the reach of transnational capitalist economies into intimate life has increased. Malls like MBK provide an important stage and resource for contemporary urban identities and for a range of social interactions, especially for younger Thais. As a major arena for social life, the market economy of shopping malls influences identities and relationships in a number of ways.

Modern consumer markets profit from the intimate economies of daily life, particularly by servicing and incorporating nonmarket exchange relations. Numerous shops in MBK sell the kinds of little gifts that are popular for the frequent exchanges between friends or sweethearts: figurines, cards, ornamental notebooks, and decorated pencils. One can even buy a coupon entitling the bearer to flirting. Seethong 555 is a shop selling decorated paper and envelopes to write notes; I often saw it filled with schoolgirls. Corporate retail has inserted itself into a host of relationships by providing and defining the goods and experiences that are their currencies.[21] Beginning with department store efforts, retail has reconfigured the gift exchange of the winter holiday season—the period of greatest sales—for example, by adding the elements of Christmas and organizing wrapped gift baskets.[22] Supermarkets sell saffron-wrapped offerings to Buddhist monks as well as the incense and items involved in routine offerings to shrines, spirits, and ancestors. By provisioning and staging relationships, capitalist retail influences intimate arenas, yet it does so in a way that not only allows for but fosters consumer diversity.

One day during my 1994 stay, a group of women associated with the Thai lesbian group Anjaree met at the new Wendy's fast-food outlet in MBK's cavernous first-floor atrium. MBK was hardly the group's regular meeting place, but it was a convenient place to rendezvous before going to see a movie there. One woman, a journalist, remarked that MBK is interesting because "all kinds of people come here; it's not just one type." With its variegated structure, accessibility, and continuity with Thai-style markets, MBK does invite a diversity of customers.

Whereas previously shopping complexes were accessible mainly to the elite, for example, the Thai and international students who frequented Siam Center in the 1970s, the explosion of malls brought a wider spectrum of young people to these spaces. The retail revolution invited spending of the growing middle-class population as well as of the populations that had previously been excluded from "modern" transnational consumption: lower-middle-class and working-class Bangkok residents, including even migrant workers from the countryside. MBK offers goods at a wide range of prices. On the upper floors, one finds counterfeit versions of expensive imported brands sold on the first two floors. In the 1990s, the Domon shop, popular with gay men, offered imported T-shirts for the equivalent of U.S.$20 while the upper floors sold Thai-made shirts for the equivalent of U.S.$2.

Shopping complexes and department store chains generally target specific class ranges of consumers, demarcated into "upper" (often considered the new professional class) and "lower" segments, or A-plus, B-plus, and C-plus consumers. Many stores such as Zen Central and particularly Japanese chains such as Isetarn or Daimaru target the "upper" segment of wealthier Thai or foreign customers. However, relying on this segment is not always a viable formula, as the Tokyu Department Store discovered. Opening in MBK in 1985, Tokyu management found that the desired elite consumers produced disappointing sales. Tokyu management turned to middle-class and lower-middle-class customers, a group that more closely matched the consumer base of the MBK mall. It offered more moderately priced goods by substituting household goods and clothing made in Thailand for imported items.[23] Tokyu's shift represents the expansion of transnational cosmopolitan consumption to lower-income Thais and hence to a wider band of the population, a segment of the city that was growing at the time.

Here, I apply a class lens to consider the effects of a delimited cross-class economic citizenship on youth identity. The cross-class diversity produced by investment and retail economies and supported by state visions in turn promoted other forms of consumer diversity.[24] Shopping malls' expanding class base incorporated a diversity of market niches and subcultures, a diversity that is evident in and made possible by consumer culture. Spaces for modern consumption like MBK are predicated on a pluralistic consumerism, an ideology of consumer freedom, which promotes a diversity of goods, styles, and identities.

One can see the diversity of MBK in the range of fashions presented by visitors and stores. A few people are wearing work outfits, the ties and shirts of clerks or the uniforms of other service jobs. Working-class customers join more elite customers, evident from the uniformed wage laborers strolling past well-heeled patrons at gold shops and sleek young professionals in expensive import stores. Although rare, I have seen Buddhist monks and nuns in the mall, and Buddhist paraphernalia are sold in at least one stall. In the Tokyu Department Store, I saw a man in a heavy metal T-shirt and black boots holding hands with a woman in denim jeans and jacket. Many of the younger visitors wear baseball hats, and even more are in T-shirts decorated with brand logos such as Harley Davidson and Calvin Klein, team insignia, and English phrases, which at times could appear random, such as the safe-sex message worn by a tom vendor one day. The styles presented are defined in relation to international fashions heavily weighted toward American themes, such as "heavy," from heavy metal and Harley Davidson style, and "young professional." There are no T-shirts with Thai writing.

MBK patrons shop for computer software (fourth floor), in-line skates (sixth), books (third), gold jewelry (second), or furniture (fifth). They eat in fast-food chains or from numerous stalls in the food court. They have their hair cut; get a fake tattoo, a real tattoo (at least by 1998), or a nipple tattoo; and wax their legs and eyebrows. They have their fortunes read, play video games, and sing in the karaoke booth. This diversity is facilitated by the differentiated, fragmented, and subleasing rent structure of the mall. The multifaceted form of MBK and similar complexes is intended to appeal to a wide range of preferences and needs and to cultivate a spectacular quality. MBK services many of the identities required by the upwardly mobile and modernizing classes of Bangkok, including the accoutrements of self-presentation, of education and career, and of peer and intimate relationships. In this diversity, the shopping complex economy makes space for, and perhaps even fosters, the presence of tom and dee.

Couples of all genders stroll through MBK, coming to watch a Hollywood or Thai movie, to window shop, to smoke cigarettes and drink coffee in Mister Donut on the third floor, or to eat a meal at one of the restaurants or the food court on the sixth floor. Side by side in the TCBY shop sat two couples: a man and a woman, his hand on her thigh; and two women, a dee with her hand on the tom's shoulder. The food court, offering inexpensive food that can be purchased with coupons, was often crowded with these groups as well as with young male-female couples with a child or two.

By staging urban identities and relationships for consumers representing upper and lower socioeconomic classes and by emphasizing a spectacle of diverse consumption and consumers, MBK quietly incorporates a diversity of sexual and gender positions and liaisons. Some young men's comportment, nail polish, lipstick, and hair clips identify them as kathoey, although one does not see full male-to-female drag or cross-dressing in the mall.

As I noted above, among the throngs of MBK consumers I saw were a good number of tom. They came in groups of girls, in coed groups, or in couples, with dee on their arms. I saw tom strolling through the "Madison Avenue" aisle of the mall section named Times Square. Riding down the escalator one day was a group of four young women, all in blue work shirts. Three of them had short, bobbed hair and wore single earrings and mod sneakers. Their haircuts and dress style could mark them as tom. The fourth had long hair and was wearing chinos with the cargo pockets on the side and plastic sneakers. She could be read as dee, although she was in virtually the same outfit as the tom but for an additional earring, her long hair, and feminine manner. I frequently saw tom and tom-dee pairs in the Siam Square area as well, at the A&W fast-food chain, and walking to the British Council hand in hand.

The presence of tom here, as elsewhere, was subtle, probably imperceptible to most observers. But those connected to the tom or lesbian world identify the mall as a site popular with tom. Indeed, one Thai colleague, when hired as a research assistant for an American graduate student studying lesbians in Thailand, chose MBK as a fruitful site to interview a large number of tom.[25] Tom and tom-dee appear amid the cross-class diversity of the shopping mall.

INTIMATE ECONOMIES OF THE TOM

Let me back up and elaborate on the persona of the tom, particularly the economic dimensions of this identity. As I argue in this book, the identities and social relations that constitute gender and sexuality are intertwined with economic institutions and principles. My economic focus here is not on the class nature of the tom role but on the relation of the tom to market economies, particularly modern consumer economies, as a rich example of the articulation between capitalist markets and gender and sexual identities.

In speaking of the tom identity, I am referring to the ways of moving through the world as a boyish female: appearance, acting in relation to others.[26] The most obvious way that tom is realized and demarcated is through appearance. The typical tom attire consists of male slacks or chinos—often hooked with a metal keychain—a loose-fitting men's button shirt over an undershirt, and men's shoes or sandals. This was the general outfit worn by tom I saw at two weddings, for example. Key to the tom persona is the short haircut, often a bob. Short hair counters the general cultural value placed on long hair as a marker of femininity (itself a twentieth-century development, but reflected in the fiercely competitive shampoo industry). In the context of stronger institutional and informal codes for clothing, however, short hair takes on more importance. Since schools and most colleges require skirts and forbid all female students (as well as female faculty) to wear slacks, short hair becomes an important marker of identity for tom students. Civil servant positions also mandate that female employees wear skirts, a point I revisit below. Thus, short hair is often particularly salient for middle- and upper-class tom. Like all gender (and possibly sexual) identities, the tom persona is established through comportment and mannerisms, costume, and, especially important, social interactions within and through relationships, notably with feminine sweethearts, or dee, but also with family, friends, and in public. Individual tom vary in their means of identifying, in their gendered comportment, and in their affiliations with masculine or feminine identity.

Being a tom means deviation from, or escape from, female gender norms, particularly widespread expectations of labor-intensive femininity and an asymmetrical model of heterosexuality.[27] This deviation—or refusal—naturally attracts commentary, criticism, and coercion. At an NGO meeting, for example, one elite woman remarked with alarm that if boys and girls were brought up similarly, the girls would become tom (clearly a negative outcome in her mind). Another NGO worker whom I met during Thailand's first AIDS conference told me that tom were unnatural. Thai homophobia is a mixture of Western and transnational influences (such as the anti-gay column in an American Christian newsletter at a language school I saw) with local interpretations.[28] Yet at the same time that the tom role is evaluated negatively in mainstream society, tom appear more embedded in many realms of Thai society than they do in other societies. Many tom are seamlessly integrated into their families and communities. This integration is connected with gendered economic roles.

In many peasant, poor, or middle- to upper-class Thai families, young tom's identifications and intense romantic relations are often accepted as long as tom remain appropriate in other realms—in reputation, work, and support for the family: in their obligations to others. In particular, if a tom earns a respectable amount of money, she also often earns her family's toleration of her peccadilloes.[29] Matthana Chetami, in her research on "women who love women" in Bangkok, finds that tom reproduce many ideals about family relations and, in particular, continue to fulfill the daughter's role of providing support and care for parents.[30] (It is possible that tom daughters experience this role as a way to compensate for transgressing other gender ideals.) In addition, tom interpret their romantic role as taking care of dee. Thus, the folk economies of gender obligations—where daughters nurture and provision their families—still underwrite the expanding sexual possibilities for women (as the case is for women working in go-go bars).

However, the acceptance of tom and tom-dee relations varies according to individual families and typically differs among the upper classes. Tom and dee from the nobility and Sino-Thai communities typically (but by no means always) face less acceptance and often take greater pains to mask or minimize their preferred style or their intimate relationships. Many Thai families compel, urge, or advise heterosexual marriage, but others never even mention marriage, and some explicitly accept their daughter's tom-ness.[31] In general, the nonnormative position of tom often makes the economic arena particularly important to them, as a realm away from home and an arena in which they can measure up to some social norms and family values.

These factors help explain the prevalence of tom workers in various markets. A number of tom work at MBK and Bonanza stalls. Vendors selling bags on the third floor, cassette tapes (probably bootlegged) on the fourth and fifth, mobile phones on the fourth, belts on the second, lingerie in a shop named Pak in Bonanza Mall—all were clearly marked as tom by their short hair, clothes, and manner. Their visibility as vendors in MBK is representative of many informal retail venues in Thailand. Tom are often found selling in outdoor markets, small stalls, shops in local markets, and occasionally, although not typically, in lower-status department stores (see figure 7). Selling at this scale is generally a working-class or lower-class occupation. This association between occupation and gender role suggests that there is a class dimension to the tom identity, based in the trading- or service-classes, in the way that certain lesbian "butch" identities remembered from the 1950s appeared mainly in working-class communities.[32] And gender combines with class to shape the meaning of the tom: their identity is experienced and interpreted differently

Figure 7. Tom in the Wororat Mall in Chiang Mai City, 1993.
Photo by author.

according to class. Nonetheless, the category itself crosses class. I met middle-class and wealthy self-identified tom. I attended a small gathering of tom and dee in the garden of a tom's suburban home; the tom, with beepers clipped to their belts, drank top-shelf whiskey with Pepsi at one table, while the dee sipped mainly soda at another. In another case, a tom and dee couple prominent in the media world ran a chic bar that catered to Bangkok's paparazzi.

Nonetheless, living as a tom often impacts one's work life and occupational options, not simply because the employer might be prejudiced, but also because of the gender discipline embedded in many forms of work. One middle-class tom, persuaded by her parents to pursue a degree in the United States, chose to study business, because, she explained, "I want a job where I can wear pants." Her stipulation was shared by many tom. It ruled out working for the government—Thailand's largest single employer—because, as already noted, civil servant positions (including that of professor) require that female employees wear a skirt. Work in much of the corporate world, in the service sector and many offices, also requires or encourages wearing skirts and increasingly pantyhose and makeup. Hence, commerce often provides a preferable workplace for tom of different classes, especially from the middle- and upper-classes, away from the regulatory regimes of states and corporations. Working in markets or in a stall in MBK continues the widespread orientation of women to markets but also bears particular weight for tom, which explains the relative frequency of tom as vendors in the MBK mall.

The presence of tom and dee in shopping malls entails other political and economic dimensions as well. Western scholars have traced the relationship between capitalist development and modern gay and lesbian identity.[33] Capitalist development in the United States, according to John D'Emilio, propelled people out of families and into wage labor, consequently creating the individual sexual autonomy that fostered the development of a gay identity and gay community.[34] Thailand presents a different context, with lower wages and no comparable welfare system of social security, unemployment, and the like. In general this situation makes children and grandchildren—hence, heterosexual marriage and reproduction—materially necessary. Also, most tom—like most unmarried women from Bangkok—do not earn enough to rent their own apartments and so continue to live at home. They therefore do not enjoy the autonomy D'Emilio describes for America, particularly for forming households with their lovers. But individual wages or rising family incomes allow young women to participate in contemporary urban consumption, including commercial leisure. Just as this consumption is critical to heterosexual femininity, it is also important for the tom role and in ways that remain gendered.

Tom have no spaces dedicated to them. Bangkok is famous as a gay travel destination because gay men and kathoey have numerous locales available to them: bars, saunas, restaurants, and discos. The social geography of the city includes gay cruising sites and specific lanes associated with gay leisure, such as those near Patpong. In addition to the places for recreation, Bangkok offers stores catering to the accoutrement of gay male life, selling clothes for club going and necklaces and paraphernalia in rainbow colors, a commercially created U.S. image that is now an international symbol of the gay community. There were at least two such shops at one time or another near MBK: 0101 in Siam Square and a small shop in the Siam Center shopping complex. (There has even been marketing research on gay men.)[35] The spatiality of tom-dee or Thai lesbians is different. No stores cater specifically to tom-dee. A number of tom and dee opened restaurants oriented to a mixed clientele, including tom-dee patrons, but all of these closed after a short time. Over the past few decades, a few bars specifically catering to tom and dee have come and gone quickly.[36] The sexual landscape of the city reflects a gender system that constrains female mobility while entitling men and born-male kathoey to public eroticized spaces.

Tom and dee make do with more generic spaces. In leisure, tom mainly socialize in the same pattern as other girls and women, in homosocial groups or coed clusters. The public spaces, therefore, are much the same as for other women: restaurants and shopping areas. As a result of this gendered geography, within the throngs of young people in MBK are numerous tom. Malls are significant to the tom identity and relationships as a space of consumption and leisure. They are spaces away from home and kin, where tom can learn, or polish, the accoutrements of tom identity and conduct relationships. The shopping mall is not an empty stage, however, but a structured commercial zone dedicated to motivating and eliciting desires and identifications, particularly those associated with heterosexual relations and identities.

COMMERCIAL HETEROSEXUALITY

Capitalist market economies explicitly and indirectly construct their population of consumers. I have already noted how department stores target particular consumer classes. In addition, consumer industries like advertising and retail have actively constructed a "Gen X" and "teen" youth market that provides the contours for young consumers' identities.[37] Corporate marketers and store managers work with intertwined visions of class, age, and also race, gender, and sexual identities. For example, to construct images considered effective across Asia, marketers rely on a pan-Asian aesthetic that today is often conveyed by mixed-race Euro-Asian models.[38] Consumer economies are also installing new transnational norms of gender identities and sexual relations, including the reconfiguration—or perhaps the invention of—heterosexuality.[39]

Consumer economies construct heterosexuality in large part through their powerful visual culture. Companies targeting youth, such as fashion or music companies, rely on depictions of romantic relationships and erotic identities to market their brands and goods. Commercial visual culture circulates images depicting male-female relationships and associates modes of masculinity and femininity with romantic or sexual relationships. Decorative covers of notebooks and cards often feature male-female couples, typically white, and Japanese- and Korean-imported stationery and bric-a-brac often feature cartoon depictions of heterosexual romance. In the 1990s, a popular style for New Year cards was color-tinted black-and-white photos of a little boy and girl posed holding hands or a bouquet of flowers: coded, that is, in precocious heterosexual exchange. Between 1988 and 1992, I saw the images adorning commodities for school-age youth change from depictions of single-sex (especially female) friends to more heterosexual themes, for example, young male-female couples, or pop icons such as the music group New Kids on the Block.[40]

The visual displays in malls, on objects, or in advertising are increasingly explicitly erotic. Photographs of male-female couples locked in passionate embrace appear on placards for brand-name jeans. In the early 1990s, an advertisement for Robinson's Department Store showed a couple in bed, while Nescafé's in-store and citywide promotions featured a highly sexualized portrayal of a woman with that company's beverage. Collectively, such images have a far wider reach than a single example has at the point of sale.

In Bangkok, local entrepreneurs make high-quality copies of advertising images, reproducing them on any variety of goods. The evocative black-and-white photographs of a partly clad man and woman embracing, for example, are mechanically reproduced (minus the ad copy) on posters, cards, T-shirts, and the covers of photo albums. This process of turning transnational marketing imagery into decorations is widespread throughout Thailand: trademark logos such as Pepsi's adorn gasoline-powered rickshaws (the tuk-tuk), motorcycle helmets, and even the sign of one police station I saw. Advertising ends up being a commodity itself, the images circulating beyond their original point-of-sale source and increasing their aesthetic and symbolic influence.

The "retail revolution" has been intertwined with the proliferation of these visual texts. Television, radio, and film also have been crucial to this new consumer economy, illustrating this commodified aesthetic and portraying new urban lifestyles for a broad-based audience nationwide. Broadcast images pervade the malls, too, in videos playing in the windows of "VDO" rental stores and in Thai and imported films in the mall's movie theaters or on sets in other shops. (I saw thirty men clustered around the front of a hair salon, watching the Thai international snooker champion play on the shop's television set inside.) While the Arnold Schwarzenneger action film *Terminator II* was a perennial favorite, romantic films such as *Ghost* and *Sleepless in Seattle* were also popular during my stay.[41] Popular transnational imports have visually legible plots and recognizable characters, qualities that promote formulaic structures, whether in romance, action, or Chinese dynastic tales. Most commercially produced imagery privileges male-female heterosocial relationships over same-sex relations. In the accumulated representations of transnational consumer culture, romantic and eroticized discourses of a male-female couple are a staple feature. As other work on consumer culture in Asia has shown, such pervasive images and narratives, however multiple their interpretations might be, consolidate into discourses about intimate relations and identities that construct heterosexual gender and sexual norms.[42]

The construction of heterosexuality in consumer culture is not confined to the commercial visual culture of movies, consumer goods, and advertisements. It also takes place at an institutional level, through the practices and management of the malls. In defining consumer groups as particular targets, retailers' considerations of class are explicitly and implicitly inflected with gender and sexuality, particularly through a focus on the family. Tokyu Department Store imagined its ideal consumers to be young families, "especially couples," heterosexual pairs, according to the chief executive. Other retail sites try to "lure . . . trendy family people" and "capture families and working-class people," offering "a one-stop shopping campaign aimed at families." Robinson's Department Store philosophy is "total family happiness," while those at Pata say, "We try to provide an environment here that will attract the whole family to spend as much time as possible on our premises. We want them to feel at home." Thailand's *Business Review* noted that shopping centers "offer fun for all members of the family. Not only are mothers satisfied with the choice of household items, food, and clothes, but fathers may also enjoy themselves in other sections such as sports, books and music, while the children can have fun in the amusement area or in the toy section."[43]

This family-focused strategy reflects the orientation of department stores to households, heterosexual families, and adults. Shopping complexes offer recreational activities for couples and families through cinemas, playgrounds, even ice skating rinks and miniature zoos. Commercial leisure invites consumers by providing what it calls family entertainment, particularly with amusement parks, which at least eight shopping centers offered in the 1990s, including the Leo Land amusement and water park on the roof of a branch of Central. These additions, which represented high investments but usually low returns, were considered crucial to draw in suburban families.[44] Even downtown MBK constructed its Magic Land amusement center on the eighth floor, although it was never successful. To draw in Thais at leisure and insert commerce into their social lives, companies rely on concepts of "family" and courtship that are not timeless and traditional but emerge through and in relation to commercial discourses and institutions. As Maila Stivens notes for industrializing Asia, "The development of elaborate new femininities based on the consumer/wife/mother and the consumer/beautiful young woman in the region can be seen as central to the very development of these burgeoning economies."[45]

Capitalism shapes the "nonmarket" realm of domestic life by staging urban kinship relations, including courtship, marriage, and parent-child relations. The historian Kathy Peiss has documented how, for the early twentieth-century U.S. working class, the emergence of affordable commercial recreation reformulated gender identities and social relationships. She proposes that forms of entertainment such as the dancehall, amusement arcade, and boardwalk changed the venues for, and importance of, leisure for the working class. These venues supplanted women's homosocial, female-centered social worlds and kin-based identities with more heterosocial worlds, pairing more young women and men in romantic and sexual relations. This entertainment fostered greater social freedom, heterosexually, than was available in the confines of the household. Such freedom, however, introduced heterosexual modes dependent upon commercial establishments.[46]

I see evidence in Bangkok of a pattern similar to the rise of a "heterosocial" world through early twentieth-century American working-class pastimes. Conventionally in Thailand, private heterosexual relations were subsumed within mixed-gender groupings.[47] Now, in the malls, there are more male-female Thai couples strolling together, holding hands and displaying affection. While reflecting norms of transnational commerce, the heterosocial dating found in malls is actually unconventional in Thai society. Such displays of intimacy are noteworthy because public affection between men and women is still considered somewhat taboo, although less and less in the city. These heterosexual hand-holders are appropriating commercial spaces for a new expression of relationship and identity, one that suits, and is indeed encouraged by, the mall. The sexual expression is subdued in these performances but represents—particularly for women—a departure from standard norms.

Capitalist markets present multiple and often contradictory norms of heterosexuality, however. As Tokyu Department Store celebrates young nuclear families, MBK revels in eroticized interpretations of male-female relations, particularly interpretations of women's comportment. Representationally, there is a rupture between sexualized passion and the young couples oriented to reproduction and domestic life. The explicitly sexualized vision found in the shopping mall contradicts elite narratives of courtship and marriage as well as rural conventions. New modes of heterosexual kinship, articulated by department store management in terms of young families, are juxtaposed with an eroticized (rather than reproductive) interpretation of male-female relations in the adjacent mall.

The mall's spectacular diversity allows for, perhaps fosters, alternative modes of sex/gender. The presence of tom, who transgress gender and sexual norms for women, makes clear that commercial (or kinship or state) norms are not necessarily realized in people's practices in a straightforward or top-down manner and also that mall-goers selectively interpret, and at times contradict, prevailing norms. In their consumption of transnational commercial culture—that is, in tom, dee, and heterosexual women's practices in the context of the infrastructure and discourses of consumer culture—these young Thai women recast conventions for social positioning and relationships, helping to generate new modes of gender and sexual affiliations.

TOM AND CONSUMER CULTURE

The presence of tom and dee in Bangkok malls continues in the gendered nature of recreation. The leisure practice of tom, more than heterosexual dating, follows the convention of homosociality: of women socializing together, rather than male-female couples in heterosociality. The fact that tom and dee reproduce long-standing norms for young people's same-sex intimacy in part explains the frequent lack of family censure. Indeed, these pairings may be less problematic than heterosexual pairings. Because same-sex physical affection is the norm in Thailand and because of the preponderance of same-sex leisure, tom-dee romantic couples walk hand-in-hand or sit entwined, camouflaged in a way that they would not be in most of the Anglophone world. This invisibility in part explains the lack of attention to female homosexual relations in Thailand and many similarly homosocial countries. Tom and dee enjoy the anonymity provided by an overflowing urban mall. They do not attract attention or commentary strolling along or shopping in stores, but blend in among the mavens of heavy, young professional, or hip-hop styles.

Tom and dee courtship re-creates homosocial traditions, drawing on prevailing cultural discourses about love and romance, which are heterosexual and often commercial. Some observers have suggested that, in the United States, particularly in the years before the gay and women's liberation movements, butch lesbians of the 1950s emulated ideals for heterosexual masculinity more closely than men did, since the butches derived their models more consistently from idealized representations of romance and gender, such as those found in Hollywood movies.[48] A similar process seems to be underway in Thailand, where definitions of gallantry and courtliness—opening doors for ladies, offering flowers or Valentine's Day gifts—are presented in American movies or in Japanese cartoon images of young romance found on stationery. At the same time as the sex/gender system of the tom and dee is predicated on homosocial patterns of leisure, tom-dee relationships are also shaped by discourses of heterosexuality. These relationships and identities realize same-sex recreation and (heterosexual) romance in a new form. Intimate exchanges (for example, of the gifts and cards that MBK sells in abundance) recast homosocial bonds among women friends in romantic or erotic ways. Thus, the tom's presence in the mall occurs in conjunction with, not despite, the prevailing heterosexual codes of consumer culture and public culture in Thailand.[49]

Instead of seeing the tom and dee as simply taking advantage of the relative freedom of the shopping mall to realize their identities, I consider how these identities flourish in a consumer culture that generally enshrines heterosexual norms. To use the classic performance metaphor, the mall functions as a theater providing imagery and scripts, props, and space for enactment of relational identities that are especially significant to women.[50] Consumers realize various identities through commercial venues, using consumer goods and drawing on the imagery of capitalist popular culture and commercial marketing campaigns. Enacting social identity through market economies, they reformulate definitions of the female gender. Heterosexuals, tom, and dee draw on romantic imagery from a variety of sources: from transnational commerce (or "modernity") as well as from Thai conventions (or "tradition"). Heterosexual dating transforms sociality from groups (usually single-sex) into conjugal coupling, which seems increasingly sexual. Tom combine a relatively recent, consumer-based transnational romantic model with Thai homosocial practices. In other words, it is the version of romance, not the same-sex character, that is "imported" in the tom and dee phenomenon.

Interestingly, English informs the contemporary expression of intimacy in Bangkok: "take care" and "I love you" are common utterances. These derive from exposure to foreign visitors (sex workers use a wide range of English relational phrases) and from international texts, including advertising and consumer goods. I heard Thai women use the term *spec* to describe their specifications about what kind of partner they wanted (in general, the final criterion was someone nice). In a conversation about identity with the lesbian group Anjaree, one woman identified herself as neither tom nor dee but rather "two in one," she said, borrowing the English marketing slogan for a shampoo-conditioner.

Constructing a tom persona through one's appearance also relies on commercial products as much as it does on postures or attitudes, and in this way the tom role, as with other identities, takes place through commerce. Living as a "real" Thai woman requires as much construction through commodities—probably more, given exacting standards of femininity and the growing importance of cosmetics, pantyhose, and hair-care products for Thai femininity. But tom's and tom-dee couples' articulation with commercial gender and sexual codes from image-laden consumer culture differs from that of heterosexual women and gay men because urban consumer culture offers one of the few significant social arenas available to them.

In an interview with an MBK visitor that I undertook with Sila (the reluctant tom and former Avon Lady whom I discuss in chapter 5), we spoke to a twenty-eight-year-old college student, a tom, who often came on weekends from her home in Thonburi, across the river, to shop, eat, and stroll at the mall. She liked buying clothes from MBK and the adjoining Bonanza Mall because they sold "new, modern" apparel: at that moment, she was in fact wearing a black shirt from Bonanza and Nike shoes from MBK. She also liked the mall because it was fun to walk around and was convenient (when you're hungry, there's food). That day she had come to rendezvous with a sweetheart (faen). She explained that it was normal to be with her and walk around holding hands at MBK, because that mall was full of such couples; other stores had some (she mentioned Central's Lardprao branch), but MBK had a lot.

The tom identity achieved a certain prominence in the mid-1980s, in part because of their increasing use of, and presence in, urban consumer culture. Two very popular pop singers of this period were known to be tom: Alice and especially Anchalee. Anchalee, according to a recent interview, "came across as pure butch and was a major influence on at least half the teens attending all-girls schools."[51] The representation of foreign lesbians matters less to most Thai tom or dee. For example, while the Canadian pop singer k. d. lang's "coming out" was significant on many fronts in North America, it was mainly irrelevant to Thai consumers or to Thai tom, although the news that k. d. lang was a tom was reported in a Bangkok music magazine. A Thai company used one of her songs for a TV commercial when the use of an out lesbian's music would have been daring in the United States or Canada. During the period of my fieldwork, another Thai tom pop singer, Om, became the darling of the 1990s teenybopper set. Girls bought laminated wallet-sized photos of her and of male heartthrobs from stalls in MBK. Pop singers' tom style was important to tom and to young female fans. A concert video showed scores of young women screaming when Om entered the stage. These crushes attracted little attention and were taken for granted as part of popular culture in Thailand, but they reinforce the link between the tom-dee identities and consumer culture.

In the 1990s, fashion magazines occasionally featured layouts with boyish, or at least short-haired, women, inspired by the images of necktied, suited women that crop up in international and Western media. In contexts of compulsory or presumed romantic heterosexuality and heterosexual norms of femininity, the availability of the image of female masculinity can offer significant information and inspiration for tom and pleasure for dee.[52] In some cases, ideals of tom style drew on commercial culture. Hence, tom role models validate and educate as much as explicit discussions about tom or lesbianism do. Commodity images, such as the pop star, can and do fulfill this purpose.

In a 1997 interview, the 1980s pop star Anchalee renounced her tom past in favor of new Christian morality.[53] Anchalee presented her earlier tom appearance as both mistaken identity and as an insignificant style that became almost a brand: "'People always think of me as a *tom*. But I've always felt more comfortable in really casual clothes. I wear jeans, a man's shirt. It's my character. When I released the first album and it did well, I had to stay with that character because that's how people wanted to see me. I needed a style of my own,' says Anchalee who today no longer has that tomboy look."[54]

Anchalee's explanation of her earlier persona resonates with a pervasive association between tom and modern styles. In practice and in the public eye, the tom identity is intertwined with modernity, perceived as one symbol of the (negative) changes underway in Thai society. In public discussion, the existence of tom is sometimes ascribed to "fashion" (using the English word), meaning that youth adopt the identity as a cute and au courant style and that, of course, it is temporary. Thai gay men told me that the prevalence of tom in public is due to fashion, although they never said this about gay men. At the time MBK was opening, a Thai women's magazine wrote, "The world of fashion is the source of this problem. The *tom-dee* fashion is disseminating everywhere. Many young women are leaping onto the new fashion band-wagon."[55]

One obvious implication of tom-as-fashion is to render it asexual: the tom we see are not motivated by sexual desire for other women, the interpretation goes, but by style. Such an asexual interpretation of tom fits nicely with the norms for female sexuality. But it also points to a distinction made between surface style and real identity. Practicing tom themselves differentiate among tom performances. As Sila said of this kind of tom, "They're not real, they're just dressing like that." But the reading of surface style and the link with fashion also associate tom with commercial and Western modernity. This association differs from the equation of homosexuality with Western modernity; tom and tom-dee are seen as a stage that some young women go through because it is fashionable in contemporary urban culture and a reflection of the increasing materialist orientation of younger generations.

Despite—or perhaps as a by-product of—the pervasive display of heterosexuality in consumer culture, a display of tom style is to be found in the malls: among the pedestrians, in depictions of masculinity, and in the occasional tomboyish image appearing in pop music and glamour magazines. Observing people, images, and fashions provides would-be tom with an education in tom style and a shopping list. Malls and markets offer a display of tom in person, in the existence of tom consumers and sellers and in men's fashions and the occasional tomboyish styles available for women.

Tom and dee integrate themselves in existing spaces and occasions. Generally, they do not seek out a broader group of other tom and dee to create "community" defined by orientation and gender. In keeping with the patterns of women's social relationships, most tom have developed little community beyond local friendship networks, a situation perpetuated by the lack of explicit tom (or even female) commercial leisure. The organization of "women who love women," Anjaree, was founded in Bangkok during the 1980s economic boom by women who were involved in women's organizations. It subsequently grew to a large cross-class organization with groups in every province.[56] Anjaree provides an important clearinghouse for tom, dee, and women who love women, but it has not saturated the small localized networks of tom and dee.

Overall, tom and dee lack the usual resources associated with organized resistance. They use contemporary consumer culture, which itself propounds a specific model of romantic, increasingly sexual, heterosexuality. This pervasive imagery reinterprets local compulsory heterosexuality in an open, yet hegemonic, form. In general, Thai women enact a sexualized and romanticized heterosexual script while continuing homosocial leisure practices, at times in a transformed mode of tom-dee. The enactment of gender scripts through folk and market economies creates uneven or incomplete reproductions of homosociality and heterosexuality.

To summarize the interaction of consumer culture and the tom identity: because malls produce a diversity of consumers to match the diversity of goods and services, they allow for, and even promote, a populist inclusion of different styles. The promotion of eroticized heterosexual imagery in these malls legitimates and inspires youth romance, dating, and sexual relations in relation to cosmopolitan modernity. This dimension, the instruction in romance and erotic desire, impacts the homosocial tom-dee relations by providing a context resonating with erotic and romantic discourses, which allow intimate homosocial relations also to be interpreted along these lines. By defining social identity in relation to consumption, malls underwrite the construction of a variety of personae, including the tom role, through the democracy of consumption.

MBK, department stores, and go-go bars all offer influential spaces for the realization of modern sexual and gender identities. Grounded in real estate and corporate economies, the consumer pluralism of the mall allows for, perhaps fosters, tom-dee and heterosexual expressions at the same time as it reinforces an economic citizenship predicated on consumption. The operations of the shopping mall and the preponderance of tom in its spectacular spaces illustrate some of the ways that the market economy articulates with and affects sexual and gender identities. Bangkok's retail revolution has underwritten identities that transgress gender and sexual norms yet are constrained and shaped by the infrastructure, discourses, and operations of the capitalist market economy.

This chapter has explored young women's sexual "deviance"— commercial, heterosexual, and homosexual—in relation to the expanse of the market economy in Bangkok. Just as a public conception of Thai female identity has come to be linked with domestic familial or heterosexual feminine consumption, so too is female sexual excess configured in relation to excesses of commercialization and materialism. In the next two chapters, I explore the personnel behind transnational markets (in a cable TV office and direct sales), considering the different ways these "professional" marketers attempt to negotiate a modern Thai entrepreneurial identity, which is at once appropriate and mobile, cosmopolitan and Thai.

CHAPTER FOUR

The Flexible Citizens
of IBC Cable TV

In January 2001, a prominent businessman and politician, Police Lt. Col. Thaksin Shinawatra, Ph.D., was elected prime minister as head of the Thai Rak Thai (Thais Love Thai) Party. Thaksin (or Taksin) Shinawatra, with his wife, founded one of the largest and most powerful telecommunication empires in Asia in the 1980s, the Shinawatra Computer and Communications Group (SC&C), generally known as Shinawatra. Among its many subsidiaries was a subscriber television company known by three English initials, IBC. During a year of IBC's boom-era growth in the early 1990s, I worked part-time at its marketing office. This site offers a view of one of the leading "modern" conglomerates in Thailand and an inside look at the mundane operations of transnational markets in media, information technology, and telecommunications. In this chapter I explore the intimate economies—the identities, relationships, and cultural affiliations—involved in Shinawatra, in the figure of Thaksin, and in the work and affiliations of some the professional marketers operating in the background of Thailand's globalization.

Media mogul and statesman, Thaksin exemplifies Thailand's modernizing economy, representing a new mix of government and business, of transnational, Thai, and Sino-Thai identifications. He is the most powerful and best known of the "culturally flexible corporate subjects" of

Thailand. These are the executives, managers, and professional workers at the upper echelons of Asian economies, who travel across national boundaries and cultural worlds fluidly, as described by Aihwa Ong in *Flexible Citizenship*. They are the stars of most contemporary media depictions of globalization.[1]

Most of the workforce in the global corporation does *not* undertake this high-level executive or managerial work, however. The success of Thaksin's corporation is underwritten by the labor of a range of workers who face the possibilities and limits posed by the intersection of transnational and local forces in markedly different ways from the leading players of the global economy. In this chapter, I consider the relatively new, sizable group of professional workers who staff companies like IBC and Shinawatra. Such industries require people who can design and operate technology, create products, manage modern workplaces, and sell to—or create—new consumer markets. This work is done by "knowledge" workers, many from the new middle classes and many of whom are women. As more or less cosmopolitan Thais—"flexible corporate subjects" in their familiarity with international culture—they are essential to the company's traffic with telecommunications and the information highway. As professional marketers, they embody a different role from that of the historical sellers in Thailand, especially the ethnic Chinese merchants or lower-class Thai women vendors. They represent the kinds of worldly identities that are required by and, to some extent, produced by the market in transnational culture and the corporate forms that traffic in the new technologies of globalization.

SHINAWATRA

The Shinawatra corporation represents the pinnacle of modernization of Thai corporations: its products (cell phones, pagers, and mainframes), its significant role in building and privatizing the national infrastructure, and its business strategy of decentralized operations all signal the cutting edge of a modern economy in Thailand. Although a Thai business, the corporation displays transnational qualities and is active across Southeast Asia and beyond. The company's slogans, keywords, and pitches reflect U.S.-based international corporate discourse. Terms such as *reengineering, globalization,* and *business concept development* (BCD) all appeared in English or Thai in the pages of Shinawatra publications. Most of the company's divisions and products have had English names, such as Symphony, Matchbox, and IBC, and its yellow-pages phonebook is described in English as the Encyclopedia of Buying. What the company sells is global culture and technology. When IBC was in operation, most of its content came from beyond Thai borders—from CNN, Hong Kong movies, and HBO among others. As a Shinawatra publication notes, "With the advanced communication technology of today's Information Age, distance is no longer an obstacle."[2] Shinawatra appears to be a generic version of a transnational system that happens to be housed in Bangkok.

Yet Shinawatra is a Thai company, and this locality is intrinsic to the functioning of the firm. As many ethnographic investigations of globalization have shown, transnational phenomena are far more grounded and localized than prevailing images of borderless worlds or homogeneous Westernized culture make them appear.[3] The prevailing corporate form in Thailand is not the Western-based multinational corporation but, in fact, a hybrid form, created by Sino-Thai business families' strategic responses to shifting domestic, regional, and global contexts. In this way, the cosmopolitan empire of Shinawatra remains quite local. Based on family money and local investments, it operates in relation to national and regional laws and social conditions. Shinawatra is grounded in Thai and Asian networks, in domestic consumer markets, and in a local workforce. A brief overview of the origins and growth of the company and the strategies of its founder, Thaksin, shows how the development of a modern, global firm unfolded within local conditions and involved local relationships and identifications, an ethnic and kin-based economy similar to that of Central's department store, Mah Boonkrong, and other Sino-Thai family firms.[4]

Though the corporation has gone through several incarnations and changed its name three times, it has been firmly associated with Thaksin and the Shinawatra family. Thaksin hails from a well-known Sino-Thai family in Chiang Mai, the descendants of a nineteenth-century male immigrant from China with the surname of Coo. His son, Chiang Coo, worked as a cotton weaver and traded textiles between northern Thailand and colonial Burma. He started a silk weaving and dying business in 1929 and then a silk factory. During this time, in the midst of Thai nationalist policies, the Coo family changed their name to Shinawatra. Chiang's children (Thaksin's grandfather's generation) continued silk manufacturing while expanding into bus lines, real estate, movie theaters, and politics. Thaksin's father, Boonlerd, was a successful businessman, and his uncle Suraphan was a politician who became a deputy minister when provincial politicians gained more power at the national level. The Shinawatra family also was probably immersed in the northern creole Sino-Thai community. Evidence for this affiliation is suggested by the name of Thaksin, which is from the half Chinese king who founded the new capital in Siam and which is used more by Sino-Thais than ethnic Thais.[5] The Coos/Shinawatras, already active transnationally in the region, parlayed provincial, cross-border, and ethnic links into a familial power base.

As in many success stories in Sino-Thai business families, Thaksin excelled both in enterprise and at school. Educated in his family's businesses, at sixteen he was managing a movie theater (presumably his family's). He was the top graduate of the police cadet school in 1973 and won a state scholarship to study abroad, earning graduate degrees from the United States. In 1974, he married his wife, Potjaman (or Potjamarn) Damapong, who joined him in Texas, where she worked at a job; they had a son and two daughters.[6] Back in Thailand, Thaksin became a police lieutenant colonel and worked in the police department for fourteen years. One of his responsibilities was overseeing the department's computer systems. While a civil servant, Thaksin also began investing in several businesses, including a profitable movie distribution company in Chiang Mai and a failed condominium project in Bangkok.

In 1983, Thaksin and Potjaman founded Shinawatra Computer Service and Investment (SC), selling mainframe computers and software to the Thai police department and government. (The collaborative nature of this business is typically forgotten in accounts of the firm, which often fail to mention Potjaman's role in building it.) After Thaksin left government work, the company expanded its operations to include mobile phones, pagers, data technologies, and IBC Cable TV, which began broadcasting two channels in Bangkok in 1989.[7]

Over the last few decades, numerous Sino-Thai businesses have shifted family wealth into new investments, away from manufacturing and retail and toward the growing areas of real estate and high-tech telecommunications. Thaksin chose high tech. Shinawatra catered to the technological infrastructure of a growing economy, providing computer, satellite, and fiber optic technologies to governments and businesses and new consumer technologies to wealthy and middle-class denizens of Bangkok and the provinces. Shinawatra was the emblem of globalization, characterized by technology, urban consumption, the growth of global markets and the global factory, and the reconfiguration of state-business relationships. This transnational telecommunication empire emerged through the interactions of family capital, domestic businesses, national government, and international networks.

In building the corporation, Thaksin combined his Sino-Thai base (and capital) with government connections. His start in telecommunications took advantage of access to state spending. As one business writer notes, "Connections with government circles were the key to his success and subsequent wealth,"[8] connections that included his uncle, well-placed in the national government, the police department, and colleagues at the Communications Authority. Thaksin was expert in winning government concessions, typically with a clause allowing a long-term monopoly in the field. (In Cambodia, he momentarily held a ninety-nine-year monopoly for IBC Cable TV.) Shinawatra benefited from the privatization of government-controlled telecommunication industries, which allowed for generous licensing terms, control of Thailand's satellite, and a monopoly on its transmissions to the country.[9] Given the centrality of the government to this field, it is not surprising that Thailand's information-technology sector as a whole has exhibited strong links to politics; in the 1992 elections, telecommunication firms made more donations to parties than finance or industry did. Shinawatra expanded in the region by negotiating with the Laotian, Vietnamese, Cambodian, Indian, and Philippine governments and has undertaken joint projects with U.S. and multinational corporations.[10]

Shinawatra's relations with the Thai state and neighboring governments signal the changing boundaries between state governments and businesses taking place in Southeast Asia and worldwide. Aihwa Ong concludes that, under globalization, governments now exhibit a "graduated sovereignty" in which they "cede more of the instrumentalities connected with development as a technical project to global enterprises"; that is, Asian governments delegate the project of national economic development to business (although they "maintain strategic controls over resources, populations, and sovereignty").[11] Shinawatra has taken over the government role of developing Thailand's technological infrastructure. Its annual reports and other corporate texts cast the company as the gateway between the world and Thailand and the key to "accelerating the Kingdom's development as a whole."[12] Winning the contract to build Thailand's first communication satellite in the 1990s "meant that Shinawatra . . . would represent Thailand" worldwide while also enhancing the company's domestic reputation and access to credit.[13] The Shinawatra empire constructed itself as the two-way broker between Thailand and the globalizing world, representing Thailand's modernity in the region (and in orbit) and transferring transnational knowledge and resources into the nation.[14]

The cable television concern, IBC, headed by Potjaman, was just one corner of this vast corporate empire. The IBC company slogan read, "We

Bring the World into Your Home." Its profit derived mainly from sub-scribers paying for having the world brought to them in the form of tel-evision programming.[15] IBC's cable television outfit repackaged and translated transnational media and cultural forms alongside Thai pro-gramming for local consumption. It sold five channels of twenty-four-hour programming, which was considered of higher quality than "free TV," the regular television channels owned by branches of the state. Al-most all of IBC's programming came from elsewhere, purchased from media network distributors: little content was actually produced by IBC itself. (A Shinawatra division, Symphony, produced *Trendsetters*, a lifestyle show, *Bangkok Catwalk*, a fashion show featuring local designers, and IBC's promotional spots.) The main work of IBC was selecting, repackaging, and selling a bundle of round-the-clock entertainment and information. Not incidentally, IBC lent the luster of Hollywood, CNN, and interna-tional sports events to the parent Shinawatra corporation, which was ap-parent in the ample use of American and international media images in the company's annual report. As a business, however, IBC did not prove hugely profitable.

MIDDLE-CLASS CONSUMERS

The Shinawatra corporation grew by marketing "the world" first to the Thai police force, followed by the Thai state and business elites, and then a wider swath of Bangkok's and the nation's population—the "new rich" and the diverse middle class enhanced by economic growth in the 1980s. *Middle class* is a catch-all term ("a residual class category") that includes a wide range of incomes, jobs, and subclasses (including professional, technical, administrative, executive, managerial, clerical, service, and sales categories). The new middle classes in Thailand are a product of the ex-panding market economy, generated by the need of businesses like Shi-nawatra for workers with professional, technical, and cultural qualifi-cations and for a consumer market to buy their goods.[16]

Management understood IBC's main consumer base to be this Thai market,[17] increasingly interpreted as average and common; in this way, it understood "Thai," particularly provincial Thai, as a market niche. According to company records, average viewers were the middle-class urban Thai family.[18] While many working-class people owned televisions, the cost of subscribing placed most viewers among the relatively well to do. At that time, the total start-up for all five channels for one TV set was the equivalent of about U.S.$300, and monthly fees were nearly U.S.$40.[19] Almost half of IBC subscribers earned more than U.S.$1,600 a month compared with many professional workers' salaries of below U.S.$1,000 a month; my IBC coworkers, for example, earned about U.S.$400 monthly in 1993.[20] Most of IBC's young knowledge workers did not subscribe to IBC; as ever-practical Bee, who developed IBC's print ads, pointed out, IBC programming is censored, and you could easily buy an uncensored, inexpensive pirated video version on the street. Nonetheless, lower-paid workers partook of widespread consumer markets in transnational media and technologies that Shinawatra cultivated.

The ability to appeal to "average" middle-class Thais was critical to IBC's growth in Bangkok and especially when it expanded services to the provinces of Thailand.[21] Language was an important part of this populist appeal. IBC Cable TV began by broadcasting two English-language channels, but once Thai-language programming began, subscriptions soared. Most of the English-language movies, American television series *(Beverly Hills 90210, Roseanne)*, the cartoons, and Hong Kong imports— most imported programming (besides news)—were broadcast with two soundtracks, original and dubbed in Thai (reception of which required special equipment). Movies were subtitled in Thai. To repackage international material for Thai-speaking audiences, IBC hired freelance translators for the subtitles and employed in-house teams for dubbing. International media therefore undergo a process of localization for the Thailand market.

Ong suggests that the corporate role in cultural life is connected to the ways that globalization and privatization have changed governments. She suggests that Asian governments are letting "market rationality" take over more of the "cultural regulation of society—especially of the middle classes," through the ways that it regulates workers and through the invisible limits on (i.e., the apolitical nature of) consumer culture.[22] In this light, Thaksin's investments both in information technologies *and* in the technologies of middle-class culture, like the former IBC Cable TV, represent a reassignment of state powers to the market economy. Commercial media play a crucial role in defining Thai national identity and in educating Thais in global citizenship, for example, through IBC's broadcast of international financial news and CNN alongside Thai programming. It is not accidental that children's educational programming, including early instruction in English, is an important part of privatized subscriber television on the weekends. Brokering transnational flows for Thailand in these ways, corporate institutions influence intimate spheres of life for Thai consumers, as I showed in the previous discussion of shopping malls.

If consumers' intimate arenas are intertwined with transnational markets, what of the personnel working in the businesses that are globalizing Thailand? How does packaging and selling global culture in Thailand involve and shape the affiliations of those who do it? In the next section, I consider the intimate economies of one of the elite "flexible citizens" in Thailand, Thaksin Shinawatra, followed by some his employees, the "knowledge workers" in IBC Cable TV. Going behind the scenes of the hybrid corporate-kin Shinawatra conglomerate, I show how participants' identities and relationships are formed at the intersections of domestic and international social worlds and the juncture of capitalist and folk economies.

THAKSIN SHINAWATRA

Thaksin's person exemplifies the changing social worlds of Thailand. He embodies the transformation from Chinese merchant to ethnic Chinese tao kae businessman to "Thai" tycoon, representing the Thai nation in the region and on the global stage. His management style, as described by the business press, recalls Central Department Store's Samrit Chirathivat: "Thaksin likes to hear opinions and suggestions and encourages his team to speak up and reach the same strategy."[23] (This management style did not appear to filter down to the middle levels of IBC, however.) Even more than the second generation of Chirathivat businessmen, Thaksin represents a new mode of elite Sino-Thai masculinity, the cosmopolitan tycoon who productively combines corporate, state, and kinship connections. He shows himself at home with transnational cultural codes, a demonstration of his cultural and ethnic flexibility. A Sino-Thai boy from the provinces who rose to power in the nation's capital, Thaksin proved himself fluent in multiple social worlds within Thailand as well.

The fact that the former police lieutenant Thaksin became involved in business is hardly startling in Thailand, where government and military figures have been included on Sino-Thai company boards since the 1950s. What is interesting is that Thaksin consolidates in his person the two interest groups involved in business: the militarized Thai state—typically the realm of Thai men—and Sino-Thai commercial families. His connections to the government dating to his school days and civil service allowed him to assimilate smoothly into realms historically associated more with ethnic Thais than with Sino-Thai populations.

Entering politics in 1994, Thaksin followed his uncle into a domain that had long been virtually monopolized by ethnically Thai men. He adopted a populist stance, expressing concern with poverty and rural issues, and promised to clean up politics from the corruption for which it was famous. Not without controversy, he took a place on the slate of the reformist Buddhist party, Phalang Dharma, headed by the ascetic, vegetarian, former governor of Bangkok. Thaksin then headed the newly formed Thai Rak Thai Party. In January 2001, despite scandals about his assets, he easily won the race for prime minister. Thus, crossing business and government, Sino-Thai and Thai worlds, and domestic and transnational arenas, Thaksin combined a tycoon persona with a nationalist Thai identity—a Thai-loving Thai—positioning himself as a key facilitator in the nation's negotiations with the processes of global-ization, for example, brokering linkages between Thai businesses and global capital after the Asian economic crisis. Thaksin individually em-bodies the strategic flexibility of the corporation.

However transnationally oriented, Thaksin and his corporation remain embedded in specific networks of kin and associates. As with Central De-partment Store and other Sino-Thai family empires, many of the people filling executive roles of Shinawatra companies have been closely con-nected with Thaksin. His wife and brother-in-law, in particular, have oc-cupied positions of power and have controlled a good share of Shina-watra's assets: Mrs. Potjaman Shinawatra, for example, was president of SC&C and director of IBC. (Typical of the gendered accounts of kin-based firms, an article describes Thaksin's wife as "of help in running Shinawatra when he is focusing on politics.")[24] Together, the couple owned roughly U.S.$204 million in cash and more than U.S.$2 billion in total assets in the mid-1990s, including holdings in the Grand Cayman Islands and the state of Delaware.[25]

The kind of hybrid corporation that Shinawatra represents is not without its critics inside Thailand and internationally. While Thaksin's business operations underwrote his political success and bid for prime minister, they also provided a constant source of critique and friction, particularly in terms of ongoing commentary about the familial nature of the Shinawatra corporation and the misleading nature of his and Pot-jaman's assets, including enormous "loans" to family members. (For ex-ample, the year of his election, their maid's reported income made her one of the wealthiest people in Thailand, having suddenly had Shinawatra stock listed in her name. Thaksin explained the stock transfer as a mis-take.) There was concern that if Thaksin were to hold political office, he would still maintain control of the businesses through his wife and brother-in-law, a clear conflict of interest. When, after being elected prime minister, Thaksin was investigated and tried over questions of his accounts, the case focused on the role of his wife's businesses and assets. (Thaksin was found not guilty.)

The 1997 Asian economic crisis radically altered the climate for Thai-based businesses (i.e., for those that did not close). Shinawatra was not destroyed by the crisis, because most of its loans were from local Thai banks rather than flighty international money, and thus benefited from Thaksin's close associations with bankers and politicians. With mounting criticisms of "crony capitalism" (a label that points to the enduring place of kinship and ethnic ties in such businesses, as previously noted) and with Thaksin's increasing prominence as a politician, the corporation changed its title to the Shin Corporation in an effort to distance it from the family name and restructured its board in the name of "transparency."[26] Overall Shinawatra has been considered professionally run. Professionalizing family firms means redrawing the border between capitalist and kin economies, thereby changing the intimate economies of the market economy. Hence, part of this restructuring meant reducing the formal role Thaksin's wife, Potjaman, who gave up chairmanship of the company. At the same time, professionalization allows for the participation of other women professionals at high ranks. In the course of pursuing a noncrony-capitalist image, the new Shin Corporation divested itself of IBC Cable TV (headed by Potjaman), which became UBC through a merger with a subscriber television rival. Thaksin and Potjaman, who remained billionaires, continued to invest family money in new projects.

KNOWLEDGE WORKERS

Part of the "flexibility" of modernizing corporations like Shinawatra (contra the "centralizing" vision of earlier business ideals that influenced, among others, Central Department Store) lies with the impermanent and varying ways that they employ people, including subcontracting, part-time work, out-putting, subsidiaries, and other legal-financial arrangements.

Thaksin's corporation, Shinawatra, relies on the large semiconductor manufacturing industry in Southeast Asia, an industry that has famously employed the eyes and hands of young women in a new global division of labor, well-documented by feminist scholars.[27] Additionally, the offices of Shinawatra employ a variety of wage laborers, often through subcontracted service companies: male security officers, cleaning women, phone operators, delivery men, messengers, and serving staff. They represent the growing numbers of laborers, many from the northeast Isan region, who staff the lower levels of the service sector of Bangkok. At the IBC marketing office, one example of a subcontracted worker was the woman who prepared beverages and managed the kitchen. (She also sold Amway on the side, an example of marketing that I discuss in the next chapter.) In Bangkok's dizzying consumer culture, at the intersection of global capital and local economies, the members of this working class attempt to integrate new urban orientations with their rural community personae.[28]

The motor of firms like IBC and Shinawatra is its salaried knowledge workers: the managers, professionals, and white-collar employees. Their presence crystallizes a number of shifts in corporations, class, and culture in Bangkok. During the 1960s, to fill executive and management positions, international and "modern" companies in Thailand employed mostly foreigners, especially Westerners. This was especially true of the advertising business.[29] Firms like Shinawatra and Central continue to employ a number of "overseas experts" as high-level managers and consultants and low-level English writers and editors. The ranks of Bangkok's Western ex-patriot ("expat") community are filled with migrants from Europe, Australia, and North America, making their living at these types of work. But overall, this employment pattern has changed. Changes to Sino-Thai corporate economies have transformed the composition of business offices. Given language needs, a nationalist context, and lower wages, modernizing Thai corporations have increasingly drawn on Thai workers to fill technical and professional jobs. IBC's office reflected the shift in Sino-Thai business practice from relying almost exclusively on family or ethnic networks and Western expertise to drawing more on the emerging middle and professional classes of Thais.

At IBC, the constellation of professional workers represented a differentiated mix of backgrounds: minor royalty, business families, government functionaries, even people from the countryside, and a few farang, like myself. Some of these workers, such as Bee, emerged from Bangkok's Sino-Thai trading families: her family had sold dishware. Others, such as Kop and Noi, come from middle classes, often the children of government workers. A few emerged from the older Thai elite, the aristocracy now maintaining their social status through corporate channels: Wit is an example from this group. One or two temporary workers were the children of politically important figures. More of the office workers were women, and there were female executives and marketing managers at IBC—the marketing division was supervised by two women in turn during my term—but men occupied a disproportionate number of leadership roles and controlled the actual television programming. The demographic diversity points to the complexity of the new "middle class" and suggests that new professional affiliations are being forged in offices throughout Bangkok.

The task of the marketing office was to encourage new subscriptions, to keep current subscribers renewing, and to ensure IBC's image as the leading cable television provider. Marketing IBC was accomplished mainly through advertisements, publicity, promotions, and special offers. (Most of the day-to-day work at the hub of globalization was, I found, rather banal.) Kop handled promotions and special events; Noi, publicity and press; Wit, the television guide; and Bee, the advertising. To ensure regular coverage in the business press, Noi generated a never-ending stream of press conferences and press-oriented events at the prestigious new Shinawatra headquarters across town; one day we all helped her tie plastic strings into pom-poms for an event announcing a new sports show. IBC undertook a variety of promotions: sales on the cost of subscriptions, "special" screenings for subscribers (Madonna's "Girlie Show" concert), and tie-in promotions (for example, with Citibank and department stores). When I first joined IBC, Kop was developing a promotional contest (the grand prize, a trip to Australia) to accompany the launch of a new Batman cartoon dubbed in Thai. Advertising was placed in newspapers and print media. Bee developed IBC's advertising campaigns. She

worked with SC Matchbox, another Shinawatra company. IBC used a Shinawatra subsidiary, Rainbow Media, to design ads and contracted research
on television viewing patterns from one of Bangkok's twenty market-re-
search firms.[30] My official work, which was well paid relative to Thai
salaries, involved writing English descriptions for the programming
guide, marketing materials (such as a promotion for *The Lion King*), and
the company's promotional spots that were broadcast between shows. I
also served as consulting translator for English-language letters and faxes
to HBO-Singapore and the Batman people and so forth. Because people
knew I am an anthropologist, they made it a point to educate me on aspects of Thai folklore and customs, ranging from old superstitions to vulgar slang. Noi, of the pom-poms and press releases, particularly embraced
the role of informant.

As I show in the next sections, these workers' engagements with global
and Thai cultures illustrate the interaction between the changing market economy and intimate arenas in ways that are significantly inflected
with gender and sexual dimensions.

KOP AND WIT AS FLEXIBLE CITIZENS

Aihwa Ong's discussion of flexible citizens focuses on the Southeast Asian
descendants of the Chinese diaspora, such as Thaksin Shinawatra, who
were versed in Western business worlds and connected to governments
and networks that crossed Asia while operating strategically in Southeast Asia.[31] If Thaksin Shinawatra and other executives, managers, and
elite professionals of the Asian diaspora exemplified flexible citizens, IBC's
marketing staff can also be read as having been culturally flexible citizens
on a smaller scale. A mix of ethnic Thai and Sino-Thai, educated in international culture and technologies, they too traveled across national and
cultural boundaries with more or less fluidity, although with significant
differences. Here I consider two of the more cosmopolitan of IBC's
knowledge workers, the Anglophile Wit and the Americophile Kop, who
most resemble Ong's culturally flexible corporate subjects. I am inter-

ested not only in how they identified but also in how they understood
and used both their global and local affiliations. Kop and Wit, who got
along very well with each other, represent a new class of Thai knowledge workers schooled in foreign material and symbolic technologies.
Comparing how each applies his or her worldliness in their local settings
reveals how class, but also gender and sexuality, impact their negotiations
of the juncture between Thailand and the world.

Kop was in charge of special promotions for television shows and
movies. Her father was a civil servant, and she described her family as
comfortable. After attending a Thai college, Kop studied for an advanced
certificate in radio and video broadcast at an art school in the United
States. Among the staff, she was the one who knew the most about broadcast technology. Over one of our group lunches, at an outdoor northeast
(Isan) food stall, she discussed the merits of satellite and fiber optic developments in broadcast, preferring the clarity of the cable image. She
explained with some disdain that our company was not truly cable, as
billed.

Wit was minor royalty, his status indicated by a title at the front of
his name. His paternal grandmother was one of the daughters of King
Rama V (r. 1868–1910). His paternal grandfather was also a child of
Rama V (Wit noted the "incest" of half siblings marrying) but of a lower-
ranked wife; this lesser ancestor did not enter Wit's narrative except to
establish that half of his blood was royal.[32] He liked being royal, he said
(and clearly he enjoyed using his title), but he wanted the freedom to move
in and out of its worlds selectively. He did not appreciate the uptightness
associated with its events or protocol requirements. For Wit, royalty was
an appealing personal identity more than a structured social position.
Wit's mother was half Vietnamese; Wit thus calculated himself to be only
a quarter common Thai. (But when out with our colleagues, Wit identified as true Thai in contrast with being Western.) Wit went to England
for high school and technical college. He was part of an elite social cir-
cle in Bangkok, mingling with models, aristocrats, and other prominent
young Thais.

Wit identified with England, although in ways inflected with Americanisms. His royal identity was infused with a British cast, from his and his father's British education to his fountain pens and his ring and cigarette case engraved with the family crest. The first day I met him, for breakfast in the McDonald's below the modern office building in which IBC was then housed, he remarked, "Thailand is so bush." He fancied English turns of phrase and spelling. In a lifestyle magazine feature, which Kop teasingly read aloud, Wit was quoted as saying that he used to be a hippie, but now he prefers the "Gatsby style," invoking the American novel to describe a dapper British style. (He complained that the magazine put words in his mouth.)

Kop, on the other hand, was more oriented toward the United States, where she had studied for two years. She had a mastery of American slang and accent and would call to me, "Hey, man." One time, Barry Manilow appeared on the TV set playing at work. Kop dashed over and began singing along in best karaoke style, explaining, "I love Barry Manilow!" In the United States, she fancied New Jersey above all, for its shopping and desirable suburbs. She admired American dressing for the way clothes match in color and pattern.

These flexible citizens are comfortable in different cultural contexts. Interestingly, it is the most powerful flexible subjects, such as Thaksin, whose strategic orientation is Asia; in politics and business, they actively mobilize their connections in East and Southeast Asia. Thus, for significant projects, Asian states and elites represent the privileged transnational orientation. For most ordinary professionals, the touchstone remains the West, because the West is most relevant for providing the credentials and know-how to be competitive *within* Thailand. The well off try to prepare their children for this fluency by sending them to study abroad when possible—Australia, England, and increasingly the United States for university and even high school.

In Thailand, the foreign, the global, the Western, are not one homogeneous "other" but are affiliated with different inflections and applications for Thais. Ties to England, a long-standing orientation of the aristocracy, inform the symbolic elements of upper- and middle-class popular culture in Bangkok. In commercial visual culture, elite Thai history and tradition are often evoked through nostalgic sepia images from the British Empire, such as a brown-tinted photograph of wire glasses on a pile of leather-bound books. Thus, Thai history is imagined in dialogue with the British high colonial era in Asia. As the United States stepped into economic, technical, and popular culture dominance, it provided a reference point for the new middle classes in particular, such as Kop's family, as well as symbolizing modern modes of business and cutting-edge trends. England remains the aristocratic favorite.

Kop's ability to sing along with Barry Manilow and quote American popular culture and Wit's performance of Thai and English aristocratic culture with fountain pens, family crests, and sports cars were part of their informal résumé and class positioning. Wit applied the trappings of English colonial signifiers to reproduce his class and status position in Thai cultural hierarchies. Kop's skills in American English and cultural references helped her career and her urban credentials. They both parlayed their cultural flexibility into economic and social resources. Their use of foreign references reflects not only global hierarchies (such as the dominance of the Anglo West) but local hierarchies as well. Knowledge workers' ability to mobilize cosmopolitan discourses is significantly shaped by Thai contexts, particularly the enduring systems of class, status, and gender. Local constraints on worldliness are especially clear when the subject is sexuality.

SEX IN THE CITY

Sexuality crept into the informal banter and private conversations of the office.[33] When Boon, a gay man from Isan, joined our party, he injected a dose of playful commentary, for example, noting the appeal of the Amerasian movie star Keanu Reeves; one day he joked that he was Keanu's wife. When the office recognized someone's birthday, the celebration included a ribald birthday song that wishes the recipient to become a prostitute and her husband a pimp (to the tune of our "Happy Birthday"). Colleagues posted a handwritten sign saying "no flirting" by a popular woman's desk.

The content of IBC included its own share of eroticized materials, tame by American cable standards and censored for nudity and explicit sex. Shows like *Baywatch* and romantic movies included sexualized imagery that is taken for granted in Western urban cultures. Part of the modern cosmopolitan identity that goes along with marketing global culture involves a liberal attitude toward sexuality, one that perhaps fits with habitual Thai tolerance of others' behaviors. However, people's casual acceptance of sexual possibilities found in media or in a gay colleague's banter did not necessarily translate into open sexual freedom for them.

The intimate relations of family and romantic life provide the starkest contrast between Wit's and Kop's worldliness. One day, as Wit drove me in his red convertible MG to visit the subcontracted printers, he told me that when he was fifteen, his father bought him an appointment with an expensive prostitute, a model. His father told him what to do: you touch here, there. After the first time, the woman called Wit and showed him the red-light strip of Patpong, he said, laughing, and then they spent the night in a motel. His father said to him, "Far out, you're far out!" clearly pleased with his son's autonomous success. The story presented an update on a fairly common rite of passage for many Thai young men, where fathers and male relatives take a teenage boy to a brothel. It constructed male sexual expression as something not distinct from, but articulated with, parent-child relations.

On returning from England after schooling, Wit asked friends to introduce him to, as he said, "a clean girl, you know what I'm saying, a virgin" who was also shorter than he. A friend fixed him up with a biracial Thai-European model. Wit was then in his hippie, long hair, and drugs phase (before the Gatsby phase), and, he explained, she was not interested at first. Since then they had become constant companions. Even though she is Eurasian, Wit explained, she did not model in Europe, partly because of her height (she was considered too short), but also because she would have had to take off her clothes, and Wit would not allow that. Instead she modeled for products and magazines in Thailand; I saw her face in a number of magazines. (I once ran into her in the hip lane of bars near Patpong. Wit had not wanted to come. "He thinks too much," she said.) Wit's worldliness made him familiar with different regional notions of propriety, which is probably what encouraged him to talk to a Western female such as myself about explicit sexual matters. At the same time, his flexible citizenship did not seem to modify his understanding of the established double standards for male and female sexuality in Thailand.

When Kop returned from the United States, she told me, she was easily angered. The heat made her irritable, something I could sympathize with. It seemed that she was chafing at aspects of her life in Thailand, as many Thais who have lived abroad have reported. Kop's mother worried about her and was anxious that the time in the United States would damage Kop's well-being. She expressed this concern as the fear that Kop would become an atheist and go crazy. She enjoined Kop to become a lay nun for a few days, which meant living in the temple, following the basic eight Buddhist precepts, and generally adhering to the ascetic tempo of the monastic life. Kop did. Kop's and Wit's different reentries from the West into Thailand illustrate the ways men and women confront various family situations and public constraints, notably in the realm of sexual expression.

Not that Kop lacked an active social life. She would wheel her chair over to my desk to talk about her long-term boyfriend or her second special friend, an older policeman. (Speaking in English, she felt our neighbors, who were not nearly so fluent, would not follow the conversation.) She participated in the teasing office banter about romance and sexuality. She also told me that living away from home would be better because of privacy, because neighbors and such would not see whoever came to visit. One of the items Kop contemplated buying from colleagues selling for direct sales companies was a brown teddy and shorts ensemble she studied in a lingerie catalog.

Yet, in contrast to Wit's light-hearted and brash recollections, and like most Bangkok women I knew (including most sex workers), Kop was circumspect about her sexual experience and feelings. Even though she understood U.S. sexual mores, she never mentioned or even alluded to sexual relations as explicitly as Wit did, and she was willing to have me assume (or have me appear to assume) that she had never had them. (I was circumspect myself, and I may have missed clues about, or invitations to ask for, greater revelations. Or I may not yet understand the codes for discussing sexuality.)

Unlike Wit, Kop discussed her future plans in relation to her natal family and social judgment. Kop lived at home, like almost all of the professional women whose situations I knew about. Her father drove her to work, and her long-term boyfriend drove her home. Unmarried at twenty-eight, Kop said that marriage was "a big thing" that required a lot of thinking: sex is important, she said, but they had to think about money for a house, a car, a comfortable standard of living. Her main boyfriend was the son of a wealthy general who, she explained, "did well on investments." (The nature of these investments was not clear, but high-ranking military personnel often forged profitable arrangements with Sino-Thai companies.) Kop said that her boyfriend's mother looked down on her because, as child of a middle-class family, she was too poor. Particularly in weighing the potentiality of marriage, Kop considered the possibility that her boyfriend (i.e., her potential husband) was philandering or would, and she suspected him of having other girlfriends. She did not care whether her "special friend" dated other women; he was clearly in a different, nonmarriageable, category. Kop was thinking a lot about money, security, fidelity, and family.

Wit lived in his family's compound, which was a common practice among nobility and old-money families with large parcels of Bangkok land.[34] Yet while Wit lived in a separate house, his sister lived in the family home. Wit told me that he did not care so much about family— "they're going to die someday"—and was more focused on life with his girlfriend. His mother, herself not born of nobility, disapproved of the relationship because his girlfriend was not nobility, yet she did not interfere. However, she was strict with his sister, he noted.

Interestingly, despite Wit's rather convincing heterosexuality, he was sometimes the subject of teasing and gossip for "acting like a gay," perhaps because of his attention to clothes or his English affect. Indeed, Kop told me that Wit's royal grandfather had been reputed to be homosexual, noting that Wit had gay relatives. (Kop linked the ancestor's purported sexuality to his insanity, associating homosexuality with mental illness. Perhaps this association derives from her time in the United States, but a medicalized view of homosexuality had also been present in Thailand for some years.)[35] Thus in ways, Wit's aristocratic English-Thai identifications destabilized his Thai heterosexuality, at least in this new Americanized middle-class Thai milieu.[36] These insinuations did not seem to perturb him.

For Wit and Kop, class, gender, and sexuality informed each other. As a wealthy man, Wit was more mobile than Kop: driving his MG or Porsche around Bangkok, he could negotiate sexuality, work, residence, and future plans without as much thought to the obligations of attending to his family or to public commentary. The global cosmopolitanism to which Wit and Kop adhered involves a sense of worldly experience that includes an awareness of sexual diversity. IBC's popular culture abounded with references to sexual practices and identities, and, more generally, a contemporary worldly identity implies familiarity and comfort with sexual affairs. Such public displays of intimate life should not be read solely as modern or Western. In Wit's case, his surprising comfort at discussing his sexual history with me might reflect a long-standing erotic prerogative for aristocratic men, an entitlement to sexual pleasure and release, which is now a pervasive entitlement for Thai men in general (except when ordained as monks). Wit's display of sexuality is not necessarily a reflection of globality, in this case, but its expression takes place at the junctures of Thai and English elite, of Gatsby and Thai heterosexuality, and of Bangkok and the world. In Kop's case, her sexual expression was more contained, most likely circumscribed by Thai expectations for women and by the pressures of immediate social relationships of family and intimates (perhaps as well by the spirit world: Kop was attentive to spirit shrines at our office). Gender structured their navigations of transnational and domestic worlds more, in fact, than it appeared to shape the project of marketing cable television.

THE SEGMENTED AD

Discourses about gender and sexuality were pervasive yet muted at the IBC office. It was rare that promotions and press releases explicitly raised questions about gender. Even the most marked examples of gender in this work turned out to be less revealing about the symbolic construction of gender than about the nature of marketing global culture for these professional knowledge workers.

One day, Bee asked for feedback on a mock-up of an advertisement from several of us in the office. The text said, "and today IBC makes women extraordinary." The image was a painted sketch of a woman divided into four parts, like the drawing game called exquisite corpse in English: the head with a beret, the torso with a turtleneck, the legs with yellow pants and a hand holding a microphone, and on the feet, sherpa boots. It was intended to illustrate relevant shows of IBC: the English arts show (the beret), CNN fashion (the turtleneck), CNN news (the microphone), and travel shows (the boots).

Kop, Bee, Wit, and I discussed the image, invoking professional judgments and vocabulary but also more ad hoc commentary, giving our individual reactions. One immediate concern was the potentially repetitive or derivative nature of the form. Some pointed out that similar pastiche images had been used in other ads—for bed sheets, a hotel, and IBC itself, in a collage that combined U.S. president Bill Clinton's face with cartoon drawings.

We critics also assessed the formal qualities and visual effectiveness of the draft. The message was not clear, we said, and the picture was poor quality. Kop and Bee stressed the importance of visual, rather than textual, qualities in an advertisement: "You have to *see* it and understand, and it has to be attractive." Pointing to the artist's head and turtleneck, Kop joked that it could be more X-rated (*po*, indecent or erotically revealing). We proposed other possibilities: how about one showing "before" and "after" IBC? No, Bee balked at the idea of criticizing anybody with a negative "before" image. One of the group members asked, "Who is the market—who is the customer?" Bee explained, "It's working women, career women, who are interested in art, news . . . knowledge: women who know about these things." Kop, trying to be positive and not criticize anyone, suggested creating an image of a woman who looks happy with her life: modern, pretty, well dressed, and healthy. Bee reiterated the objective: the ad would pitch shows targeting women to the women's segment of the market, to "women who want to improve themselves."

When the ad's designer from Shinawatra's advertising subsidiary, SC Matchbox,[37] called, Bee said, "Don't even 'good afternoon' me [*may tong sawasdee*], because they aren't *buying* the ad." She said "buying" in English as well as "concept," "explain," and "attract." Ultimately, IBC executives did not run this ad. Instead, they chose to advertise Chinese movies, which, on the basis of their undeniable popularity with Thai viewers, were believed to involve a wider audience than the female market.[38] Most of the ads and promotions that IBC undertook were not so explicitly gendered as the segmented woman effort. While this discussion showed that "career women" is considered a social category and a potential market niche, workers hesitated to distinguish a female market. None of the participants in the discussion invoked her or his own gender in the evaluation. In this case, the content of the draft—the text itself—was not very significant; what was more interesting was the workers' process of evaluating the market.

This crit session illustrates a number of qualities found in the work of marketing global culture at IBC. First, the scene conveys the range of knowledge that professional marketers draw on in their evaluations, which includes formal concepts (e.g., about visual qualities) and a facility with English phrases as well as more informal dimensions, including their own conceptions of the tastes, incomes, desires, and identifications of various populations. No one invoked market research to define the audience, for example. Second, and relatedly, this interaction displays the informal nature that I found in much of the work in the office. We often participated in other people's projects, whether tying pom-poms, filling in the audience of a sparsely attended press conference, selecting prize winners for a promotion, posing as viewers and writing letters to *Spectrum*, the cable TV guide, or helping develop an advertisement, even if it was not part of our formal job description. This scene captures some of the blurred boundaries between different job functions and different kinds of knowledge involved in the office work of professionals. These qualities are another illustration of the "flexible" nature of work in modern industries, particularly the application of dispersed knowledge to a shifting range of tasks.

Finally, the discussion of the market for the segmented woman advertisement captures the participants' own aspirations. Bee's image of a niche of "women who want to improve themselves" speaks to professional women and also men who, in their work and social lives, are engaged in ongoing efforts to educate themselves, to develop, and to remain knowledgeable and relevant in a rapidly changing society. Such an orientation entails an ideal of personal management and self-help that resonates with discourses about entrepreneurial identities. Vital to their job and to their membership in the new Thai professional class, self-improvement and education are linked to changing political economic conditions. In the final section, I consider the ways that workers' knowledge, consumption, and identity are integral to their work and professional role.

KNOWLEDGE WORK

IBC was not a market fixed in space, as a store is, and its selling strategies were symbolic and mediated. It represented the professionalization of marketing into a class position and a public identity that differed dramatically from low-class, gendered, and ethnic forms of vending. But a professional role did not translate into incomes that easily underwrote middle-class consumption. Salaries for workers in our office were not very high compared with some other businesses—the person in press or special events earned about ten thousand baht (U.S.$400) a month. Low pay but high status from connection to the glamorous field of television.[39] While a few well-born staff could view their IBC job as a temporary apprenticeship, others without family resources, like Kop, worried about achieving their aspirations for a house, car, and family. Nonetheless these workers viewed their work as part of a creative or fulfilling endeavor, perhaps even part of a career. The job represented a strategy for navigating the fluctuating economic and social worlds of Bangkok. (Other strategies included living at home, starting a business on the side, and changing jobs; a number of IBC's workers were looking for or found new positions during my brief tenure.) Working at the transnational frontier of Thailand positioned these flexible subjects at the cutting edge of Thailand's development.

Because IBC's business depends on knowledge about global culture and Thai media, it requires workers familiar with these arenas. Professional marketers' work thus hinges on their formal qualifications and also on their knowledge of and participation in global culture, which together can be seen to constitute significant cultural or symbolic capital.[40] This work thus intimately binds their identities with the changing labor regimes of globalization.

The fields of information technology and global media require a complex set of knowledge, including facility in English and formal instruction in marketing or communications. While Kop, Wit, and a few others had studied abroad, most had earned degrees in Thailand. Some freelancers at IBC had graduated from Chulalongkorn's prestigious media department, and much of the office staff had studied at private business colleges in Bangkok, while currently enrolled college students majoring in advertising worked in the office part-time. Corporations such as IBC draw on a pool of educated Thais, a pool that has been increasing, particularly since the 1960s. In the last four decades, greater numbers of college graduates have pursued careers in business rather than government, which had long provided the secure and prestigious route for Thai men (as opposed to Sino-Thai men or any women). Women born after the mid-1960s and able to study beyond high school have increasingly chosen university or vocational education rather than teaching or nursing.[41] This shift has affected higher education. Communications is an increasingly popular college major. To address the growing need for credentials for professional work, business colleges and a variety of certifying programs have sprung up around Bangkok. Knowledge workers such as those at IBC obtain the most prestigious or applicable formal qualifications they can afford. The awareness to do so is an important part of urban middle-class families' repertoires.

The knowledge required for marketing jobs includes areas that are not necessarily conveyed through formal degrees. Vital but less defined qualifications for this work included basic creativity, a grasp of Thai tastes, and a thorough familiarity with global (mainly American) popular culture. The work requires, even necessitates, the workers' knowledge of transnational mass media in addition to certificates and technical knowledge. IBC workers were fluent in American culture, having been raised in a cultural mélange of Western and pan-Asian movies, television, and music. Most of the office staff grew up with television, which from the 1960s on played a mixture of dubbed American and Thai programming: *Dragnet, Mission Impossible, Big Valley, and Please Don't Eat the Daisies, Bewitched, Tom kap [with] Jerry, Leave It to Beaver,* and a game show called *Nathi Thong* (Golden Minute).[42] Coming up with copy for a promotional showing of the American action movie *Speed,* Kop employed knowledge about the movie and the stars as well as current Thai slang.

Marketing IBC involved a working conception of the audience, specifically the tastes, capacities, and identities associated with Thai viewers. In synthesizing the Thai with the foreign, office staff identified themselves as familiar with transnational culture and cosmopolitan tastes and able to grasp farang tastes, but viewed their charge as calibrating such cultural products for a more general Thai audience. Workers understood

Thai viewers as a specific non-Western niche with partly modern, partly conservative tastes, and they differentiated Bangkok from provincial audiences. For example, the evaluations of a market for women's programming, seen above, incorporated a sense of Thai women's sensibilities. Similar negotiations also arose in programming. The easy-going man who selected movies and variety shows for IBC told me that *Reservoir Dogs* and *Who Framed Roger Rabbit?* were seen as too violent for Thais, even though IBC broadcast violent suspense films such as *Cape Fear* and *Killer Instinct.*

All of the IBC staff would have been academically educated in English at school, and some such as Kop and Wit were quite fluent. Comfort in English, particularly in speaking with or writing to foreigners, was particularly prized. As Bee's use of *concept* and *buying* in her exchange with the advertising subsidiary showed, much Thai discourse is interspersed with English phrases. Hers was a typical mix in professional contexts, and in daily life in Bangkok, where term such as *shopping, take care, no problem,* and even *sur* (from *surreal*) have entered the general vocabulary. Familiarity with specific English words is assumed in commercial culture, for example, in the use of English for the title and calendar of IBC's *Spectrum* guide.

Most of IBC's print materials for subscribers were produced in English and Thai,[43] written in a casual manner that seemed to fit with the relaxed mode of much of the work in this office. The Thai writer gleaned descriptions from distributors' information, from Thai film magazines, and also from her substantial knowledge of popular culture. She wrote, in Thai, the section titled "Backstage," which offered information on select stars from American sitcoms and films. The focus of these texts was on the actors, the "stars" as they were called in both English and Thai, rather than on directors' visions or the films' narratives. I wrote the English-language descriptions of movies, documentaries, television shows, and star gossip, probably not very well, focusing more on the plots than on actors or awards. Wit and an assistant who had been educated in England used British spelling, such "programme"; I used American spelling. Thus,

IBC's marketing texts featured both American and English spelling, a mix that did not disturb anyone.

Thus, marketing and media work depended on workers' own knowledge and also on their own consumption of popular culture, while their ongoing consumption of global and Thai culture qualified them in part for the job. This blend of consuming and working characterizes professional work in the information age. When our office had a television, it was set to the HBO movie channel all the time.[44] IBC workers were enthusiastic consumers of media products, avidly watching movies and skimming magazines. One woman had an Aladdin toy on her desk, one of Disney's commercial tie-ins to its cartoon version of the classic tale. Because of the steady stream of gift giving, I asked her who it was for: "It's for me," she said, laughing.

CONCLUSION

Thailand has achieved its position in the global economy in part through projecting its national culture in the tourist industry's images of exotic Thai culture and also through the transnational projects of firms like Shinawatra. At the same time, Thais employ aspects of the global to navigate changing social worlds. Knowledge workers like Kop and Wit maneuver themselves by using foreign, global symbolism: their mastery of English, their media savvy, their comfort with foreign employees. Their ability to mix the local and the global in knowledge and in their identities is part of their profession. Bee's notion of "women who want to improve themselves" speaks to the ongoing efforts of the professional classes to stay knowledgeable in relation to being modern Thai subjects, urbane consumers, and flexible workers—efforts that immerse them further in contemporary global consumption. Such navigations occur in specific contexts and social relations that continue to be shaped by class, ethnicity, gender, and sexuality and thus constrain corporate subjects like Wit, Kop, and Thaksin Shinawatra differently.

This chapter has traced some of the ways that global markets, realized through institutions such as IBC Cable TV, involve and affect the social identities of class, ethnïcity, gender, and sexuality for elite and professional personnel. These culturally flexible identities, forged in relation to transnational culture and knowledge, are also articulated with the infrastructure and operations of changing capitalist economies. In the next chapter I turn to the corporate version of old-time market selling and consider the engagements of market form with local identities and relationships that recast the worldwide figure of the "Avon Lady."

CHAPTER FIVE

The Avon Lady,
the Amway Plan, and the Making
of Thai Entrepreneurs

In the IBC marketing office discussed in the last chapter, there was a woman, Suranee, whose job was to prepare the beverages for office workers and guests (ice water, instant coffee, hot tea made from iced tea mix, and cocoa) and who happened also to be an enthusiastic Amway distributor. Amway is one example of what is called "direct sales," a hundred-year-old American merchandizing approach that has been spreading around the world.[1] Through the course of living and doing research in Thailand, I encountered a number people who were or had been distributors for Avon, Tupperware, Mistine, Vienna, or other direct sales companies: a university librarian, workers at the sex worker NGO, and civil servants all turned out to be connected with this transnational industry.

It took my untrained eye a while to recognize the pervasiveness of direct sales in Thailand. Once I learned to see them, I found Amway stickers everywhere: a market stall, a Chinatown noodle restaurant, a bag at the airport, a car in traffic. I noted that Avon sponsored the 1994 Miss Thailand pageant. I spotted a YMCA staff member selling Avon to cleaning women, both crouched on a hallway floor. Catalogs and product samples from American or Thai companies (such as Mistine) appeared in IBC, go-go bars, NGOs, a chiropractor's office, and open-air market stalls of mostly Thai-made beauty products. Staying with the bride's family at an up-country wedding, I was served Amway coffee. Direct sales is mobile and pervasive.

Direct sales expanded into Thailand during a period of intensifying global flows and rapid economic growth. These powerful forces, combined with the accompanying social flux characterized by transforming class, status, ethnic, and gender codes, shape needs and wants, income and consumption. The expanse of direct sales into Thailand means that people buying Avon, Amway, and Tupperware products are engaging the companies' transnational regimes of consumption and culture. This consumption traffics in globalizing images of gender, race, sexuality, and economic identities. By distributing goods this way, through vast networks of ordinary people, companies extend their reach into intimate spheres and personal relationships. Yet it is this mode of distribution, rather than the products or their consumption per se, that distinguishes direct sales. The selling, the sellers, and the operations of this industry provide a perhaps more embedded and subtle picture of the workings of gender within and through this market form.

Direct sales use an army of salespeople, who (at least in principle) sell cosmetics, coffee, household products, and so forth, using catalogs to take orders from, and later deliver to, their own local network of buyers. Amway, Avon, and other companies cast these salespeople as autonomous agents, entrepreneurs, even independent business owners, signaling this difference by naming them distributors, representatives, or beauty consultants (as with Mary Kay). With an enlistment fee and a start-up kit (the sale of which provides a steady source of income to companies), such distributors become independent retailers and receive a commission of 25 to 50 percent of the retail price of goods they sell to customers. In the case of network marketing or multilevel marketing, a distributor also receives a commission on the sales of those she has recruited into the company sales force (and she earns more income from and focuses more energy on recruiting and motivating these "downline" sellers).[2]

The direct sales industry offers distributors a supplemental income, one potential component of the economic bricolage necessary in a changing, cash-based world. The forms and businesses connected with direct sales expanded in Thailand during the height of a speculative economic boom, a time when privatization policies and international rhetoric celebrating entrepreneurship in general were increasingly powerful worldwide. The global expanse of direct sales marketing combines notions of entrepreneurial self-help with a corporate system, cosmopolitan American modernity with local neighborhood networks and mundane sales. In this chapter, I investigate the multifaceted rhetoric, practices, and identities of direct sales on the part of both participants (distributors) and corporations. I consider the meanings of Thais' engagements with this American-born industry, giving particular focus to two ethnographic portraits, one of a reluctant Avon Lady and the other of Suranee, an eager Amway recruit. These situated examples denaturalize the transparent and universal claims for the promise and methods of direct sales.

DIRECT SALES IN THAILAND

Direct sales have been in Thailand at least since the 1970s and took off during the economic boom years of the later 1980s and early 1990s. In the early 1990s, more than half a million people—roughly six hundred thousand—registered with direct sales companies as distributors.[3] Because their entrepreneurial distribution system is decentralized, transspatial, and expansive, direct sales have been able to grow as an industry in Thailand (at least until the economic crisis of 1997): an impressive feat considering that the markets for personal care and beauty products are notoriously competitive. Avon and Tupperware established operations in Thailand in the late 1960s. Amway entered in 1987,[4] and in 1988 the Thai direct sales company Mistine began a successful career rivaling Avon; it was founded by a former manager of both Avon Cosmetics (Thailand) and Coca-Cola (Thailand). Mary Kay entered the fray in the 1990s.[5] Some of the success of direct sales marketing lies in its ability to escape the well-known traffic conditions that impede conventional retail (fixed stores) in the city.

The growth of the direct sales industry depends on the participation of hundreds or thousands of registered distributors. Many enlist for only a short time, quickly deciding that they have saturated their immediate consumer base, or have become bored, or that the practice would not live up to the promise. (Some people also enroll as a direct sales distributor simply to purchase favorite products at a discount.) A few sell for many years. Direct selling in Thailand has recruited a diverse array of participants—many women (including tom), some men, and some third gender kathoey. Sellers come from many classes and social worlds: office workers, sex workers, university and NGO workers, as well as farmers, bureaucrats, professionals, wealthy Sino-Thais, and the occasional spirit medium.[6] A Thai enthusiast prosaically described the variety of distributors: "Amway has an army general down to meatball sellers." While his handy phrase betrays the rhetorical nature of Amway pitches, the sellers of direct sales products are diverse; wealthy, middle-class, and poor people are employing direct sales as one self-determining tactic to earn extra income. One of the first clear distinctions among this population is between those who already sell goods, the established vendors, and those who do not. While this difference may have to do with class, it is a critical general difference in the way direct sales are enlisted, practiced, and imagined in Thailand.

Some of the already experienced vendors enlisting with direct sales companies simply integrate direct sales products with other wares. In Thailand, there is a ready population of vendors, local women and Sino-Thai individuals and families in particular, who remain alert to new products and outlets. One stall owner in a market near Patpong sold Vienna lingerie from catalogs alongside a range of clothes and other merchandise. Direct sales offer those already oriented to selling an additional resource, one holding the cache of modernity and America.

Although they may welcome direct sales products, these vendors do not necessarily adopt the official methods or discourse of the direct sales industry or identify with the company image. Vendors will stock up on goods at a sale price to sell from their neighborhood market stall or from bags they carry to the office. A large number of officially registered distributors do not follow direct sales protocol but rather sell these new products according to time-tested, locally calibrated marketing practices.

Yet not all or even a majority of people adopting direct sales have selling experience or identify with selling. The recruitment of ordinary people regardless of experience is a hallmark of the industry worldwide, characteristic of its populist aura. A major vector of direct sales' appeal in Thailand lies in these discontinuities with vernacular forms of marketing. Because direct selling is cast as something anyone can do and learn, but also as different from ordinary vending, it holds appeal for a large number of recruits. Direct selling is presented and viewed as accessible, viable, and potentially lucrative—that is, a potential source of increasing income and upward mobility. This is the version of direct sales trumpeted by the corporations, their agents, and business media as a new opportunity for Thais. In Thailand, this also means that recruits come from social groups not conventionally associated with the class, ethnic, and gender groups identified with common selling.

Such cross-class diversity indexes the widespread ramifications of economic flux—both well-placed and poor people need extra income. What is noteworthy is that direct sales attracts very different groups of people. Typically, people's livelihoods are sharply divided by class and other social differentiations. The direct sales form of marketing appears more feasible and appealing than ordinary, small-scale selling precisely because a wider range of people have been willing to take it up. According to corporate rhetoric, such popular appeal testifies to the universal nature of the entrepreneurial spirit and to the quality of the company's products and methods. As an ethnographer, however, I am interested in examining this appeal, by exploring the interpretations and identifications that inform Thai people's engagement with this version of marketing. Their engagement is invited and realized through descriptions, images, and the figure of the entrepreneur, as well as through a ready-made system of selling and delivering goods—through discourse, practice, and system. In the pages that follow I turn first to a rather reluctant Avon Lady, Sila, who participated in direct sales during their early growth in the 1980s, and then to IBC's Amway seller, Suranee.

THE RELUCTANT AVON LADY

At the sex worker advocacy group I worked with in Bangkok, a number of people sold, or had sold, through direct sales. There was Chiraporn, a neighborhood vendor who sold lingerie and who availed herself of the center's very inexpensive English and informal education classes. Mistine wares were displayed at one of the advocacy group's branches. One of the agency's workers, Sila,[7] had sold Avon as a teenager in the 1980s. A more unlikely Avon Lady than Sila would be hard to find. She had a degree in social work from a leading university with a progressive reputation and was a long-term organizer and activist, with years of experience, particularly in communities of Thai sex workers in Bangkok and in beach resorts. She also worked in a chic bar on Silom Soi 4 (across from Rome Club Disco), which was partly owned by her uncle. Sila was called (and sometimes called herself) a tom.

Avon began full-fledged operations in Thailand in 1978. As a teenager in the early 1980s, Sila had seen Avon advertisements for some time. Sila's stint as an Avon Lady began not too long after this launch and before Amway had even entered the country. When she was seventeen, she answered an ad that read, "If you want income in your free time . . ." Sila was part of a business-oriented family identified as Chinese or Sino-Thai. Her maternal grandfather had migrated from China and run a rice mill in the provinces before moving to Bangkok. Before Avon, Sila had had some work experience: she had sold confections made by her mother and performed sundry tasks in her family's battery factory. But she welcomed the chance to earn her own money, prove her capacities, and stretch the circumscribed spheres of family, factory, and school, to which her guardian aunt confined her. Speaking to me in English mixed with Thai,

Sila said of her maternal aunt, in whose custody the family had placed her, "I felt bad she had to give money." This bad feeling, on one hand, refers to the deeply felt obligation one incurs to a caretaker, which is experienced as acute indebtedness, and, on the other, to the specific inequalities within her own bourgeois Sino-Thai family. Although all family members were cared for, resources were distributed unevenly within the household; for example, Sila noted that while her aunt had money, her mother did not. Her uncle, though junior in age to his sisters and gay, had the highest status within this family formation, through a conflation of the status attached to his income and his gender.

"I hadn't worked for outside," Sila said, and therefore the meeting with the Avon representative offered a chance "to meet someone with responsibilities outside the world of school and work, who was professional." The Avon Lady, the embodiment of the modern public world, fulfilled these expectations: "She came by car, wore business clothes, and she explained clearly in a short time." Direct selling exposed Sila to a business she found more organized and professional than the family firm or the occasional selling of homemade sweets. (Later, in the margins of an article about direct sales that she mailed to me, Sila noted that her mother had also sold Tupperware but did not specify when. Tupperware entered Thailand in 1969.)

At Sila's first "training," the agent asked questions about Sila's interest and resources. She explained their products and procedures, instructing Sila from catalogs, and offered guidance for selling: "speak nice, *'riaproy narak suphap'*—proper, sweet, and polite." Though this advice could hardly have appealed to her temperament, Sila signed on, paying the equivalent of U.S.$14 to enroll and some more dollars for the start-up kit of an Avon bag, catalog, and product samples. Sila did not use the Avon bag: "It was ugly. Yellow, pink, brown-tan, colors I don't like. All their things were these colors," she said, waving her cigarette at the pastel-colored wallpaper that covered my flat.

Sila enjoyed the catalogs and used them to sell. "The big one had color," she remembered. "It had so many things in it, all kinds of things."

A chief function of Avon's texts in settings such as Thailand is to provide an education about a transnational system of femininity. Direct sales materials provide lessons for achieving through consumption white, American-style heterosexual femininity and domesticity. The catalog—that English word is well-known—served as an instruction manual for the use of cosmetics, she recalled: "Use with X and Y, this color goes with these colors, shades. You could study a little about makeup: methods for makeup." Catalogs offered a field guide to the new technologies of self-presentation. They also offered an important tool to distributors, as a critical component of sales and perhaps especially for those who did not identify with the catalogs' images. Sila was not herself engaged in the utility of Avon products for achieving femininity. Hence, the catalog was particularly helpful in selling the apparatus for a femininity she herself disavowed. "It's funny," she said, "they'd ask me, 'Is this pretty? How do you use this?' and I'd give them the catalog, saying: 'Here, look.' I couldn't tell them."

Sila appreciated the irony of a tom selling as an Avon Lady. She gathered that the Avon representative was surprised to encounter her as the would-be distributor. Yet in Sila's world, no one made much of the gender contradiction of a tom Avon Lady. "No one said, 'Oh, a tom is selling,'" Sila explained, "but they wondered how I can sell it. That's *Sila* selling cosmetics?" Her contradiction of the feminine Avon image was noted but did not generate conflict or anxiety for her or her family.

Sila's household may have been comparatively neutral about gender deviance or homosexuality (more so than about transgressive female heterosexuality, in fact), but, as discussed in chapter 3, such relative tolerance is not unique. Within many Sino-Thai and Thai families, earning income and fulfilling family duties can overrule the costs of inappropriate gender or sexual behaviors. While males were clearly favored, what most determined status in Sila's household was fiscal, rather than normative gender, achievement: "My aunt was happy because I'm trying to make money," Sila said.

The income was good "for a kid," according to Sila. In the beginning, she sold well, making U.S.$12 to $20 on an order from the 25 percent commission she received. Later, she said, she might occasionally sell $40, $80, even $120 worth for one shipment. Lipstick, but more often perfume and white face powder (the latter at U.S.$4), were the staples Sila sold to the women around her: the female members of her extended family and her mother, the women workers in the family factory, and the girls at her school. The power of direct selling lies in its ability to tap individuals' social worlds and so enter extremely local markets. Sila was generating consumers in her locale who may not have purchased those items from other venues.

Yet even as this selling mobilized social relationships, it was also contained by them. For example, Sila might allow for payment on delivery (rather than on ordering), "depending on how close we were." She would ask herself, "Are we close? If it's your mother, you don't get [the money up front]." In fact, one reason that Sila abandoned selling was the difficulty of collecting the payments from her intimates, especially her mother. Selling within intimate locales generates ambivalence, which is compounded by the ambiguous meanings associated in Thai culture with profiting from the sale of goods.

Moreover, in her teen years Sila was a precocious social critic and, she said, uncomfortable with the profit structure built into sales: "I didn't like selling. I feel like I'm cheating every time I sold. That was the first experience I got selling not-good-enough things." Sila criticized the products that she sold, saying that she never accepted their promotional claims to improve skin and hair. She noted that she did not know about the origins or contents of products (the labels were in English, which at that age she could not yet read easily). Thus, she did not have the ideal relation to the knowledge involved in the creation, use, value, and effectiveness of the products to sustain her participation as an Avon Lady. Sila said that she found herself uncomfortable with the exploitative nature of the price markup. Recuperating payment from her mother proved awkward. She stopped selling Avon.

It is intriguing to consider what Sila, who went on to become a radical community organizer and social worker, remembers as appealing about Avon. Her initial interest was to earn income, certainly, but earning income is not without meanings, valences, or interpretations. In Sila's case, income was a way to prove herself to her aunt and her family. Direct sales offered a bit of cash and some leverage or respect in her male-favoring family for being competent and responsible. Sila had already modified one facet of her social position—her ascribed gender; another means to otherwise modify her position in the social hierarchies around her was through earning money. In this regard perhaps, direct sales' entrepreneurial narrative was important in eliciting her participation.

Yet as an adult, Sila manifested an aversion to accumulating or even displaying a concern with money. While perhaps this attitude might partake of some strands of Buddhist critique, it should not be seen as a reflection of the teachings of the official Buddhist order, and in fact Sila (like most NGO workers and lesbians I knew) criticized the religious orthodoxy and state religion in Thailand. Sila's antimaterialist orientation did fit her radical critiques of capitalist development and the increasingly consumerist feel of Bangkok. It is possible as well that this disinterest in money also expressed a reaction to her family's monetary measure of social position, a priority which had stigmatized her mother in their household and by extension herself.

Neither the income nor the entrepreneurial spirit—nor clearly Avon's beauty projects or the Avon Lady image, let alone the pastel tote bag—fully explains all of her engagement with the company. Sila did not identify with or through the respectable or modern figure of the Avon Lady or the transnational regime of femininity posited by the corporation. What the adult Sila, the organizer, found memorable—in fact, enviable—about direct sales was their transparent and methodical system. This system articulated even the smallest sales with a large, global organization. Avon, like many direct sales companies, holds motivational meetings. Having attended a few, Sila had observed the professional grooming of Avon representatives and witnessed a highly organized and motivated network of women drawn from different worlds.[8] In this way, affiliating with the direct sales company was a connection to a larger world beyond kin ties, which is especially significant in young women's more circumscribed lives. The knowledge of another system perhaps represented the possibility of escape and of worlds beyond the confined orbit of a teenage Sino-Thai daughter. Sila, like many other Thais at this time, prudently pursued not only cash but also connections to extrafamilial and nontraditional vehicles with which to traverse the rapidly changing economic and social landscape. While marketing goods has offered a conventional source of income for Thai and Sino-Thai women, Avon offered the authority of an external and foreign system, couched in American modernity.

Sila temporarily applied Avon's system to some modest goals in the context of her family, her world, even her tom identity, and was drawn to the promise of systematicity (perhaps especially to such a predominantly female system, though she did not say so). She remained selective about the various other kinds of knowledge and training imparted by the industry. For the young incipient radical and tom, Avon's accessible methods and expansive affiliations provided not so much escape from as respectable leverage within local hierarchical worlds.

THE ENTHUSIASTIC AMWAY DISTRIBUTOR

The direct sales mode of marketing is composed, unevenly, of American-derived discourse consisting of meanings embedded and conveyed in catalogs, sales techniques, inspirational meetings, promotional materials, and advertisements. Perhaps the most obvious discourses are those connected to the desires of consumers to create modern Thai homes and selves. But as I am suggesting here, direct sales hinge on discourses surrounding the seller. Of course, participants embrace or engage with these discourses to different degrees. Some Thais adopting direct sales engage with these discourses more seriously than Sila or the local stall keeper. Many are motivated by the kinds of knowledge and training—or the new kinds of subjectivity—that transnational direct sales companies offer. To greater and lesser degrees, direct sales offer membership in a larger organization, a professional identity, a model for action, and in some cases a vocabulary of self-advancement and self-help. It is here that direct selling contributes to a discourse about the self in a changing social world. To those who embrace it, direct selling can provide a learnable system for working independently, as the case was for Sila, and compelling templates with which to narrate one's possibilities in a shifting social order. The case of Suranee, the novice working-class Amway distributor at IBC, illustrates the salience of direct sales as a narrative about self-actualization.

Suranee is one of many Thai working-class women taking up direct sales as a part-time (rarely full-time) source of income. She grew up in the poor northeast region of Isan, and her childhood mixed the simple pleasures of playing and boating during the monsoon floods with the demanding work of rural life. Her family farmed rice, raising a few ducks, chickens, and pigs for their own table. They might occasionally sell extra produce to neighbors, but there was "no market," Suranee said, and prices were low.

Suranee, like many country girls, grew up confined to the environs of her local community, more so than her six older brothers. She finished only the minimum education, the sixth grade, and from the age of ten to twenty worked her widowed mother's fields. One brother was ordained as a novice monk. His extended novice monkhood brought him a respected status and moreover allowed him to leave home, study through high school, and finish a degree at Bangkok's open university. Before moving to Bangkok, Suranee had barely been outside her district, going to the provincial capital Khorat but twice and, as a teenager, traveling once with a brother to Ratburi, another provincial city.

Suranee and most of her brothers headed to the nation's capital for work, boarding the same buses and joining the same flows as the women who work in the go-go bars. Most of the cab drivers in Bangkok are men from Isan, and three of her brothers took up this work. Suranee first worked in a textile factory. After four years, the company moved out of Bangkok, following the decentralizing flow of many primary industries and leaving workers, including Suranee, unemployed. Suranee then started work for a subcontracting service company and was assigned to our marketing office. Her take-home pay was the equivalent of U.S.$144 a month. Her college-educated brother, no longer a monk, also worked in marketing. He, however, had arrived in a different class. While Suranee worked as a subcontracted service worker, this brother worked as a marketing professional for a golf resort. As in Sila's situation, in Suranee's family, while money and resources might be given or shared, they were not pooled.

A friend from Suranee's residence introduced her to Amway, telling her, "Here's a way to earn money that's not risky—and it's legal!" Legality is a significant criterion for a peasant woman working for low wages in Bangkok. Suranee paid the membership fee of U.S.$24 and began selling in February 1993. She said she had no experience selling—interestingly discounting her farm experience—but emphasized that Amway trained you. Moreover, she said, "friendliness is the starting point and the main requirement," clearly quoting corporate rhetoric. On the one hand, Amway's populist approach provided a means with which to name and shape the cultural competence in marketing she and many Thai women already possess; on the other hand, this naming in turn diminished their relevant experience in deference to Amway's impressive and enabling system. That is, rather than crediting any local traditions or available kinds of knowledge such as those provided by the long-standing orientation of Thai women to markets, Amway credits its own instructions, albeit in combination with behavioral traits like friendliness, with instilling the confidence and skill to sell and build markets.

Suranee understood that she had to study and learn not only about Amway's procedures but also more about economics in general. The income, she said, was good; like Sila, she received 25 percent of the good's selling price. She could increase that percentage and her Amway income if she recruited other distributors from whose sales she would receive a percentage in a system called network marketing. Amway demarcates categories of distributors according to sales volumes, and members memorize the different commissions that accompany each rank. Once you get to the level of selling U.S.$6,000 worth a month, Suranee explained, you become a "direct distributor," receiving goods directly from the company's warehouse rather than from your sponsor. (There were approximately eight hundred at this level in the country at the time, a high-level Thai distributor told me.) After nine months, she had four satellite sellers and soon added two more. She was, for the first time in her work life, in a position to more or less manage and motivate others.

Suranee exuded enthusiasm for the methods and principles she had learned and more than once explained Amway's lineage structure and selling operations to me. She attended trainings, read the monthly Amway magazine AMAGRAM, and used her Amway date book. To illustrate the advantages of the approach, she put pencil to paper, using the "Artistry" pad promoting Amway's new cosmetics line, to chart a comparison between conventional retail and Amway on one side of the page and, on the other, to sketch her plan (called simply the Plan in Amway lingo): her goals for future sales volumes and profit percentages. I found such schematic sketching rather atypical for people's everyday planning and suggestive of the extent to which she had studied and absorbed Amway's teachings. For Suranee, the weekly visits to the distant Amway center were important to improving her knowledge and her skills, and she encouraged her satellite sellers to go as well. As an example of such learning, she held up a container of throat spray and explained its nonpolluting aerosol pump, pointing out its money-back guarantee.

One day during one of our conversations, I said, "I hear Amway is preparing to enter China." (I had learned this from a conversation with a couple who were among Thailand's earliest distributors.) "Yes," she said, countering, "but *why* did Amway choose China?" According to Suranee, Amway is entering China because there is an abundance of resources (she mentioned mountains and people) and because "not all the people there are poor." But Suranee's question—*why* did Amway choose China?—was rhetorical: I was not expected to provide an answer. Such rhetorical form of questioning is, in my experience, more representative of formal contexts, above all the monastic order or party politics—male-dominated institutions empowered with particularly effective language and speech. Employed by Suranee, this rhetorical question hinted at some sort of inspiration and model. Likely, it was informed by the extensive training offered by Amway (which, of all the direct sales companies, brings the most far-reaching and exuberant pedagogical approach to its ranks).

AMWAY'S ARTISTRY

Frequent training sessions and special Amway events in the major provinces of Thailand are listed in the Amway magazine. Suranee said about a hundred people attend three-hour workshops on problem solving, which are held every Friday evening. She and I independently attended one special event, a huge, well-advertised gathering to launch the new Artistry line of several "systems" of face care and cosmetics products, for example, the revitalizing night treatment system, consisting of progressive emollient cream, moisture essence serum, and hydrating masque.[9] During the hour I spent at the all-day event, hundreds of people milled earnestly about the convention center, which faced Bangkok's major slum. The visitors studied the instructional boards and display cases, underwent "skin analysis," and watched on stage or on video monitors the schedule of events—such as the talk-show-style discussion "How do you sell your way to wealth?" This meeting provided Suranee with the training and enthusiasm necessary to promote the Artistry line for dry or oily skin types. Unlike Sila's experience with Avon, but like other Amway sellers, Suranee identified with the products and the methods of her parent company.

Amway provides the rhetoric and narratives through which the seller can discern and construct clear goals, meaningful motivation, and a comfortable professional identity. The company teaches sellers how to talk not only about products but also about their plans and objectives. Helpful affirmations fill the margins of its bilingual monthly magazine. Once, at a loss for words to convey her frustration with the subcontracted job as coffee server, Suranee pointed to a photocopied Amway motivational statement she had taped to the partition, saying, "It's like this." Amway offered both a strategy to change her situation and a vocabulary with which to articulate her frustrations—in particular through the available role of the Amway entrepreneur. Suranee would rehearse this discourse with me: "You can have a better life. This is not all there is. In the future, you can have better if you want it. If there's an opportunity, take it."

In an industry focused on the distributor, companies need to recruit and fashion motivated sellers in ways that mesh the corporate image with individual aspirations and cultural conceptions. Here is where the narratives of self-advancement and self-help become important. Emphasizing a productive and empowering relationship between company and distributor, Amway, Avon, and other direct sales companies teach personal management (defined as how to clarify goals or establish plans). Suranee said of the income she earned, "You have to know what you are using the money for." The companies helpfully provide definite milestones marking individual achievement, for example, the clear rankings accorded to sales volume.

In fact, as Amway enabled her articulation of herself as an economic agent, Suranee became increasingly frustrated with her subcontracted job as coffee server for a number of reasons—the high percentage taken from her earnings, the regulations and corruption, the lack of potential for advancement, and the lack of training. One day Suranee spoke critically about Thai society to me; she criticized the hierarchy and limits, the expectation that one will stay in one's place, and the way superiors treat subordinates. Thai society is small, she said, indicating the smallness with her hands. She spoke enviously of the on-the-job freedom of her taxi-driving brothers and bitterly remarked that at least her former seamstress job involved skill.

Amway's entrepreneurial self-help discourse was rooted in an appealing egalitarian narrative—all one needed was friendliness, hard work, and a Plan. Suranee did not yet earn enough from her Amway sales to leave her subcontracted work, but she was cultivating more satellite sellers (although she was unsuccessful in recruiting me) and aspired to leave the service job. She wanted to be self-employed at forty or fifty years old. She talked about returning home to engage in agriculture, but, with Amway's training in mind, she stipulated that it would have to be on a commercial scale, with capital for fertilizer and for hired help. Direct sales promised not only a potential income but also a method to escape the confines of low-paid work in a ranked bureaucratic office. In selling for Amway, there are no rules and no limits on what you earn, she said: "You're free." She said that direct selling offers workers the liberty to set the time themselves, to think whatever they want, and follows the precept of "work little, get little; work plenty, get plenty" (or reap what you sow).

Suranee periodically sent home part of her service-work salary to her mother in the northeast and brought cash, clothes, and Amway products home as gifts during Buddhist Lent or New Year visits.[10] As a good Thai daughter, she wanted to fulfill her ongoing filial duty to provide and care for her mother.[11] It is interesting, however, that she used the Amway income for herself. Some months she bought clothes, and some months she saved. For her brother, the monkhood provided an avenue of education and mobility (and by and large fulfilled his filial duty to reciprocate his mother's care); for Suranee, Amway offered an individual program for self-help, involving her goals and her voluntary training.

WHAT'S GREAT ABOUT DIRECT SALES?

Direct sales have achieved such a presence in Thailand that they invite attention, remarks, and at times criticism. Avon and its Thai incarnation, Mistine, have entered popular culture in Thailand; Mistine's version of "Dingdong! Avon Lady"—"Mistine's here!" (*Midteen maa leew*)—is well known and a source of raw material for jokes. In one of the comic books that are ubiquitous in Thailand, a cartoon shows a young servant girl walking by a television set during a commercial for "Midteen" (this spelling reflects the Thai pronunciation but is not the actual spelling: Mistine). The blonde corporate announcer asks a rhetorical question similar to Suranee's "Why is Amway entering China?": "What's great about selling Midteen?" The girl responds, "Oh jeez, oi. What now? I just walked in and already you're asking me something. It's not like I'm just free to answer you. Someone has to sweep the house. Miss Lady over there asks a question. Huh, she knows everything." The low-status wage-worker grumbles at the facile enticement of the Mistine Lady, in this case represented as a presumably white, schematically pretty professional (middle- or upper-class) woman. The cheerful optimism of direct sales recruitment is here juxtaposed with the drudgery of commonplace work (and the bad attitudes that presumably accompany it). Perhaps more indirectly, the cartoon raises the foreign nature of direct sales, even in the form of a Thailand-based business, juxtaposing foreign farang femininity with working-class Thai female life. The parody thus hints at potential criticisms of direct selling.

Explicit critiques of the direct sales industry, however, are uncommon. There have been insinuations about resemblance to pyramid schemes or lack of consumer protection measures, for example. A few newspaper articles in the liberal English-language paper raised questions about the risks and accountability of this new, diffuse form of marketing.[12] More rare are Sila's indictment of the system of profit making. In Thailand, direct criticism of capitalist developments has been muted by government repression, a Cold War climate, and pressures against publicly criticizing the more powerful.

Yet as with other enterprises expanding or injecting commodity exchange into less commercial relations or realms—most obvious in the sex industry—direct sales venture into problematic territory. Anxieties about the impact of economic growth and the intrusions of commodified exchange generally take indirect forms, experienced and expressed through the cultural associations with profit, commerce, and the overlap of market and nonmarket realms. (These implicit critiques often center on the condemnation of less powerful groups: materialist youth or mercenary sex workers.)

While I did not hear people criticize Amway or Avon per se, I did witness people's wariness about a seller. After Suranee was relocated to another office, the marketing staff she left behind complained that she had charged an extra fee to tend to plates and mugs used in daily snacking. (She had not charged me.) They criticized an inappropriate introduction of material exchange into their relations with her and ascribed it to greed. The accusation of greed is a liability of selling. In another work place, when a wallet was stolen from the office, it was a vendor of several direct sales brands who was the prime suspect, a suspicion based on her personality but also associated with her assertive salesmanship, which was considered a sign of avarice and materialism. Even if direct sales suit the tenor of the times, their agents are vulnerable to public suspicions about selfishness and excessive individualism and to concerns about individuals' and corporations' profiting from social networks. These suspicions take particular cultural casts: they are imagined through certain personae and behaviors and in relation to a transforming but strongly felt moral economy.

THE IMAGE AND IDENTITY
OF THE DISTRIBUTOR

In going global, direct sales enter social fields where marketing, especially individual or small-scale trading, has particular moral weight as well as gender, ethnic, class, and spiritual connotations. As anywhere, there is a certain hierarchy of trade, commerce, and retail in Thailand. Hawkers, vendors, peddlers, and petty-commodity traders are low on this scale. Associated with females and ethnic Chineseness, the vendor occupies a gendered and/or ethnicized role of "other" to Thai men. Marketplaces are cast as neither masculine nor nationalist Thai spheres, although by no means are off-limits to Thai men.[13] This construction of social space is to a large extent underwritten by the Theravada creed and everyday practices of Buddhism,[14] which, although it definitely accepts this-worldly, material concerns, nonetheless interprets profit and money in social life in contradictory and ambivalent ways.

As a kind of mobile market, the practices and identifications associated with direct sales represent both continuities and discontinuities with already existing forms of marketing in Thailand. Direct selling, after all, is peddling goods at a rather small-scale and local level. In some ways, then, direct sales practices simply continue the long-standing, face-to-face marketing of so many Thai and Sino-Thai women. The same goods—talc, shampoo, and plastic storage containers (some common direct sales items)—are sold by street vendors, itinerant merchants, in market stalls and small shops, in addition to supermarket and convenience store chains.

Yet although they resemble and are absorbed within old-time neighborhood trade, direct sales are discontinuous with the established modes of trade in Bangkok. Among the greatest differences are the field's self-representations and especially the conception of the role and practice of selling. Both face-to-face vending and direct selling involve "dialogical" relations between seller and buyer, but the transnational corporate model stresses universality and transparency in ways that differ—or try to— from the customary mores of the marketplace.[15]

Worldwide, the industry's strategy is to differentiate itself explicitly and implicitly from both established corporate retail and local market traditions. Books about this industry make much of its difference from both department stores and provincial forms of hawking. (The Thai-language texts are mainly literal translations of English-language volumes.) Thus, the self-representations and discourses of direct sales are crucial to establishing this distinction, above all the figures and process of distribution— the equipped and trained salespeople who approach acquaintances in a friendly manner. The promise of training and cultivation is vital to its value as a distinct, and superior, mode of work and business, one that is middle-class or upwardly mobile and cosmopolitan.

Just as departments stores did in the 1950s and 1960s, capital-intensive forms of corporate retail such as direct sales have attempted to change the status and connotations of selling. The industry addresses the stratification of retail in Thailand. To render direct sales as modern, professionalized, and even prestigious in Thailand, the *identity* of seller as well as the *form* of selling must be distinguished from its low-status predecessors. The American-based, global form of peddling goods (re-)creates vendors through the figure of the distributor and through training in corporate sales approaches.

Here the universal, American-cast version of the entrepreneur has local salience and ideological purpose. First, it presents a distinct alternative to the cultural persona of the Thai vendor: the lower-class provincial market woman or the ethnic and accumulative Sino-Thai merchant. For Thai and Sino-Thai women (and Sino-Thai men), direct sales allow them to continue to employ marketing as an economic recourse but in a form redefined—or refined—along the lines of a cosmopolitan, Western model. Moreover, as select modes of selling become "professionalized" and more high-status, they are simultaneously rendered into an acceptable practice for Thai men in particular.

The local connotations of selling within Thailand also point to a logic underpinning direct sales corporate narratives: the need to address the moral or social compunction about selling through personal relations. The clean-cut and codified identity of the distributor can be read not only as a sales strategy but also as a tactic designed to counter local distaste for, or suspicion of, the small-scale profit making of neighborhood merchants found in Thailand and elsewhere. The image of the direct sales distributor is presented as generic and even universal, but emerged from a twentieth-century U.S. context, in relation to changing models of class, gender, and citizenship.[16] At least in Thailand, this figure potentially helps recast the problematic blurring of personal and market networks or market and moral economies posed by direct sales. In corporate rhetoric, the Avon Lady or Amway Diamond Distributor is presented not in terms of vulgar individualism but in terms of compliant membership in society as a gendered citizen.

Finally, the distributor, representative, or consultant embodies a self-help ideal which is rapidly becoming hegemonic under global restructuring. For leading companies such as Avon, Tupperware, or Mary Kay, this emphasis partakes of women's empowerment discourse, for example, "offering the tools of opportunity especially to women from all walks of life."[17] Direct sales' self-help rhetoric parallels and reinforces powerful global projects of free-market privatization. Where direct sales operate most profoundly as discourse is in the representations and enactments of flexible entrepreneurship. These representations are crystallized in the figure of the distributor, such as the world-renowned Avon Lady, and in the systematic method for selling and self-help, such as "the Plan" for Amway. Direct selling has cultivated the autonomous distributor-cum-entrepreneur role as a profit-generating and ideological tactic. This role is critical to the material and symbolic operations of direct sales for the industry as a whole but also for individual distributors. It constructs public identities and shapes individual subjectivities in line with these ideological visions, even when participants do not embrace the corny representations of the perkily successful distributor.

In practice, direct sellers operate through both Thai and international discourses about selling. Direct sales recast selling as an acceptable role of entrepreneurial distributor; they can also articulate people's goals and desires and narrate the possibilities for an individual's self-refashioning. Such personal progress narratives do not result solely from enlisting with direct sales companies, but at times they offer one of the key motivations for doing so. However, the engagement with direct sales narratives is tactical and strategic on the part of participants as well. The complex interactions between direct sales rhetoric and people's practice are shaped by and inform the realm of gender and sexuality.

NORMS OF SEX AND GENDER

Amway holds motivational meetings with regularity in every region of Thailand. I dragged Sila through monsoon rains to one such event at a Bangkok hotel, where a zealous distributor tried to recruit her (not noticing when Sila used the masculine particle *khrap-phom*, a playful habit of hers) and where she again marveled at direct selling's impressive organizing capability. This revival-style meeting recognized the successes of various levels of Amway distributors. The honorees, mostly heterosexual couples but also some single women, came onstage to the applause of the multitudes of participants—we estimated two thousand—to receive a pin marking their distributor status, after which they stepped to the front of the stage and waved at the crowd. I was not the only person tape-recording the event; the mixed audience was full of Filofax-type datebooks and mobile phones but also included turbans, tattoos, and chadors.

After the recognition ceremony came the main inspirational speaker. A successful distributor, nattily dressed in a double-breasted blazer, presented his rehearsed story delivered in a light-hearted and natural style that often involved the audience. (When he asked how many of the audience had been to Amway's U.S. headquarters, approximately a hundred hands went up.) He also presented a slide show illustrating his progress from a long-haired hippie youth to an Amway seller, ending with images of the rewards of motivational trips and material possessions: a picture of him at the Michigan Amway headquarters, with Mickey Mouse at Disneyland, and, finally, in front of his car and house.

The plot organizing his illustrated biography revolved around his struggle to overcome the obstacles to success, one being the skepticism around him. This skepticism came even from his mother! He explained that he had had to prove his mother wrong and go against her advice in order to succeed, a posture that departs from the usual deference to mothers shown in this somewhat matrifocal society. This distributor's professional, Western-inflected identity as a successful distributor allowed, and compelled, a redefinition of family duties from filial obedience to individual (financial) achievement. For this Amway speaker, the rejection of maternal control was a way of remaking himself as a man according to the international, entrepreneurial narrative supplied by Amway.

Direct sales draw on gender imagery in the framing of distributor identities. The "modern" and "professional" nature of direct sales, associated with America and clearly distinct from old-time Thai marketing, renders it more suitable for Thai men in particular. But direct sales are most famous for their cosmopolitan, yet gender-appropriate, female roles, the Avon Lady or the Mistine Lady. Through their representations of professional female sellers, the companies avoid the problematic associations with conventional commercial women—the independent and rough market woman selling in unruly street markets as well as the selfish, autonomous career woman pursuing her own desires (or the mercenary sex worker). In their advertising and promotions, direct sales also draw on family imagery as well, defined according to Thai conceptions. One television campaign for the Thai company Mistine, for example, portrayed a seller using the money to buy a house to live with her mother. (This image resonates with the Thai ideal of the youngest daughter remaining in the family home and caring for her parents.)

Distributors' engagements with gender norms involved a complex set of motivations and interpretations. Suranee, after asking if I were a "Miss" (using the letters *naw saw*, initials for *Nang Sao*), told me conspiratorially that she was unmarried too. She said she was *choey choey* (blasé, indifferent) about marrying: if the time is right, and it happens, okay. She said that thinking about marriage is different from the old days; now, a wife and husband help each other. When I asked her if Thai men believe this, she said, "If they don't, I won't go for them"—adding "no" in English. Like Kop in IBC marketing, Suranee felt that people should have children when they are ready, and she was not ready: ready meant having time, money, and an education. One reason she was not ready to have children (and presumably to marry) was that she had to work at a job she didn't like. Planning her future life, including relationships and reproduction, was already informed by the globalizing rhetoric of this American corporation.

Amway in particular defines responsible profit making through conceptions of gender, including norms for marriage and sexuality. Part of the Amway motivational speaker's joking also involved his single status, which was explained—and justified—through humor. Former U.S. distributors have reported that Amway pressures the unmarried, at least those in the upper ranks, to marry.[18] The bachelor Amway motivational speaker, the tomboy Avon Lady Sila, and Suranee, who was deliberately unmarried, suggest that in Thailand sellers sidestep the industry's connotations of normative sexuality. Even in the Mistine commercial featuring the dutiful daughter, there is no husband in sight.[19] It is possible, in fact, that alternate income and foreign self-help methods from direct sales may enable participants' deviations from the very idealizations that underwrite the success of those corporations.

In Thailand, as in the United States, direct sales allow a kind of acceptable resistance to frustrations with low wages, bureaucracy, and exploitations as well as with limits of local social hierarchies. Direct selling can offer a means to re-create oneself and one's station through economic exchange and a means to hedge the confining limitations of wage work or family labor. The possibilities of autonomy from, or leverage within, confining work or kin obligations are important in the narratives of many Thai direct sellers. Such obligations are heavily gendered, creating a common setting where the motivations and means for earning income are differently weighted for women and men.

The direct sellers in Bangkok, especially at the lower levels, use direct sales as a tactic in economic bricolage. Thai participants modify virtually every facet of direct sales operations: practice and system, image and identity, discourse and rhetoric. The stall-keepers who add some Mistine and Avon talc to their table are using direct sales companies as a stable source of product supply without engaging the corporate promise of financial mobility. Like the tomboy distributor, they need not traffic in the middle-class femininity of the Avon Lady or Mistine Lady figure or necessarily partake in any of the gender ideals conveyed through the catalogs and products, including normative heterosexuality. Yet many of the sellers are engaging more than the possibilities for income when they enlist with direct sales. By choice or necessity, through their participation with this marketing industry, they engage the self-help model: the idea that people as individuals (or, for Amway, as heterosexual couples) carve out solutions to economic conditions that are nationwide.

LOCAL ENTREPRENEURS

Following the onset of the economic crisis in July 1997, discourses about economic strategies for individual and national development became ever more pronounced. Business pages of the *Bangkok Post* ran articles pointing to the possibilities of selling Avon, Amway, or other direct sales brands "as workers look to extra jobs to keep their income steady."[20] In 1998 and into 1999, Amway and Avon posted declining profits in Thailand, suggesting that the strategy of entrepreneurial sales of goods paid for in U.S. currency might not work when a nation's currency has plummeted to as much as a half of its former value.[21] Tellingly, the direct sales companies' core crisis strategy was to recruit new sellers. The industry's fiscal failures by no means suggest that entrepreneurial discourse itself is flagging. Instead, the rhetoric of entrepreneurship prevails, providing a key frame for narrating individual and national possibilities in Thailand and the emerging markets of the global economy.

What does it mean for Suranee, Sila, or the Amway inspirational speaker to learn corporate rhetoric forged in the United States? The international, American-modeled version of an entrepreneurial distributor promises the ability to expand beyond a confined world, one especially circumscribed for women. It makes the role more palatable to many by distinguishing Avon representatives and Amway distributors from the common market vendor. At the same time (and through this imagery), transnational direct sales legitimate material or social aspirations that can be locally problematic. The extent to which direct sales' cheerful discourse and methodical practices are taken up or interpreted is affected by the individual's temperament but also by larger cultural and social contexts, such as how selling, profit, and corporations as well as self-help are all interpreted in particular social settings. From different class positions, Suranee and Sila used transnational models of self-help to navigate the economic flux and local hierarchies in their worlds. Together, they illustrate one form of the emerging intimate economies of global capitalism in Bangkok.

CONCLUSION

The Intimacy
of Capitalism

These chapters have shown different intersections between intimate lives—personae, subjectivities, relationships—and the expanding capitalist economy in Bangkok. Through concrete examinations of department stores and shophouses, go-go bars and the sex market for tourists, shopping complexes, professional corporate marketing, and direct sales, these case studies reveal how the increasingly global market economy integrates and remakes social worlds, cultural meanings, and local economies in Bangkok.

This book argues that the ongoing and dynamic interaction between market economies and intimate realms of life is critical to understanding how global capitalism involves and affects social life. Capitalist markets interact with other economies—with folk, kin, and moral economies. These alternate economies are not timeless but have transformed alongside and informed modernization in Thailand. They provide a symbolic and practical counterpoint to capitalist exchange. Capitalism draws on and profits from existing social systems and local economies. In turn, identities, relationships, values, and practices play a significant role in the global economy. As markets stage more and more of daily life in Bangkok, people realize their identities and relationships through commercial venues, and capitalist systems recast intimate life. Let us consider these points in more detail.

Capitalism has depended on and integrated the intimate realms of culture, relationships, and identity. In Thailand, capitalist markets and "modern" corporations emerged from and drew on the older economic forms of shophouses and village trading. The role of ethnicity in Chinatown's commerce and in subsequent Sino-Thai businesses, such as Central Department Store, MBK, and Shinawatra, makes clear that social relationships and identities have been integrally involved in Thailand's capitalist economy. Central Department Store built on gendered kinship and ethnic networks to develop capital for investment, to provide essential unpaid labor, and to train the next generation of executives. Not only did successful Sino-Thai corporations like Central, MBK, and Shinawatra rely on diasporic networks in the country and in the region, they also cultivated relations with powerful ethnic Thai families, seeking opportunity in the changing nature of the Thai state in the postwar period, even during nationalist anti-Chinese periods.

Direct sales such as Avon and commercial sex work also rely on existing social systems and local economies. Direct sales distributors activate their immediate social worlds for profit, while sex workers are recruited and sustained by village networks, at least in part because, as daughters and as mothers, they are oriented to the economic support of their families. The sex trade for foreigners profits from domestic configurations of kinship, heterosexuality, and gender in which male sexual activity is a natural entitlement, and, other things being equal, men are considered senior (phi) and treated with deference. The integral role of intimate realms in modern market venues belies the common image of global capitalism as neutral and homogeneous.

In turn, as much ethnography and critical social theory has shown, the expanse of capitalist economies remakes intimate worlds: indeed, this remaking is experienced as one of capitalism's most disruptive components when it expands into new locales or new arenas. Just as factory work (or wage work) produces the proletariat, global markets produce new identities and relationships in a number of ways. This book has explored several examples of this process.

The expanse of the market economy has been accompanied by changing ideologies concerning identity, culture, and intimate life. Capitalist development comes with its own figures, personae that represent new modes of work and new styles of being that accompany economic modernity. Some examples found in Thailand are the Avon Lady and a Thai variant, the Mistine Lady (Sao Midteen); the globe-trotting "Chinese" or Sino-Thai business tycoon, what Aihwa Ong calls the "flexible citizen," such as Thaksin Shinawatra, who represents successful overseas-Chinese corporate capital in Southeast Asia; but also the sex worker in the go-go bar and the enthusiastic teenage consumer of Generation X or Y. As I have shown, these symbolic figures condense gender, ethnicity, and class, often with sexual associations, into embodied symbols of the promise and problems of new economic realities.

Capitalist economies have generated powerful ideologies about tradition and "private" life. The emergence of a Western-style "housewife" role, for example, is a by-product of market capitalism. Drawing on older elite Thai, Chinese, and European worldviews, the ideologies accompanying capitalist development have propagated a widespread image of "traditional" Thai femininity as noneconomic and oriented to the home (rather than household) and husband (rather than kin group). This image, connected with a feminized vision of consumption, simultaneously defines images of "modern" Thai femininity and domesticity (provisioned by corporate retail) as well as traditional femininity. Although the department store was underwritten by women's labor in the home, back office, and factory, the symbolic logic of this form of retail meshed with a vision of economic citizenship based on consumption. From the 1950s on, increasingly widespread discourses of modern Thai female identity emphasized women's roles as wives, mothers, and consumers rather than as the workers who underwrote Thailand's development.

This book has linked such ideologies and discourses about identity to the material dimensions of capitalism—to the infrastructure, operations, and practices of markets—and has emphasized the effects of this material level on intimate life. Capitalist commerce has played an important part in Thailand's changing class structure, particularly by influencing the meanings and interpretations of class positions in the country and city. As either workers or consumers, Thais across classes affiliate with new social identities and subtly modify their patterns of relationships through their engagements with capitalist systems. This process is especially apparent in sexuality. Amid the array of cosmopolitan consumer-based identities, tom, heterosexual women, and sex workers all realize emerging sexual identities at the same time as they navigate local judgments. Capitalist development has also transformed work identities. The profession of selling, now defined by advanced degrees and transnational linkages, has become a higher-status identity than when associated with floating-market vendors, local hawkers, and Sino-Thai shopkeepers. Articulating with capitalist markets refashions people's self-understandings and public presentations. Transformations in intimate life are a core feature cosmopolitan modernity: cultivating a modern identity to some extent reconfigures sexual, national, ethnic, and gender identities.

Markets are often associated with individual freedom and choice; a variegated space like MBK offers consumers and vendors certain freedoms. Yet when people engage with markets, they are not simply exercising their preexisting desires through a neutral medium. Markets are greatly shaped by economic, social, and cultural systems. In Thailand, market arenas have long carried gendered and ethnic associations, and marketing work has remained an important economic recourse for women (and recently for tom). After the 1997 economic crisis, as a way to make ends meet, many women—but now Thai men as well—sold all manner of goods in the informal and impromptu market venues that sprouted up around the city. People's ability to use particular market resources is constrained by class and also by gender, sexuality, and status, particularly as marketing has become more professionalized. The contrast between IBC's male and female worldly knowledge workers reveals key differences in their capacities to leverage cosmopolitan experience and business opportunities.

Markets are not simply opportunities for exchange but are powerful influences on social life. The engagement with capitalist markets educates and disciplines participants, training them in public presentations of self, in modern values and reference points, and in appropriate behavior. This education is clear in the transformations of rural young women in the go-go bar but takes other forms in department stores, shopping malls, telecommunication offices, and direct sales training sessions. Markets stage more and more of Thais' work, leisure, and self-expression. The realization of intimate lives through capitalist venues both reproduces and transforms aspects of identity, social relationships, and cultural meanings.

I have argued throughout this book that one way to see the impact of capitalist development on "private" life is to consider a broader range of economic systems and to locate intimate life at the juncture of folk (or kin, or moral) economies and market economies (themselves varied). Thais' encounters with the global economy are motivated by and often perpetuate the meanings and practices of their folk economic systems. Thais commonly integrate consumer goods and marketplaces into ongoing cultural practices: spiritual offerings, support for parents, and gifts to friends all rely on the products of retail, often handily packaged for that very purpose, as in the saffron-wrapped temple donations sold in supermarkets. Bangkok's social worlds are still shaped by enduring status hierarchies, and workers use transnational corporations, commodified intimacy, and knowledge of Western culture to leverage their status and power in their worlds. Thai women and Sino-Thai men, for example, engage with the market economy in order to fulfill kinship and gender obligations. Not surprisingly, the Chinese ethnicity and the Thai female gender are still connected with marketing, just as the realm of markets remains subtly tinged with femininity and ethnicity—"other" to masculinist Thai culture.

From day to day, people partake of both capitalist and folk economies, frequently navigating the boundaries between them. The examples in these chapters show how, in the context of global capitalism, identities and relationships are often realized at the changing junctures of market and nonmarket economies. Considering intimate realms in relation to plural economies recasts the question of how the global economy is affecting intimate life. It moves from an image of an external penetrating force to a view of transformations unfolding within Thai society.

As local exchange systems have interacted with an increasingly powerful and global market economy, they have reconsolidated in new forms. The changes to folk economies wrought by international political economic developments have accordingly transformed practices and meanings associated with sex, gender, and kinship relations (which are considered "traditional" and "natural"). Heterosexual relations, for example, have altered over the twentieth century: the migration from China to Siam/Thailand of married couples instead of mainly single men; the inflation of bridewealth; the emergence and sexualization of dating couples; and the crystallization of a suburban nuclear family as the emblem of modern Thai citizenship—all represent significant transformations to the practices of heterosexuality in Thailand.

At the same time that folk economies have changed, the borders between folk and market economic systems have been redrawn, or often eroded, with notable consequences for social identities. As examples in this book have shown, there are material and systemic differences between capitalist markets and local economic systems. But in public life, more often it is an imagined border that is symbolized and defended. Capitalist development has constructed a separation between the economic world and cultural, traditional, and private realms. The images and infrastructure of capitalist markets, such as the shopping complex or direct sales, cast these intimate arenas as noneconomic, by minimizing their historical and ongoing links to current economic operations and by presenting capitalist systems—like direct sales—as a neutral and benign medium. The material and symbolic boundaries between capitalist and moral economies play a significant role in evaluating and enacting identities and relationships in Thailand. Exploring these borders illuminates some of the subtler ways that transnational economic developments are shaping intimate life there.

In daily life and in public discourse, the differentiation between the values of the market and those of kin, community, and Thai culture has become a noticeable source of anxiety. Sexuality, gender, ethnicity are often key to such ideological demarcations of the border between capitalist and folk economies. The concern over the separation of market and nonmarket exchanges can be seen in the judgment of the sex worker, who embodies the transgression of this boundary. The mainstream association of tom with "fashion" offers another ideological distinction between modern commercialized style and "authentic" social relations.

Everyday life in Bangkok is realized more and more through capitalist venues, allowing transnational flows of capital to refashion social worlds at the most intimate levels. This book has critically examined these processes by exploring the identities, relationships, and values located at the fraught and changing intersections of capitalist and local economies; in turn, these textured examples illustrate the "local color" of modern commerce, in other words, the intimacies of global capitalism itself.

NOTES

INTRODUCTION: INTIMATE ECONOMIES

1. M.S.S. Tour Trans Co. Ltd. http://www.google.com/search?q = cache: 2XK4xw3I4A4:www.awebspace.com/mss/bkk/croc.html+%22floating+market% 22+history&hl = en [accessed October 10, 2001].

2. In the 1990s, foreign investors looking for quick returns poured money into Thailand. Thai banks and well-placed businesses were flush with this money, which they often invested in massive construction projects, like shopping complexes and hotels oriented to a global consumer economy. This situation was later labeled a bubble economy, contributing to the Asian economic crisis of 1997, which originated in Bangkok's banking industry and spread across the region. Most of my fieldwork took place during the boom years of the mid-1990s; however, I visited Bangkok in 1998 and 2000 and draw on observations from those times in some chapters here. For more information about the crisis, see Ara Wilson, "Bangkok, The Bubble City," in *Wounded Cities: Destruction and Reconstruction in a Globalized World*, ed. Jane Schneider and Ida Susser (Oxford: Berg Publishers, 2003), 203–26.

3. The reference to the predominance of women in markets appears in an enormous number of works on Thailand, but some more in-depth studies include Napat Sirisambhand and Christina Szanton, *Thailand's Street Food Vending: The Sellers and Consumers of "Traditional Fast Foods,"* Women's Studies Programme, Social Research Institute, Chulalongkorn University, Bangkok, 1986; and Preecha Kuwinpant, *Marketing in North-Central Thailand: A Study of Socio-Economic Or-*

ganization in a Thai Market Town (Bangkok: Chulalongkorn University Social Research Institute, 1980). One classic piece on the sexual division of labor in Thailand that points out women's prevalence in markets and sales (as opposed to government bureaucracy, for example) is Thomas Kirsch, "Buddhism, Sex-Roles, and the Thai Economy," in *Women of Southeast Asia*, ed. Penny Van Esterik, Northern Illinois University Occasional Paper no. 9 (Dekalb, Ill.: Center for Southeast Asian Studies, 1982), 16–41. On markets and the female gender in Indonesia, see Suzanne A. Brenner, "Why Women Rule the Roost: Rethinking Javanese Ideologies of Gender and Self-Control," in *Bewitching Women, Pious Men: Gender and Body Politics in Southeast Asia*, ed. Aihwa Ong and Michael Peletz (Berkeley: University of California Press, 1995), 19–50; and Suzanne A. Brenner, *The Domestication of Desire: Women, Wealth, and Modernity in Java* (Princeton, N.J.: Princeton University Press, 1998). Certain types of markets and marketing systems involve more male sellers—for example, Buddhist amulets and icons; prepared fruit stalls; wholesale produce markets at Paak Naam; stamps; junk markets, or "thieves markets."

4. James C. Ingram, *Economic Change in Thailand since 1850* (Stanford, Calif.: Stanford University Press, 1955); Katherine A. Bowie, "The Alchemy of Charity: Of Class and Buddhism in Northern Thailand," *American Anthropologist* 100, no. 2 (1998): 469–81.

5. "News for Nang and Nangsao," *Bangkok World*, June 16, 1963, 10.

6. An example of a tourist guide depiction of Chinatown is Steve Van Beek, *Bangkok* (Hong Kong: Insight CityGuides, 1988).

7. I am grateful to the University of California Press reviewer who suggested I include this example.

8. "Intimacy" has recently been employed as a rubric by a variety of authors. The title of a recent ethnography of northeastern Thailand by Andrea Whittaker is *Intimate Knowledge: Women and Their Health in North-East Thailand* (St. Leonards, NSW, Australia: Allen & Unwin, 2000). Examples of critical theories of intimacy include Lauren Berlant's trenchant analysis of intimacy in relation to the public/private divide in U.S. culture (Lauren Berlant, "Intimacy: A Special Issue," in *Intimacy*, ed. Lauren Berlant [Chicago: University of Chicago Press, 2000], 1–8). Her use of the term addresses a range of issues connected with the subjectivity beyond those conveyed by the term *identity*. For the changes in concepts of intimacy with modernity, also see Anthony Giddens, *The Transformation of Intimacy: Sexuality, Love & Eroticism in Modern Societies* (Stanford, Calif.: Stanford University Press, 1992). One exploration of gendered exchange in the classical period is Victoria Wohl, *Intimate Commerce: Exchange, Gender, and Subjec-*

tivity in Greek Tragedy (Austin: University of Texas Press, 1997). *Intimate* in my use is meant as an umbrella term to allow for the exploration of "private" issues in "public" economic spaces, including but exceeding those connected to gender or sexual identity.

9. This project draws on an enormous body of theoretical and empirical discussions of the ways that categories and locations either assigned to or adopted by people are defined by historically and culturally specific discourses and practices. Most work on Thai gender adopts an intersectional approach, for example, recognizing the importance of region and class, and stresses the social dimensions of self-perceptions and public categories rather than intrapsychic dimensions, such as those that inform much scholarship on erotic desires and identifications.

10. Claude Lévi-Strauss, *The Elementary Structures of Kinship*, revised ed., ed. Rodney Needham, trans. James Harle Bell and John Richard von Sturmer (Boston: Beacon Press, 1969); Gayle Rubin, "The Traffic in Women: Notes on the Political Economy of Sex," in *Towards an Anthropology of Women*, ed. Rayna Rapp [Reiter] (New York: Monthly Review Press, 1975), 157–210; Marcel Mauss, *The Gift* (New York: Norton, 1967); Karl Polanyi, *The Great Transformation: The Political and Economic Origins of Our Time* (1944; Boston: Beacon Press, 1957); Paul Bohannan, "The Impact of Money on an African Subsistence Economy," *Journal of Economic History* 19 (1959): 491–503.

11. On the moral economy, see E. P. Thompson's landmark work, for example, the discussion of the term in *Customs in Common* (New York: New Press, 1993). For the ways capitalism changes the social codes of the market in Europe, see Polanyi, *The Great Transformation*.

12. Thongchai Winichakul, *Siam Mapped: A History of the Geo-Body of a Nation* (Hawaii: University of Hawaii Press, 1992).

13. On the interactions between the monastic order and the laity in Thailand, see the classic monographs by S. J. Tambiah: *World Conqueror, World Renouncer: A Study of Buddhism and Polity in Thailand against a Historical Background* (Cambridge: Cambridge University Press, 1976), and *The Buddhist Saints of the Forest and the Cult of the Amulets* (Cambridge: Cambridge University Press, 1984); also see S. J. Tambiah "The Galactic Polity: The Structure of Traditional Kingdoms in Southeast Asia," *Annals of the New York Academy of Sciences* 293 (1977): 69–97. On merit, see, for example: Jasper Ingersoll, "Merit and Identity in Village Thailand," in *Change and Persistence in Thai Society*, ed. G. W. Skinner and A. T. Kirsch (Ithaca, N.Y.: Cornell University Press, 1975), 219–51; H P. Phillips, *Thai Peasant Personality* (Berkeley: University of California Press, 1966); Charles

Keyes, "Mother or Mistress but Never a Monk: Buddhist Notions of Female Gender in Rural Thailand," *American Ethnologist* 11, no. 2 (1984): 223–39.

14. Darunee Tantiwiramanond and Sashi Pandey, "The Status and Role of Thai Women in the Pre-Modern Period: A Historical and Cultural Perspective," *Sojourn* 2, no. 1 (1992): 141.

15. Marjorie M. Muecke, "Make Money Not Babies: Changing Status of Northern Thai Women," *Asian Survey* 24, no. 4 (1984): 464.

16. My portrait of Thai women as economic agents is not found in the dominant Thai cultural vision of gender, which stresses attractive feminine appearance and comportment and the role of the "housewife" (increasingly associated, in the Western fashion, with consumption rather than with the managerial role of the *mae baan*, the "mother of the household"). Symbolically, the figure of the market woman represents a rustic, low-class position, and "market Thai" is considered a vulgar mode of speech. The dominant model of gender derives at least in part from the aristocracy, where the most elite wives and daughters did not engage in work or trade. The formation of modern Thailand popularized a model of gender from Siamese elite and European and East Asian gender symbolism, to define Thai "culture" in ways that obscure women's economic and community roles. But the history and customs of rural Thai society suggest something else: markets hold particular significance for peasant and working-class Thai women and remain class-inflected and gendered spheres.

17. See Ara Wilson, "Women in the City of Consumption: Markets and the Construction of Gender in Bangkok, Thailand," Ph.D. diss., City University of New York Graduate School, 1997, for elaboration of this point (introduction and chapters 1 and 2).

18. For the diversity of historical Bangkok, see Akin Rabibadana, "The Organization of Thai Society in the Early Bangkok Period, 1782–1873," Southeast Asia Program, Data Paper 74, Cornell University, 1969; Charles Keyes, *Thailand: Buddhist Kingdom as Modern Nation-State* (Boulder, Colo.: Westview Press, 1987). The Mon people are Theravada Buddhist, like most Thais. Indian migrants to Siam were known to be Bombay Indians, "Kling," Makassarese, Sikhs, Bengalis, Tamils, and Gujaratis (see Abha Bhamorabutr, *The History of Bangkok* [Bangkok: Mr. Somsak Rangsiyopas, publisher; printed at Department of Corrections Press, 1982]; and Zakir Hussain, *The Silent Minority: Indians in Thailand* [Bangkok: CUSRI, 1982]). The "Indian" community lived in the Pahurat area of Chinatown, built over a former Vietnamese (Yuan) quarter. The ethnic mix varied in other regions of the country; in northern Thailand, for example, the

Chinese male traders were of different ethnicities from those in Bangkok. They were the Yunnanese (Haw, in Thai) and Han Chinese, who migrated overland to trade with the northern Thai (see, e.g., Ann Maxwell Hill, *Merchants and Migrants: Ethnicity and Trade among Yunnanese Chinese in Southeast Asia*, Yale University Southeast Asia Studies Monograph no. 47, 1998, 54; Michael Moerman, "Chiangkham's Trade in the 'Old Days,'" in *Change and Persistence in Thai Society*, ed. William Skinner and A. Thomas Kirsch [Ithaca, N.Y.: Cornell University Press, 1975], 151–71).

19. See Moerman, "Chiangkham's Trade," for long-distance trading by northeastern men.

20. Jiemin Bao argues that discussions of the Chinese role in the Thai market economy tend to erase Chinese women's household and business labor. (Jiemin Bao, "Marriage among Ethnic Chinese in Bangkok: An Ethnography of Gender, Sexuality, and Ethnicity over Two Generations," Ph.D. diss., University of California, Berkeley, 1994).

21. Work presenting varying interpretations of the relationship between capitalist market economies and other economies (noncapitalist, folk, moral) includes: Karl Polanyi, *The Great Transformation*; J. K. Gibson-Graham, *The End of Capitalism (As We Knew It)* (London: Blackwell Publishers, 1996); and Bohannan, "The Impact of Money." Drawing firm conclusions about the nature of capitalist market economies' interaction with other economies—whether they form an overarching global system for capitalist accumulation, or multiple capitalisms, or some other configuration—is beyond the scope of this project.

22. Rubin, "The Traffic in Women."

23. Aihwa Ong, *Spirits of Resistance and Capitalist Discipline: Factory Women in Malaysia* (Albany: State University of New York Press, 1987); Ong and Peletz, eds., *Bewitching Women, Pious Men*; Ann Stoler, "Carnal Knowledge and Imperial Power: Gender, Race and Morality in Colonial Asia," in *Gender at the Crossroads of Knowledge*, ed. Micaela di Leonardo (Berkeley: University of California Press, 1992), 51–101; Anna Tsing, *In the Realm of the Diamond Queen* (Princeton, N.J.: Princeton University Press, 1993).

24. The many discussions of women's labor in Southeast Asia's capitalist development include Amara Pongsapich, ed., *Women's Issues: A Book of Readings* (Bangkok: CUSRI, 1986); Noeleen Heyzer, *Working Women in South-East Asia: Development, Subordination and Emancipation* (Philadelphia: Open University Press, 1986), 424–51; Linda Lim, "Women Workers in Multinational Corporations," Michigan Occasional Papers in Women's Studies, Women's Studies Pro-

gram, University of Michigan, Ann Arbor, 1978; Aihwa Ong, "Center, Periphery and Hierarchy: Gender in Southeast Asia," in *Gender and Anthropology*, ed. Sandra Morgen (Washington, D.C.: American Anthropological Association, 1989), 294–312; and Aihwa Ong, "The Gender and Labor Politics of Postmodernity," *Annual Reviews of Anthropology* 20 (1991): 279–309.

25. A recent ethnography on gender and the industrializing economy in Thailand is Mary-Beth Mills, *Thai Women in the Global Labor Force: Consuming Desires, Contested Selves* (New Brunswick, N.J.: Rutgers University Press, 1999).

26. For studies on Thai gender systems in context of modernity, see: Mary-Beth Mills, "Attack of the Widow Ghosts: Gender, Death, and Modernity in Northeast Thailand," in *Bewitching Women, Pious Men*, ed. Ong and Peletz, 244–73; Penny Van Esterik, "Deconstructing Display: Gender and Development in Thailand," Thai Studies Project/WID Consortium paper no. 2, York University, Toronto, 1989. On sexual and gender categories, see: Peter A. Jackson, *Male Homosexuality in Thailand: An Interpretation of Contemporary Thai Sources* (New York: Global Academic Publishers, 1989); Rosalind C. Morris, "Three Sexes and Four Sexualities: Redressing the Discourses on Gender and Sexuality in Contemporary Thailand," *positions* 2, no. 1 (1994): 15–43. Other examples are found in anthologies, including Peter A. Jackson and Gerard Sullivan, eds., *Lady Boys, Tom Boys, Rent Boys: Male and Female Homosexualities in Contemporary Thailand* (Binghamton, N.Y.: Harrington Park Press, Haworth Press, 1999), 1–28.

27. The research challenges and linguistic dimensions of formal interviewing are laid out in Charles L. Briggs, *Learning How to Ask: A Sociolinguistic Appraisal of the Role of the Interview in Social Science Research* (London: Cambridge University Press, 1986).

28. On the rise of "multisited" ethnographic research, see Michael M. J. Fischer, "Emergent Forms of Life: Anthropologies of Late or Postmodernities," *Annual Review of Anthropology* 28 (1999): 455–78.

29. Eric Wakin, *Anthropology Goes to War: Professional Ethics and Counterinsurgency in Thailand* (Madison: University of Wisconsin/Center for Southeast Asian Studies, 1992).

30. For examples of the Cornell studies, see G. W. Skinner and T. Kirsch, eds., *Change and Persistence in Thai Society* (Ithaca, N.Y.: Cornell University Press, 1975). Private market research began in the 1960s, providing information such as Business Research's 1966 consumer profile of Bangkok. For an intriguing 1960s travel book, I recommend glancing at an unusually homoerotic 1968 account of Bangkok: James Kirkup, *Cities of the World: Bangkok* (London: Phoenix House, 1968).

CHAPTER 1. FROM SHOPHOUSE
TO DEPARTMENT STORE

1. Before Central Department Store opened, Bangkok had earlier stores that organized into departments, such as the turn-of-the-century European stores and Tai Fah, located in Chinatown. In the northern city of Chiang Mai, the Tantrapan Department Store dates to 1942. However, these are not considered the first true large-scale department stores and did not develop other branches. Sources on Central Department Store and the Chirathivat family include: "Department Stores Getting into High Gear," *Business in Thailand*, February 1987, 83–91; "Retailing," *Business in Thailand*, March 1981, 33–37; "Central Department Store Co. Ltd.," *Business Review*, September 1985, 125–26; "Department Stores and Shopping Centres: The List Grows Longer," *Business Review* (Thailand), March 1984, 9–24; Duangporn Prinyanut, "Store Wars: The Sequel," *Nation, Year in Review* (Bangkok), December 1992, 71; Tim Harlow, "Changing Patterns of Bangkok Retailing," *Property Review*, March–May 1992, 14–17; Kevin Hewison, "The Structure of Bangkok Capital in Thailand," *Southeast Asian Journal of Social Science* 16, no. 1 (1988): 81–91; Takio Nakagawa, "Asian Retailing Revolution and Japanese Companies: The Thailand Case," International Economic Conflict Discussion Paper no. 34, Tokyo, 1987; Pasuk Phongpaichit and Chris Baker, *Thailand: Economy and Politics* (New York: Oxford University Press, 1995); Pasuk Phongpaichit and Chris Baker, *Thailand's Boom and Bust* (Chiang Mai: Silkworm Books, 1998); "Central song hua hawk radom tun khayaay sakhaa" (Central spearheading branch expansion investment), *Phujatkaan* (Manager Thailand), November 11, 1994, 1; Santi Chatterji, "Central's Plaza," *Business in Thailand*, March 1980, 33–36; Central Department Store, "History," http://www.central.co.th/web/html/aboutus/history.html [accessed November 4, 2001].

2. On department stores in Europe and the United States, see: Susan Porter Benson, *Counter Cultures: Saleswomen, Managers, and Customers in American Department Stores, 1890–1940* (Urbana: University of Illinois Press, 1986); William R. Leach, *Land of Desire: Merchants, Power, and the Rise of a New American Culture* (New York: Pantheon, 1993); Frank M. Mayfield, *The Department Store Story* (New York: Fairchild Publications, 1949); and Judith R. Walkowitz, *City of Dreadful Delight: Narratives of Sexual Danger in Late Victorian London* (Chicago: University of Chicago, 1992). Émile Zola's 1882 novel *Au bonheur des dames* (first published in English, as *The Ladies' Paradise*, in 1883) chronicles the violent ascendance of a French department store like Printemps over small shops, using gender and sexual themes to convey this history. In *Land of Desire*, Leach locates

the emergence of the U.S. department store in the context of the shift from an agrarian economy to a market economy, showing how these stores generated a new visual culture and value system.

3. Samrit Funeral Commemoration, "Chirathivat Samrit," Nangseu thi raleuk ngansob (Samrit Chirathivat, Funeral/cremation remembrance book), November 3, 1992, unpaginated copy of manuscript from Chulalongkorn University Library, Bangkok (cited page numbers added by author); and Bunsri Funeral Commemoration, "'Mae' Bunsri Chirathivat," Nangseu thi raleuk ngansob ("Mother" Bunsri Chirathivat, Funeral/cremation remembrance book), dated 2541 B.E. (1998), manuscript from Chulalongkorn University Library, Bangkok. Supecha Boughthip obtained these copies for me.

4. See, for example, Aihwa Ong and Donald Nonini, eds., *Ungrounded Empires: The Cultural Politics of Modern Chinese Transnationalism* (New York: Routledge, 1997).

5. During the reign of King Rama V (1868–1910), Bangkok featured a few European stores "on the line of the departmental stores." Arnold Wright, ed., *Twentieth Century Impressions of Siam: Its History, People, Commerce, Industries, and Resources* (1908; reprint, Bangkok: White Lotus Press, 1994), 273. English establishments such as John Samson's or Harry A. Badman and Company provided the imported accoutrements of elite living to a limited group of European and aristocratic Thai consumers. They sold furniture, silverware, carpets, and the blouses, stockings, and shoes that were elements of the emerging hybrid fashion of aristocratic Thais, which selectively combined Thai, Lao, and Western styles. Badman also specialized in naval and military uniforms, benefiting from the ceremonial requirements of the expanding Siamese state. But in the early twentieth century, broad social changes radically altered the climate for European stores like Samson's and Badman's—changes in politics (the constitutional monarchy and rise of civil-military governments); in class (the rise of a middle class of government workers); and war (World War II and Japanese occupation). These European department stores did not survive. John Samson's building was converted to the Public Works Office, a concrete manifestation of the shift from royal to bureaucratic power.

6. Larry Sternstein, *Bangkok Portrait* (Bangkok: Bangkok Metropolitan Organization, Committee on the Rattanakosin Bicentennial, 1982).

7. On return migration as sojourning, see Wang Gungwu, "Sojourning: The Chinese Experience in Southeast Asia," in *Sojourners and Settlers: Histories of Southeast Asia and the Chinese in Honour of Jennifer Cushman*, ed. Anthony Reid, with

the assistance of Kristine Alilunas Rodgers (St. Leonards, NSW: Allen & Unwin, 1996), 1–14.

8. Jamie Mackie calls the Chinese populations in Southeast Asia "mestizo" or "creole." See Jamie Mackie, "Changing Patterns of Chinese Big Business in Southeast Asia," in *Southeast Asian Capitalists,* ed. Ruth McVey (Ithaca, N.Y.: Cornell University Press, 1992), 161–90. On the complexities of overseas Chinese identity, see Bao, "Marriage among Ethnic Chinese in Bangkok: An Ethnography of Gender, Sexuality, and Ethnicity over Two Generations," Ph.D. diss., University of California, Berkeley, 1994; Reid, ed., *Sojourners and Settlers;* G. W. Skinner, *Chinese Society in Thailand* (London: Oxford University Press, 1957).

9. Samrit Funeral Commemoration, 91. Unless otherwise noted, all quoted translations of Thai sources into English are my own.

10. Khao san, which means "unhusked rice," is also the name of a lane to the north of the palace, which is now lined with guesthouses and shops that cater to backpackers.

11. James Ingram, *Economic Change in Thailand Since 1850* (Stanford, CA: Stanford University Press, 1955).

12. Banking in Thailand was monopolized by Europeans until after World War II. Chinese business families, laborers, women merchants, and Thai farmers did not use banks to save and invest. Chinese merchants had their own systems of savings and loans. Many common people used pawn shops (run by Sino-Thais) and invested their money in alternative modes of banking: gold jewelry or land. In the 1960s, the government discouraged pawn shops and promoted banks, which helped banks accumulate capital for investments in large new projects, such as manufacturing.

13. Samrit Funeral Commemoration, 91. In Singapore, Hainanese (Hailam) were associated with coffee shops such as those clustered along Hylam (i.e., Hainan) Road.

14. The Jeng's store sign read KENG SENG LEE, which, according to the Central Department Store, "History," web page, means "baskets for sale." According to Samrit's funeral commemoration, it means "Hailam samrit pol," or Hailam successful benefit. This Thai translation uses *Samrit,* which was the Thai name chosen for Hokseng.

15. On ethnic occupational niches, see, for example, Sternstein, *Bangkok Portrait;* and Samrit Funeral Commemoration. Bao notes that Hainanese were associated with sex trade businesses, while Landon reports that men from Hainan

were clients at brothels. See Jiemin Bao, "Reconfiguring Chineseness in Thailand: Articulating Ethnicity along Sex/Gender and Class Lines," in *Genders and Sexualities in Modern Thailand*, ed. Peter A. Jackson and Nerida Cook (Chiang Mai: Silkworm Books, 1999), 67; and Kenneth P. Landon, *Siam in Transition* (Chicago: University of Chicago Press, 1939), 162.

16. Pasuk and Baker, *Thailand: Economy and Politics.*

17. On retail, see Ingram, *Economic Change in Thailand*, 131. Manufacturing in Bangkok was limited at this time to fewer than a dozen major factories producing construction materials or consumer goods: cement, aerated water, soap, cigarettes, and leather goods (ibid., 133). There were also numerous small print shops and workshops making salt, beer, perfume, furniture, matches, medicine, and pottery, mainly owned by Chinese entrepreneurs. Some, like the cigarette and match factory, employed young Thai women (see Kevin Hewison, "Industry Prior to Industrialisation: Thailand," paper presented at the conference Industrializing Elites in Southeast Asia, Sukhothai, Thailand December 1–12, 1986, 8, 11). Much to the dismay of Sino-Thai entrepreneurs and foreign observers, the climate was prohibitive for serious manufacturing until the 1960s (when the government changed its economic policies to promote import substitution), and the Thai economy grew mainly by increasing rice exports and consumer trade.

18. On the shophouse, see Marc Askew, *Interpreting Bangkok: The Urban Question in Thai Studies* (Bangkok: Thai Studies Section, Chulalongkorn University Press, 1994); and Ara Wilson, "Women in the City of Consumption: Markets and the Construction of Gender in Bangkok, Thailand," Ph.D. diss., Department of Anthropology, City University of New York Graduate School, 1997, chapter 1.

19. For this view of social transformations under capitalist economies, I am drawing on Linda Nicholson and Karl Polanyi, among others. Linda Nicholson, "Feminism and Marx: Integrating Kinship with the Economic," in *Feminism as Critique: On the Politics of Gender*, ed. Seyla Benhabib and Drucilla Cornell, (Minneapolis: University of Minnesota Press, 1987), 16–33; Karl Polanyi, *The Great Transformation: The Political and Economic Origins of Our Time* (1944; Boston: Beacon Press, 1957).

20. Bao, "Reconfiguring Chineseness in Thailand." See also Cristina Blanc-Szanton, "Gender and Inter-Generational Resource Allocation Resource Allocation among Thai and Sino-Thai Households," in *Structure and Strategies: Women, Work and Family*, ed. Leela Dube and Rajni Paltriwala (London: Sage Publications, 1990), 79–102; and Skinner, *Chinese Society in Thailand.*

21. Jiemin Bao, "Same Bed, Different Dreams: Ethnicized Sexuality and Gen-

der among Elderly Chinese Immigrants in Bangkok," *positions* 4, no. 2 (1998): 475–502, quotation from 489.

22. The interview, reprinted in the Bunsri Funeral Commemoration, 73–75, was published in the women's magazine *Praew.* Lamsang Naamfeng, "Bantheuk wai nai Praew" (Notes in Praew), *Praew* 9, no. 216 (2531 B.E. [1988]): 180–181, 184–185.

23. Bunsri Funeral Commemoration, 52, 73.

24. Bao, "Reconfiguring Chineseness in Thailand," 65.

25. Lamsang, "Bantheuk," in Bunsri Funeral Commemoration, 74. The award was the National Exemplary Mother Award for Patience, Perseverance, and Diligence.

26. Sternstein, *Bangkok Portrait*, 106.

27. Bao, "Reconfiguring Chineseness in Thailand."

28. Bunsri Funeral Commemoration, 52, 56, 54, 57–59, 74.

29. On kinship labor, see Micaela di Leonardo, "The Female World of Cards and Holidays: Women, Families and the Work of Kinship," *Signs* 12, no. 3 (1987): 440–53.

30. Bao, "Same Bed, Different Dreams."

31. Bao, "Reconfiguring Chineseness in Thailand," 65.

32. Bunsri Funeral Commemoration, 74.

33. Dole Anderson, *Marketing and Development: The Thailand Experience* (East Lansing: Michigan State University International Business and Economic Studies, 1970), 70–71, 144; also see chapter 4 on IBC of this book for middle-class training and education.

34. Samrit Funeral Commemoration, 66.

35. John Knodel, *Gender and Schooling in Thailand* (New York: Population Council, Research Division Working Papers, 1994).

36. Pasuk and Baker, *Thailand's Boom and Bust.*

37. Samrit Funeral Commemoration, 138.

38. The exact amount of Tiang's investment in Central is cut off in my copy of the manuscript (ibid., 139). It appears to be 1,000 to 9,000 baht, or approximately U.S.$100 to $900.

39. The dates reported for the opening of the next few stores are contradictory. One article states 2571 (1928), which would have been too early; the Samrit Funeral Commemoration and the web page for Central Department Store, "History," writes 2460 (1917), but I believe this to be a typo.

40. Samrit Funeral Commemoration, 141. As in the chapter text, the italicized terms in the ad were transliterated into Thai from the English.

41. Perhaps Sino-Thai readers readily know which centralizing Chinese regime Tiang admired—Kuomintong, Sun Yat-sen, Chiang Kai-shek, or communist—but the text does not say. It is likely that "Tong Iang" refers to the nationalizing Chinese state. The southeastern China region from which the Jengs migrated had been rife with nationalist, then communist, revolutionary activity.

42. Samrit Funeral Commemoration, 142; see also Central Department Store, "History."

43. Tai/Thai nationalism was particularly promoted by Phibul Songkram, a dictatorial ruler from 1938 to 1944 and then again from 1948 to 1957.

44. From 1939 to 1942, under the military dictatorship of Field Marshal Phibul Songkram, the government issues a series of twelve national conventions, or Rattha Niyom, along with slogans like "Nonpatriots make the world untidy." These concerned: the name of the country as "Thailand" (a nationalist move meant to flag the ethnic Tai people over others); national security issues; the national flag, national anthem, and royal anthem; promotions of Thai-made products; nation-building projects; citizenship and language issues; the promotion of Westernized dress—hats, shoes, skirts, and blouses for women—and repression of some traditional practices (notably betel-nut chewing); the work routine; and the treatment of children, elderly, and handicapped. Phibul put forth an interventionist vision of culture that modernized conceptions of ethnic Thai culture. He promoted such modernizing measures as having husbands kiss wives before leaving the house and eradicating betel-nut chewing. See, for example, David K. Wyatt, *Thailand: A Short History* (New Haven, Conn.: Yale University Press, 1982), chapter 10.

45. In 1952, Chinese residents protested an increase in their annual fees to 100 baht (U.S.$20). See Victor Purcell, *The Chinese in Southeast Asia* (1951; 2nd ed., Kuala Lumpur: Oxford, 1980), 160.

46. Ibid., 163.

47. Pasuk and Baker, *Thailand's Boom and Bust*, 24.

48. I have no information on whether Tiang changed his name as well.

49. The introduction of surnames in Siam reconceptualized local marriage, family, and descent norms—and women's and children's public identities—in patrifocal ways that contradicted rural custom. Chinese families were, of course, well accustomed to the organizing principle of male family names.

50. Preecha Kuwinpant, *Marketing in North-Central Thailand: A Study of Socio-Economic Organization in a Thai Market Town* (Bangkok: Chulalongkorn University Social Research Institute, 1980).

51. See, for example, Keyes, *Thailand*, 156. After the 1949 Chinese revolu-

tion, sending remittances became difficult, which led to Sino-Thai investing more money locally.

52. This population figure is from D. J. M. Tate, *The Making of Modern South-East Asia*, vol. 2 of *The Western Impact* (Kuala Lumpur: Oxford University Press, 1979), 538. In 1947, the population of Bangkok proper was tallied at 889,538, and for Thonburi across the river, 281,343 (Wolf Donner, *The Five Faces of Thailand: An Economic Geography* [St. Lucia, Queensland: University of Queensland Press, 1978], table 161: 791).

53. Central Department Store, "History."

54. Ibid.

55. On haggling as a cultural mode, see Deborah Kapchan, *Gender on the Market: Moroccan Women and the Revoicing of Tradition* (Philadelphia: University of Pennsylvania Press, 1996).

56. Samrit says that the Central shopping complex located in Lardprao is based on the Japanese model (Samrit Funeral Commemoration, 154), but what counts as Japanese or American models varies. Business reports claim that Central draws on "the American concept of the all-inclusive one-stop suburban shopping center" and "the superb ambience of Los Angeles' Century Plaza," while the Japanese concept is found in "leisure centers" and "the convenience of top department stores in Tokyo" ("Retailing," 34; and "Bangkok's Major Shopping Complexes," *Business Review* (Thailand) (March 1983): 29. On the Japanese model, see Nakagawa, "Asian Retailing Revolution and Japanese Companies."

57. Suchart Prasith-rathsint and S. Piampiti, eds., *Women in Development: Implications for Population Dynamics in Thailand* (Bangkok: NIDA, 1982).

58. Dole Anderson, *Marketing and Development: The Thailand Experience* (East Lansing: Michigan State University International Business and Economic Studies, 1970).

59. Thomas Kirsch, "Text and Context: Buddhist Sex Roles/Culture of Gender Revisited," *American Ethnologist* 12, no. 3 (1985): 302–20; Thomas Kirsch, "Buddhism, Sex-Roles and Thai Society," in *Women of Southeast Asia*, ed. Penny Van Esterik, Northern Illinois University Occasional Paper no. 9 (Dekalb, Ill.: Center for Southeast Asian Studies, 1982), 16–41.

60. On training working-class clerks to match middle-class consumer culture in the United States, see Benson, *Counter Cultures*.

61. Samrit Funeral Commemoration: on appearances, 66; family principles, 114–19 and 198; business principles, 195–98.

62. Walkowitz, *City of Dreadful Delight*, 47.

63. Leach, *Land of Desire*, 76.

64. Nicholson, "Feminism and Marx."

65. Of Samrit's brothers, Vanchai has been the (titular) head of the Central Group; Suthichart has been retail business president; Suthikiati, an executive of marketing and planning. His half brothers (by Bunsri) Sudthidej and Suthitham have managed Central's business and property development as well.

66. Hewison, "The Structure of Bangkok Capital in Thailand," 85–89.

67. John Kohut, "A Cut-Price, Cutthroat Challenge," *Asia Inc.*, July 1996, http://www.asia_inc.com/index.php?articleID = 1025 [accessed November 11, 2001]. A Chirathivat son dated a daughter of a founder of Robinson's Department Store, a chain that merged with Central in the late 1990s. On the royal marriage, Pasuk and Baker, *Thailand: Economy and Politics*, 171 n. 23.

68. "Retailing."

69. "Department Stores Getting into High Gear," 97.

70. Duangporn, "Store Wars."

71. Pasuk and Baker, *Thailand's Boom and Bust.*

72. Craig Reynolds, "Tycoons and Warlords: Modern Thai Social Formations and Chinese Historical Romance," in *Sojourners and Settlers*, ed. Reid, 137.

73. On the Alien Business Law, see "Department Stores and Shopping Centres," 9–10.

74. Samrit Funeral Commemoration: 153.

75. Bao, *Reconfiguring Chineseness*, 67.

76. "Top Companies 1985: Central Department Store Co., Ltd.," *Business Review* (Thailand), September 1985, 126.

77. Samrit Funeral Commemoration, 66.

78. Aihwa Ong, *Flexible Citizenship: The Cultural Logics of Transnationality* (Durham, N.C.: Duke University Press, 1999).

CHAPTER 2. THE ECONOMIES
OF INTIMACY IN THE GO-GO BAR

1. On the trade oriented to foreigners, relevant primary research in English includes: Marc Askew, "Sex Workers in Bangkok: Refashioning Female Identities in the Global Pleasure Space," in *Bangkok: Place, Practice and Representation* (London: Routledge, 2002), 251–83; Eric Cohen, "Lovelorn Farangs: The Correspondence between Foreign Men and Thai Girls," *Anthropological Quarterly* 59, no. 3 (1986); 115–27; Eric Cohen, "Sensuality and Venality in Bangkok: The Dynamics of Cross-Cultural Mapping of Prostitution," *Deviant Behavior* 8 (1987):

223–34; Cleo Odzer, "Patpong Prostitution: Its Relationship to, and Effect on, the Position of Women in Thai Society," Ph.D. diss., New School for Social Research, New York, 1990; and Thanh-Dam Truong, *Sex, Money and Morality: Prostitution and Tourism in South-East Asia* (London: Zed Books, 1990). Analytical discussions of the Western-oriented sex business that include research can be found in Lenore Manderson, "Public Sex Performances in Patpong and Explorations of the Edges of Imagination," *Journal of Sex Research* 29 (1992): 451–75; and Ryan Bishop and Lillian Robinson, *Night Market: Sexual Cultures and the Thai Economic Miracle* (New York: Routledge, 1998). Few works study the customers' or Westerners' involvement in detail, but see Cohen, "Lovelorn Farangs"; Manderson, "Public Sex Performances"; Bishop and Robinson, *Night Market;* and Julie O'Connell Davidson, "British Sex Tourists in Thailand," in *(Hetero)Sexual Politics*, ed. Mary Maynard and June Purvis (London and Bristol, Pa.: Taylor and Francis, 1995), 42–64. Research on Thai brothels and the local trade include Pasuk Phongpaichit's classic study and foundational analysis, *From Peasant Girl to Bangkok Masseuse* (Geneva: ILO Report, 1980); Chris Lyttleton, "The Good People of Isan: Commercial Sex in Northeast Thailand," *Australian Journal of Anthropology* 5, no. 3 (1994): 257–79; Pamela S. DaGrossa, "Kamphaeng Din: A Study of Prostitution in the All-Thai Brothels of Chiang Mai City," *Crossroads* 4, no. 2 (1989): 1–7; Wathinee Boonchalakski and Phillip Guest, *Prostitution in Thailand* (Salaya Thailand: Institute for Population and Social Research, Mahidol University on Bangkok, 1994); and Susanne Thorbek, *Voices from the City: Women of Bangkok* (London: Zed Books, 1987). On the question of trafficking of women within, into, or from Thailand, for an overview, see Siriporn Skrobanek, Nattaya Boonpakdi, and Chutima Janthakeero, *The Traffic in Women: Human Realities of the International Sex Trade* (London: Zed Books, 1997); and Asia Watch's 1993 report on Burmese women into Thailand: Asia Watch, Women's Rights Project, *A Modern Form of Slavery: Trafficking of Burmese Women and Girls into Brothels in Thailand* (New York: Human Rights Watch, 1993). On child prostitution, Heather Montgomery offers a rare and thoughtful ethnographic study: "Children, Prostitution, and Identity: A Case Study from a Tourist Resort in Thailand," in *Global Sex Workers: Rights, Resistance, and Redefinition*, ed. Kamala Kempadoo and Jo Doezema (New York, Routledge, 1998), 139–50.

Much critical analysis of prostitution discusses the prevailing Thai attitudes toward sex workers, such as the following: Sukanya Hantrakul, "Prostitution in Thailand," in *Development and Displacement: Women in Southeast Asia*, ed. G. Chandler, N. Sullivan, and J. Branson, Monash Papers on Southeast Asia no. 18 (Melbourne, Australia: Center for Southeast Asian Studies, Monash University,

1988), 115–36; Nerida Cook's critique of "middle-class" projects in "'Dutiful Daughters,' Estranged Sisters: Women in Thailand," in *Gender and Power in Affluent Asia*, ed. Krishna Sen and Maila Stivens (New York: Routledge, 1998), 250–90; Parissara Liewkeat, "Theorizing 'Women,' Practicing Prostitution: U.S. and Thai Feminists Discursive Practices," master's thesis, Ohio State University, 1996; Rachel Harrison's discussion of prostitution in literature: "The Madonna and the Whore: Self/'Other' Tensions in the Characterization of the Prostitute by Thai Female Authors," in *Genders and Sexualities in Modern Thailand*, ed. Peter A. Jackson and Nerida Cook (Chiang Mai: Silkworm Books, 1999), 168–90; and Jiemin Bao's discussion of attitudes toward sex work among Sino-Thai men and women: "Reconfiguring Chineseness in Thailand: Articulating Ethnicity along Sex/Gender and Class Lines," in *Genders and Sexualities in Modern Thailand*, ed. Jackson and Cook, 63–77. Much of the English-language anthropological discussion of prostitution in Thailand has considered the relationship between the sizable sex trade and Thai culture and society, for example, Buddhism: Khin Thitsa, "Nuns, Mediums, and Prostitutes in Chiengmai: A Study of Some Marginal Categories of Women," Women and Development in Southeast Asia Occasional Paper no. 1, University of Kent at Canterbury, 1983; Charles Keyes, "Mother or Mistress but Never a Monk: Buddhist Notions of Female Gender in Rural Thailand," *American Ethnologist* 11, no. 2 (1984): 223–39; Thomas Kirsch, "Text and Context: Buddhist Sex Roles/Culture of Gender Revisited," *American Ethnologist* 12, no. 3 (1985); and Marjorie M. Muecke, "Mother Sold Food, Daughter Sells Her Body: The Cultural Continuity of Prostitution," *Social Science and Medicine* 35, no. 7 (1992): 891–901; for criticisms of this work and synthetic discussions of the English-language scholarship, see Nicola Tannenbaum, "Buddhism, Prostitution, and Sex: Limits on the Academic Discourse on Gender in Thailand," in *Genders and Sexualities in Modern Thailand*, ed. Jackson and Cook, 243–60; and Cook, "'Dutiful Daughters,' Estranged Sisters." I am not recounting here the ample and neglected primary research on sex work in Thai or the growing body of scholarship in English and Thai concerning HIV/AIDS, which often addresses prostitution; relatedly, there are a number of empirical studies on Thai sexual practices and attitudes, especially some emanating from Mahidol University, for example, Nicholas Ford and S. Kaetsawang, "The Socio-Cultural Context of the Transmission of HIV in Thailand," *Social Science and Medicine* 33, no. 4 (1991): 405–14.

2. Pasuk, *From Peasant Girl;* Truong, *Sex, Money and Morality.*

3. James C. Scott, *The Moral Economy of the Peasant: Rebellion and Subsistence*

in Southeast Asia (New Haven, Conn.: Yale University Press, 1976); E. P. Thompson, *Customs in Common* (New York: New Press, 1993).

4. Truong, *Sex, Money and Mortality;* Pasuk, *From Peasant Girl;* Siriporn et al., *The Traffic in Women.*

5. The history of prostitution in Thailand predates the Vietnam War. Brothels date to nineteenth-century Bangkok particularly and have cultural precedents in the polygyny of the aristocracy (see Pasuk, *From Peasant Girl*). The sex industry developed in relation to international trade and politics and the growth of wage labor in the country. In the 1960s, Bangkok and the beach resort of Pattaya became key R&R spots for U.S. GIs, and the United States had three bases in the country. Northeastern Thai women tended to form ongoing and longer-term relations with GIs, often living with them; other Thais called these women rented wives. After the U.S. troops were asked to leave Thailand, some of these women entered the Bangkok trade that was revamped for foreign tourists, for example, in Soi Cowboy. For more detailed history of the sex trades in Thailand, see Pasuk, *From Peasant Girl;* and Truong, *Sex, Money and Morality.*

6. Mary-Beth Mills, *Thai Women in the Global Labor Force: Consuming Desires, Contested Selves* (New Brunswick, N.J.: Rutgers University Press, 1999).

7. On customers, see Cohen, "Lovelorn Farangs," for a sympathetic evaluation of Western customers of the sex trade. More critical analyses of the racial, gendered, class, and national dimensions involved in Western men's desire and behavior in the trade are found in Bishop and Robinson, *Night Market;* Davidson, "British Sex Tourists"; and Cleo Odzer, *Patpong Sisters: An American Woman's View of the Bangkok Sex World* (New York: Blue Moon Books, Arcade Publishing, 1994).

8. Mills, *Thai Women in the Global Labor Force.*

9. The often-discussed practice of families debt-bonding their daughters to brothels or massage parlors represents a different trade from the one I discuss here. These venues, ubiquitous nationwide, are patronized mainly by Thai and, in the south, Malaysian clients. Massage parlors and especially brothels typically present much more regulated and confining work conditions than the go-go bar or beer bar. Women have virtually no ability to choose customers and limited ability to negotiate price, time, or services. Young women are recruited into brothels from the northern province of Thailand, including from hill-tribe populations, or from neighboring countries (e.g., Yunnan, Burma). These circuits involve networks of gangs and gray-market organizations, often connected to powerful Thai elites. The routes to the massage parlors are more varied. For more information on these trades, see, for example, Wathinee and Guest, *Prostitution*

in Thailand; Siriporn et al., *The Traffic in Women;* Asia Watch, Women's Rights Project, *A Modern Form of Slavery*.

10. Mills, *Thai Women in the Global Labor Force*.

11. Andrew Harris, *Bangkok after Dark* (New York: MacFadden Books, 1968).

12. The only sex-show performer I ever heard express pride in her work was a transsexual woman who proudly pointed out that these shows drew international audiences to Thailand and brought her son to see the show.

13. Megan Sinnott, "Masculinity and *Tom* Identity in Thailand," in *Lady Boys, Tom Boys, Rent Boys: Male and Female Homosexualities in Contemporary Thailand,* eds. Peter A. Jackson and Gerard Sullivan (Binghamton, N.Y.: Harrington Park Press, Haworth Press, 1999), 112.

14. Rory O'Merry, *My Wife in Bangkok* (Berkeley: Asia Press, 1990).

15. Mills, *Thai Women in the Global Labor Force*.

16. Ibid.

17. Marjorie M. Muecke, "Make Money Not Babies: Changing Status of Northern Thai Women." *Asian Survey* 24, no. 4 (1984): 459–70.

18. William J. Klausner, *Reflections in a Log Pond* (Bangkok: Suksit Siam, 1972).

19. O'Merry, *My Wife in Bangkok*, 120.

CHAPTER 3. MBK

1. Whether tom incorporates lesbianism, or female homosexuality, varies: sometimes no, increasingly yes, although Megan Sinnott points out that for tom themselves, the term implies lesbian sexuality. See Megan Sinnott, "Masculinity and *Tom* Identity in Thailand," in *Lady Boys, Tom Boys, Rent Boys: Male and Female Homosexualities in Contemporary Thailand,* eds. Peter A. Jackson and Gerard Sullivan (Binghamton, N.Y.: Harrington Park Press, Haworth Press, 1999), 97–120. A music magazine depicted the Canadian pop singer k. d. lang as a "true *tom*," which equates true tom with lesbian and suggests that foreigners are sometimes recognized as tom (but not always). On the concept of female masculinity and manifestations in the United States, see Judith Halberstam, *Female Masculinity* (Durham, N.C.: Duke University Press, 1998).

2. In this chapter, I focus more on the tom than the dee. The dee is considered by Thai society and by many tom and dee to be a "normal" woman who happens to be with a tom rather than a man. The dee is not usually considered by others as a sexual identity defined by an erotic orientation to women or to tom (i.e., a lesbian). Dee are "real" women or "natural" women, not homosex-

ual or gender deviant; it is assumed, often with resigned sadness by their tom partners, that the dee will eventually fulfill the diffuse obligation for women to marry. By most accounts (besides a few self-named dee), the dee is a temporary identity defined in relation to the tom. Thus, typically, a dee requires a tom to be a dee and does not present an independent sexual persona. The tom identity, on the other hand, stands alone. See Peter A. Jackson and Gerard Sullivan, "A Panoply of Roles: Sexual and Gender Diversity in Contemporary Thailand," in *Lady Boys, Tom Boys, Rent Boys*, ed. Jackson and Sullivan, 1–28; Peter A. Jackson, *Male Homosexuality in Thailand: An Interpretation of Contemporary Thai Sources* (New York: Global Academic Publishers, 1989); Matthana Chetamee, "Withi chiwit le chiwit khrawpkhrua khong ying rak ying" (Lifestyle and family life among women who love women), master's thesis, Thammasat University, Bangkok, 2539 B.E. (1996); Sinnott, "Masculinity and *Tom* Identity in Thailand."

3. Since my first trip to Thailand, several scholars have written about the tom: Megan Sinnott in particular has undertaken in-depth research on the tom-dee. See Sinnott, "Masculinity and *Tom* Identity in Thailand." See also Jackson, *Male Homosexuality in Thailand*, and "From *Kamma* to Unnatural Vice: Buddhism, Homosexuality and Intolerance in Thailand," paper presented at the School of Oriental and African Studies, University of London, July 1993, 25, 99; Rosalind C. Morris, "Three Sexes and Four Sexualities: Redressing the Discourses on Gender and Sexuality in Contemporary Thailand," *positions* 2, no. 1 (1994): 15–43; Kanokwan Tarawan, "Thailand," in *Unspoken Rules: Sexual Orientation and Women's Human Rights*, ed. Rachel Rosenbloom (San Francisco: International Gay and Lesbian Human Rights Commission, 1995), 203–8; Devika Singh, "Gender Benders: The Role of Masculinity in Thai Lesbianism," unpublished paper, Summer in Thailand Program, Chiang Mai, 1993; Took-Took Thongthiraj, "Toward a Struggle against Invisibility: Love between Women in Thailand," *Amerasia* 20, no. 1 (1994): 45–58 (based on an interview with Anjana Suvarnanand, a cofounder of the Thai lesbian group Anjaree). Within Thailand, there has been at least one master's thesis on Thai "lesbians" at Thammasat University (Matthana, "Lifestyle and Family Life among Women Who Love Women") as well as numerous articles in the popular press. The term *tomboy* is found elsewhere in Southeast Asia: on *tombois* in West Sumatra, see Evelyn Blackwood, "*Tombois* in West Sumatra: Constructing Masculinity and Erotic Desire," *Cultural Anthropology* 13, no. 4 (November 1998): 491–521.

4. On the tom, see, for example, Jackson, *Male Homosexuality in Thailand*; Morris, "Three Sexes and Four Sexualities"; and Sinnott, "Masculinity and *Tom* Identity in Thailand."

5. "Department Stores and Shopping Centres; the List Grows Longer," *Business Review*, (March 1984): 9–24; Takio Nakagawa, "Asian Retailing Revolution and Japanese Companies: The Thailand Case," International Economic Conflict Discussion Paper, no. 34, Tokyo, 1987.

6. Information on the Bulakul family can be found in "Ma Bulakun, Mr.," *Khrai pen khrai nai Prathet Thai 2506 (Who's Who in Thailand 1963)*, vol. 2 (Bangkok, 2506 B.E. [1963]), 245, microfiche, Ohio University Library, Center for International Collections; Pasuk Pongpaichit and Chris Baker, *Thailand: Economy and Politics* (New York: Oxford University Press, 1995), 111–12; Akira Suehiro, "Capitalist Development in Postwar Thailand: Commercial Bankers, Industrial Elite, and Agribusiness Group," in *Southeast Asian Capitalists*, ed. Ruth McVey (Ithaca, N.Y.: Cornell University Press, 1992), 35–63; and Tanom Pipityakorn, "MBK Rental Deal Good for Both Sides," *Bangkok Post*, July 13, 1995, 331. My background on MBK also derives from articles in the business press: "MBK Cuts 625m Baht Off Sirichai's Rent," *Bangkok Post*, October 15, 1994, Business, 17; "Department Stores and Shopping Centres"; "Department Stores Getting into High Gear," *Business in Thailand*, February 1987, 91; Tim Harlow, "Changing Patterns of Bangkok Retailing," *Property Review*, March–May 1992, 14–17; Kung-Nguan Sae-aua, "MBK to Go Ahead with Listing: Chanut," *Nation* (Bangkok), October 13, 1994, B13; Nuntawan Polkwamdee, "MBK Combatants Fail to Find Common Ground," *Bangkok Post*, August 8, 1994, B3; Supakana Sopittakamol, "Costly Promotions Push Up Sales," *Bangkok Post*, July 19, 1993, 51; and Supakana Sopittakamol, "Major Changes in the Market," *Bangkok Post*, July 19, 1993, 50; Supakana Soppitakamol and Kirssana Pansoonthorn, "Downtown Retail Projects to Prosper," *Bangkok Post*, July 28, 1994, 30; Tanom, "MBK Rental Deal"; "Mahbunkhrong Sirichai tong pheung 'Philip Cox'"(Mahbunkhrong Sirichai promotes "Philip Cox"), *Phujatkaan raisapdah* (Manager weekend), July 4–10, 2537 B.E. (1994), 54. For the "Asian retail revolution" in Thailand, see Nakagawa, "Asian Retailing Revolution." Annette Hamilton captures the flavor of "mall-time" Bangkok in "Wonderful, Terrible: Everyday Life in Bangkok," in *A Companion to the City*, ed. Gary Bridge and Sophie Watson (Oxford: Blackwell Publishers, 2000), 460–71. Finally, one overview of retail business in general I drew on is Clifford Guy, *The Retail Development Process: Location, Property, and Planning* (London: Routledge, 1994).

"Bulakul" (pronounced Boonlakoon) is also written as "Bulkul." According to Pasuk Phongpaichit, the Bulakul family descended from an engineer who migrated to Siam from Canton in 1888, operated rice-mill machinery, and purchased a rice mill in 1917; he also founded the Cantonese Thai association (see Pasuk and Baker, *Thailand: Economy and Politics*, 111–12). However, according to *Who's Who in Thailand 1963*, "Ma Bulakul," born in 1897 in China and educated in Hong Kong, was a leading businessman in rice mills, finance, and transport in Thailand, as well as a trade representative. See "Ma Bulakun, Mr.," 245–46. This appears to be the Mah Bulakul of MBK, who, with Boonkrong (apparently his wife), headed the Mah Boonkrong Drying and Silo Company, which operated rice mills and a granary and expanded to an integrated cluster of agricultural, finance, and shipping businesses. When the Siamese government formed a state rice company, Mah Bulakul served as its managing director, leasing his own companies' rice mills. At least in the postwar period, the Bulakul family apparently educated their daughters; one daughter born in the 1930s earned U.S. degrees and became the chairperson of Toshiba Thailand. Reflecting typical shifts from agricultural into urban projects, the Drying and Silo Company transformed into the Mah Boonkrong (MBK) Properties and Development PCL, a mostly privately held, sometimes publicly listed company. Going public lessened Bulakul family control of the business, however. The major shareholder of MBK from the Bulakul family, Sirichai, competed for control of the board with a prominent Sino-Thai businesswoman (an immigrant from Hainan); he managed, through complicated lawsuits, to exert control over the direction of the mall and its holding company.

7. See Wolf Donner, *The Five Faces of Thailand: An Economic Geography* (St. Lucia, Queensland: University of Queensland Press, 1978); and Larry Sternstein, *Bangkok Portrait* (Bangkok: Bangkok Metropolitan Organization, Committee on the Rattanakosin Bicentennial, 1982).

8. Aihwa Ong, *Flexible Citizenship: The Cultural Logics of Transnationality* (Durham, N.C.: Duke University Press, 1999), 21–22.

9. "Department Stores and Shopping Centres," 24.

10. Bangkok retail land sold for U.S.$3,500 per square meter, while residential land sold for $70 to $350 per square meter. Kevin Hewison, "Emerging Social Forces in Thailand: New Political and Economic Roles," in *The New Rich in Asia: Mobile Phones, McDonald's, and Middle-Class Revolution*, ed. Richard Robison and David S. G. Goodman (New York: Routledge, 1996), 137–60.

11. Harlow, "Changing Patterns of Bangkok Retailing."

12. The Australian feminist critic Meaghan Morris, in a provocative meditation on the epistemology of the shopping mall, proposes "pedestrian" as an organizing rubric for discussing reflexively the participation of female consumers. See Meaghan Morris, "Things to Do with Shopping Centres," in *Grafts: Feminist Cultural Criticism*, ed. Susan Sheridan (London: Verso, 1988), 193–225.

13. June Nualtaranee, "Household Consumption and Savings: Random Walk Hypothesis," master's thesis, Thammasat University, Bangkok, 1992.

14. *Key Statistics of Thailand* (Bangkok: National Identity Office, Office of the Prime Minister, 1993).

15. Pasuk and Baker, *Thailand: Economy and Politics*, 163.

16. The MBK mall still has an incomplete feel: in 1994, the top floor had a barely functioning children's entertainment center, and the fifth floor was a ghostly assemblage of shops selling Western-style kitchen and household furnishings. (Because it was so quiet, I used this floor to make phone calls.)

17. James Eckardt, "Malls: Lost in Space," *Manager* (Thailand), March 1995, 15.

18. Shopping malls are composed of layers of leasing and rents, an arrangement deriving from and contributing to real estate speculation. Built on land leased from the state, MBK leases floor space to stall owners at rates that depend on location, particularly which floor: fees on the less prestigious upper floors initially cost about U.S.$6 (147 baht) per square meter. The rent of a short-lived clothing stall amounted to roughly U.S.$800 a month, according to a worker there, a gay man from Isan (the brother of Ploi, one of the bar workers I knew in Patpong). Besides the rent, shop owners must pay fees for cleaning, security, and other services. Rent, not consumer spending per se, produces profits for the shareholders of the MBK Properties and Development PCL. Like other new shopping complexes that made up the retail revolution, MBK relies on a long-term lease to a large department store to attract other lessees. The "anchor" for MBK is the Tokyu Department Store, a U.S.$20 million investment, jointly owned by Thai investors and the Japanese Tokyu Department Store Company (which has branches in Taiwan and Hong Kong). In addition to Tokyu, the lower floors of the mall are ringed by transnational chains and franchises (Mister Donut, KFC, Pizza Hut, Tom's Quik, Watson's Drug Store, Benneton, Pata Shoes) and a few Thai chain stores (Muang Pong Music); these can afford to pay the higher rents commanded by these prime locations. Filling in the remaining spaces are countless salons, stores, and stalls, often run on a small scale by Thai entrepreneurs selling carefully selected goods, sometimes their own manufactures. See Nakagawa, "Asian Retailing Revolution and Japanese Companies," on Tokyu Department Store.

19. Pasuk and Baker, *Thailand: Economy and Politics*, 161; and chapter 1 of this book. American and Japanese models likely influence shopping mall design in Thailand as well. The shopping center form is defined by a department store anchor and by its infrastructure: "These provide an air-conditioned retail envi-

ronment, design features emphasizing pedestrian flow, proper open spaces, good lighting, and visibility of the shop-fronts[;] quality finishes, escalators and parking spaces are well managed and promoted" (Harlow, "Changing Patterns of Bangkok Retailing," 15).

20. Hewison, "Emerging Social Forces in Thailand," 151.

21. Daniel Miller, *A Theory of Shopping* (Ithaca, N.Y.: Cornell University Press, 1998); Grant McCracken, *Culture and Consumption: New Approaches to the Symbolic Character of Goods and Activities* (Bloomington: Indiana University Press, 1988); Mike Featherstone, *Consumer Culture and Postmodernism* (London: Sage Publications, 1991).

22. See Ara Wilson, "Women in the City of Consumption: Markets and the Construction of Gender in Bangkok, Thailand," Ph.D. diss., City University of New York Graduate School, 1997, chapter 2. On the role of department stores in seasonal gift exchanges in Japan, see M. R. Creighton, "Maintaining Cultural Boundaries in Retailing: How Japanese Department Stores Domesticate Things Foreign," *Modern Asian Studies* 25, no. 4 (1992): 675–709.

23. "Department Stores Getting into High Gear," 91.

24. I am drawing on such critical political-economic theories as David Harvey, *The Condition of PostModernity* (Oxford: Basil Blackwell, 1989); and Frederic Jameson, "Postmodernism, or the Cultural Logic of Late Capitalism," *New Left Review* 146 (1984): 53–92. Feminist examples include Doreen B. Massey, *Space, Place and Gender* (Minneapolis: University of Minnesota Press, 1994); and Morris, "Things to Do with Shopping Centres."

25. The graduate student's paper is Singh, "Gender Benders." The research assistant, Kanokwan Tarawan, as an NGO worker and member of the Thai lesbian group, independently wrote an overview about lesbians in Thailand. See Kanokwan, "Thailand."

26. The subject of sex/gender identities has become the grounds for an impressive body of theorizing and research that consider the cultural categories for people, the subjective or intrapsychic or psychological dimensions, or the enactment or performance that (re-)creates such social locations. My use of identity vis-à-vis tom is continuous with anthropological explorations of cultural locations and social roles and statuses. For one review of "identity," see Stuart Hall, "Introduction: Who Needs 'Identity'?" in *Questions of Cultural Identity*, ed. Stuart Hall and Paul DuGay (London: Sage Publications, 1996), 1–17. For a theoretical treatment of sex/gender identification in Thailand, see Morris, "Three Sexes and Four Sexualities."

27. Sinnott, in "Masculinity and *Tom* Identity in Thailand," reports that some

tom explicitly recognize the role as a desirable escape from (or resistance to) hegemonic heterosexual feminine ideals.

28. On homophobia in Thailand, see Jackson, "From *Kamma* to Unnatural Vice"; Jackson, *Male Homosexuality in Thailand;* and Jackson and Sullivan, "A Panoply of Roles." The lesbian group Anjaree has organized to challenge homophobic ideas about gays, lesbians, and kathoey in the women's NGO community, the press, the government, and society at large.

29. There is no formal documentation of the number of women whose family accept, ignore, or condemn tom, dee, or the relations and identities of women who love women. My impressions derive from conversations with individual women and from the evaluations offered by members of the lesbian group Anjaree. See Sinnott, "Masculinity and *Tom* Identity in Thailand," for further discussion.

30. Matthana, "Lifestyle and Family Life among Women Who Love Women."

31. Although marriage is strongly urged and compulsory in some families, there is some flexibility, and increasingly more people are marrying later or not at all; see John Knodel, *Gender and Schooling in Thailand* (New York: The Population Council, Research Division Working Papers, 1994), 43. Speaking about "traditional" central Thai ways, Suvanna reports, "Usually a person who remains single, either by choice or other reasons, is not thought of as unusual. It is generally said that if a person can earn his living without trouble and does not depend too much on other people, he should have full authority to choose his own lifestyle." See Suvanna Kriengkraipetch, "Folksong and Socio-Cultural Change in Village Life," *Asian Review* 2 (1998): 123. A number of scholars note the presence of women who resist or do not foresee marrying. See Mary Beth Mills, *Thai Women in the Global Labor Force: Consuming Desires, Contested Selves* (New Brunswick, NJ: Rutgers University Press, 1999), 160; Cristina Blanc-Szanton, "Gender and Intergenerational Resource Allocation among Thai and Sino-Thai Households," in *Structure and Strategies: Women, Work and Family,* ed. Leela Dube and Rajni Paltriwala (London: Sage Publications, 1990), 93; and chapter 5 of this book.

32. Lillian Faderman, *Odd Girls and Twilight Lovers: A History of Lesbian Life in Twentieth-Century America* (New York: Penguin, 1991); Elizabeth Lapovsky Kennedy and Natalie Davis, *Boots of Leather, Slippers of Gold: The History of a Lesbian Community* (New York: Routledge, 1993).

33. For capitalism and gay identity, see John D'Emilio, *Sexual Politics, Sexual Communities: The Making of a Homosexual Minority in the United States, 1940–1970* (Chicago: University of Chicago Press, 1983); John D'Emilio, "Capitalism and Gay Identity," in *Powers of Desire: The Politics of Sexuality,* ed. Ann Snitow, Chris-

tine Stansell, and Sharon Thompson (New York: Monthly Review Press, 1983), 100–113; Rosemary Hennessy, *Profit and Pleasure: Sexual Identities in Late Capitalism* (New York: Routledge, 2000); and Jennifer Terry, *An American Obsession: Science, Medicine, and Homosexuality in Modern Society* (Chicago: University of Chicago Press, 1999). Dennis Altman has also proposed that the internationalization of "gay" identity and culture is intertwined with global capitalism. See his "Rupture or Continuity? The Internationalization of Gay Identities," *Social Text* 14, no. 3 (fall 1996): 77–94. See also Jasbir Kaur Puar, "Introduction," *GLQ: A Journal of Lesbian and Gay Studies* 8, nos. 1 and 2 (December 2002): 1–6.

34. D'Emilio, "Capitalism and Gay Identity."

35. "Beeppheen kaandamneunchiwit le pritikaam kaanboriphok khong gay kween nay Krungthepmahanakorn" (Lifestyle customs and consumption behaviors of gay queens in Bangkok), *Waansaaw brihaanthurakit* (Saturday business administration) 11, no. 44 (2530 B.E./1987): 51–66.

36. In 1995 an American man opened a gay and lesbian bookstore-cafe and bar called Utopia. For a while in 1990s, Utopia hosted a lesbian pub one night a week in the upstairs bar.

37. The new market niche of teens and young adults in their twenties is not simply a demographic reality but is also the product of marketing discourse. Media in the 1990s described this population as Generation X or *Room X*. This group, the unmarried young with disposable incomes, was significantly constructed by the efforts by manufacturers, retailers, the advertising industry, and popular culture. The interplay among social worlds, people's practices, and corporate efforts in creating a "youth market" reveals one of the ways that the changing market economy articulates with and affects social positions. The youth market also reflects broader changes in the demographics, class structure, and kin economies of Bangkok. In the early 1980s, half of Bangkok's residents were under thirty years old, according to the royal Thai government's publication *Thailand in the 80s* (Bangkok: National Identity Office, Office of the Prime Minister, 1984). Youth spending represented significant changes in the ways ordinary families allocated resources; more youth had access to greater amounts of families' disposable income than ever before, and many parents gave their children money to spend on buying snacks, presents, and clothes. In middle-class and elite families, young people gained more control over this family money, while working-class youth used income they earned at jobs. A sizable group of teenagers had access to cash or even credit to spend on their own: as one manager of a beverage company said, "Teenagers have freedom in choosing what to buy." See Supakana, "Major Changes in the Market."

38. On mixed-race Eurasian figures, see Ong, *Flexible Citizenship*. The late Jan Weisman's Ph.D. dissertation offers the most thorough discussion of the mixed-race *(luuk kreung)* Thai. See Jan Robyn Weisman, "Tropes and Traces: Hybridity, Race, Sex and Responses to Modernity in Thailand," Ph.D. diss., University of Washington, Seattle, 2000.

39. On the "invention" of heterosexuality, see Jonathan Ned Katz, "The Invention of Heterosexuality," *Socialist Review* 20, no. 1(1990): 7–34; and Jonathan Ned Katz, *The Invention of Heterosexuality* (New York: Dutton, 1995).

40. The presence of Western versions of heterosexuality is not new, having long appeared in Thai popular culture, for example, in Thai novels that follow the models of English nineteenth-century narratives. See: Kittiwut Jod Tywaditep, Eli Coleman, and Pacharin Dumronggittigule, "Thailand (Muang Thai)," in *The International Encyclopedia of Sexuality*, vol. 3, ed. Robert T. Francoeur (New York: Continuum, 1997), 1192–265; Craig Reynolds, "Predicaments of Modern Thai History," *Southeast Asia Research* 2, no. 1 (1994): 64–90; and Craig Reynolds, "On the Gendering of Nationalist and Postnationalist Selves in Twentieth Century Thailand," in *Genders and Sexualities in Modern Thailand*, ed. Peter A. Jackson and Nerida Cook (Chiang Mai: Silkworm Books, 1999), 261–74.

41. On television in Thailand, see Annette Hamilton, "The Mediascape of Modern Southeast Asia," *Screen* 33, no. 1 (1992): 81–92; and chapter 4 of this book.

42. On consumer-based heterosexuality in Asia, see essays in Krishna Sen and Maila Stivens, eds., *Gender and Power in Affluent Asia* (London: Routledge, 1998). The scholarship pointing to the multiple possible readings in popular culture texts represents an enormous body of work. For one overview of feminist approaches to popular culture in the West, see Suzanna Danuta Walters, *Material Girls: Making Sense of Feminist Cultural Theory* (Berkeley: University of California, 1995).

43. On Tokyu and families, see "Department Stores Getting into High Gear," 91; "lure trendy family . . . people" comes from Kwanchai Rungfapaisarn, "Bt 300m Set for Major Facelift to Central/Lardprao," *Nation* (Bangkok), November 23, 1994, B2; "capture families . . ." comes from "Strategies of the Discounters Push Department Stores to High-End Niches," *Nation* (Bangkok), October 3, 1994, B12; "one-stop shopping campaign" is from "Expanding or Just Staying Competitive," *Business Review* (Thailand), January 1987, 91; on Robinson's and Pata's philosophy of department stores as fun for all members of the family, see "Department Stores and Shopping Centres," 10, 17, 18.

44. On the place of family-oriented amusements in attracting consumers, see "Suan sanuk boom" (Amusement park boom), *Weekend* (Thailand), February 11–17, 2538 B.E. (1995), 38–41.

45. Maila Stivens, "Theorising Gender, Power, and Modernity," in *Gender and Power in Affluent Asia*, ed. Sen and Stivens, 5.

46. Kathy Peiss, *Cheap Amusements: Working Women and Leisure in Turn-of-the-Century New York* (Philadelphia: Temple University Press, 1988).

47. Kittiwut et al., "Thailand."

48. For example, Faderman, *Odd Girls and Twilight Lovers.*

49. Sinnott suggests that the tom's caretaking of the dee reflects socialization in the female gender rather than performing elements of Thai masculinity (which is seen as far less solicitous). Sinnott, "Masculinity and *Tom* Identity in Thailand," 112.

50. The linguistic concept of gender performativity is not the same as the general use of the theater metaphor in social analysis, because it does not imply a preexisting or core identity to the actor performing social roles. Judith Butler, *Gender Trouble: Feminism and the Subversion of Identity* (New York: Routledge, 1990).

51. "For the Love of God" (interview with Anchalee Jongkhadeekit), *Nation* (Bangkok), February 11, 1997, http://www.nationgroup.com.

52. Halberstam, *Female Masculinity.*

53. Fewer than 10 percent of Thais are Christians, and most of these are Sino-Thai or hill-tribe minorities. However, Western Protestant missionaries, such as from the Church of the Latter-day Saints and other denominations, have been active in the country in the last few decades.

54. "For the Love of God."

55. "From Gay to Tom-Dee: The Strange World," *Phuean Chiwit* 2, no. 6 (1984): 19. Translated and cited in Sinnott, "Masculinity and *Tom* Identity in Thailand," 98.

56. For information about the Anjaree group, see Kanokwan, "Thailand." I first became involved with Anjaree in 1990 and have remained connected with the group since then.

CHAPTER 4. THE FLEXIBLE CITIZENS
OF IBC CABLE TV

1. Ong focuses on wealthy Chinese businessmen; here I extend her arguments to Thais as well. See Aihwa Ong, *Flexible Citizenship: The Cultural Logics of Transnationality* (Durham, N.C.: Duke University Press, 1999). On flexibility as part of the new "post-Fordist" economy and culture, see David Harvey, *The Condition*

of PostModernity (Oxford: Basil Blackwell, 1989); and Emily Martin, *Flexible Bodies: Tracking Immunity in American Culture from the Days of Polio to the Age of AIDS* (Boston: Beacon Press, 1994).

On the executives and managers as representative of the new global economy, see Saskia Sassen, *Globalization and Its Discontents* (New York: New Press, 1998).

2. *Shinawatra Computer & Communications Group*, a special publication of the Bangkok Post (Bangkok, 1991), 9.

3. On the emerging ethnography of global capitalism, see, for example, Sharryn Kasmir and Ara Wilson, "Introduction," *Critique of Anthropology* 19, no. 4 (1999): 376–78; and Daniel Miller, ed., *Worlds Apart: Modernity through the Prism of the Local* (New York: Routledge, 1995).

4. Another exemplary Sino-Thai family enterprise is the family-based CP group, or the Charoen Pokaphand, an often-hostile competitor of Shinawatra. A largely family-run firm, the CP group was originally based in agricultural industries—in a seed and chick shop in Chinatown—but diversified into manufacturing and retail (e.g., 7-Eleven and Makro) and property development and telecommunications (telephone lines and a joint satellite with China) while remaining under "conservative" family control (*Midyear Report* [Bangkok: The Nation, June 1994], 16). CP collaborated with the U.S. company NYNEX to install telephone lines for the government. The CP group has received particular attention for its successful forays into China and for a role in the 1990s U.S. "donor-gate" controversy about Asian or Asian-American funding to the Democratic Party. In 1998, despite mutual hostility, CP and Shinawatra merged their failing cable television concerns.

5. Information on the Shinawatra family is from the following: Yingyord Manchuvisith, "The Shinawatras," *The Nation Mid-year Review: Thai Tycoons— Winners & Losers in the Economic Crisis* (Bangkok: The Nation, July 1998), 27–29; Thailand Government Public Relations Department, National News Bureau, "Thaksin Shinawatra," http://www.thaimain.org/cgibin/newsdesk_perspect.cgi? a = 276&t = index_2.html [accessed October 24, 2001]. Other information comes from IBC and Shinawatra corporate texts and from conversations in the IBC office.

6. Thaksin received an M.A. in criminal justice at Eastern Kentucky University in 1974 followed by a Ph.D. in criminal justice at Sam Houston State University, Texas, in 1978.

7. The original business of Shinawatra was computers (e.g., mainframes and software sold to government branches). SC&C's telecommunication division included mobile phones (now an omnipresent feature of urban life), pagers, and

data technologies. Working jointly with the government, another division ran Thailand's first satellite, Thaicom 1, which provides television transmission, paging services, and e-mail to the provinces of Indonesia and Thailand. Shinawatra's international operations were increasingly active through the 1990s. The IBC Media division was composed of several interrelated concerns: IBC Cable TV; the Rainbow Media Company, which packaged programming and paid commercials for the established television networks; SC Matchbox, a marketing and advertising subsidiary; and a phone-directories division (formerly with AT&T).

8. Yingyord, "The Shinawatras," 27.

9. IBC operated under a twenty-year license from the Mass Communications Organization of Thailand (1989–2009) but merged with the CP corporation's UBC cable television company before the license ended. The Shinawatra Satellite Company joined the government in 1993 to launch the first Thai satellite, Thaicom 1, facilitating television transmission, paging services, and e-mail, among other functions, to the provinces of Thailand and to Indonesia. The Thaicom 1 satellite project gave Shinawatra an eight-year monopoly on satellite transmissions to Thailand (International Broadcasting Corporation Limited, *Annual Report* [Bangkok, 1992], 18).

10. Thai firms are taking advantage of their superiority in this Asian region by exporting their businesses to China and the recently opened neighboring socialist economies. For example, in 1993 IBC began subscriber television with TV 5 in Phnom Penh, a move that involved Thaksin's relations with various elements in Cambodian politics; he is reported as having a close relation with Cambodian's controversial prime minister Hun Sen (the agent of a coup in July 1997) as well as with Hun Sen's rival, Prince Norodom Chakrapong. See Banyat Tasaneeyavej and Nattaya Cheetchotiros, "Thaksin: I'll Step Down if Found Unfit," *Bangkok Post*, October 28, 1994, 2; and *Bangkok Post*, "Thaksin Tops PDP List in Public Wealth Declaration," *Bangkok Post*, November 19, 1994, 1. In 1994—when a bridge was built across the Mekong River, connecting Thailand and Laos—IBC opened a TV station in Vientaine. As IBC noted, at first its "international" label referred only to its programs, but after 1993 it reflected the company's scope as well (or "program delivery points") (International Broadcasting Corporation Public Company Limited, *Annual Report* [Bangkok, 1993], 20).

11. Ong, *Flexible Citizenship*, 21.

12. *Shinawatra Computer & Communications Group*, 9.

13. Yingyord, "The Shinawatras," 27.

14. On the two-way nature of globalization in relation to a nation, see Leela Fernandes's discussion of advertising in India: "Nationalizing 'The Global': Me-

dia Images, Cultural Politics, and the Middle Class in India," *Media, Culture and Society* 22, no. 5 (2000): 611–28.

15. IBC was not allowed to feature commercials in its programming (although the television guide had advertisements). As a holding company, IBC Media was also involved in commercial-"free" TV through the Rainbow Media subsidiary, which sold time slots for commercials. In addition to the revenue from this and from IBC subscribers, IBC also generated profit from paid advertising in other avenues. For example, the IBC television guide was filled with advertisements— gaping mouths in dental ads or pastoral suburban scenes for housing estate promotions—and even the dense show listings themselves featured product logos. It includes *Shopping Express* ("Shop the World by Mail"), a home-shopping catalog for mainly imported consumer goods such as elaborate gold jewelry, German coffeemakers, an Italian breast enlarger, and a U.S. stomach trimmer.

16. On the middle class in Thailand, see Kevin Hewison, "Emerging Social Forces in Thailand: New Political and Economic Roles," in *The New Rich in Asia: Mobile Phones, McDonalds, and Middle-Class Revolution*, ed. Richard Robison and David S. G. Goodman (New York: Routledge, 1996), 137–60. For the "new rich" and middle class in Asia, especially regarding gender, see Maila Stivens, "Theorising Gender, Power, and Modernity," in *Gender and Power in Affluent Asia*, ed. Krishna Sen and Maila Stivens (London: Routledge, 1998), 15.

17. In 1989, Bangkok had more than one million television sets for nearly six million people. The number of those subscribing to IBC increased from 120,000 in 1993 to 140,000 in 1994. In the early 1990s, television sets outnumbered telephones six times over. See *Thailand in the 90s* (Bangkok: National Identity Office, Office of the Prime Minister, 1992).

As IBC spread to the provinces in 1994, using the Thaicom 1 satellite and "direct to home" (DTH) technology, the company predicted that its market niche would be 5 percent of the eight million households with television sets, or four hundred thousand homes (IBC, *Annual Report*, 1993, 23).

18. Ninety percent or more of the 140,000 viewers in Bangkok (in 1994) were Thai citizens rather than foreigners. They were presumably living in families: 70 percent reported being married, in households including on average five or six viewers. Most of the subscriptions were in the name of men (75 percent in 1994), on average thirty-eight years old. For work on media consumption in Thailand, see Annette Hamilton on the place of television and other media, in "The Mediascape of Modern Southeast Asia," *Screen* 33, no. 1 (1992): 81–92; Sara Van Fleet for soap-opera viewership, in "Prime-Time Dramas: Television, Gender and Desire in Thailand's Urban North," unpublished ms. in author's possession,

University of Washington, 1996; and Mary-Beth Mills's 1999 discussion of TV use among Bangkok factory workers, in *Thai Women in the Global Labor Force: Consuming Desires, Contested Selves* (New Brunswick, N.J.: Rutgers University Press, 1999).

19. The cost of subscribing includes a deposit and installation charge and a monthly fee, with additional charges for HBO's channel 5.

20. According to 1992 figures, the average monthly wages for a man working in urban business were just under U.S.$200 in manufacturing, U.S.$230 in commerce, and about U.S.$120 in services. Government employees earned more; for example, a man in an urban government commercial enterprise earned U.S.$420 a month (Suteera Thomson and Maytinee Bhongsvej, *Profile of Women in Thailand*, prepared for the UN Economic and Social Commission for Asia and the Pacific [Bangkok: Gender and Development Research Institute, 1995], 61)—however, government employees accounted for only 14 percent of IBC subscribers in 1994. Although these are average wages, well-educated workers do not receive dramatically higher pay, as indicated by 1987 figures, when the average monthly pay of single working eighteen- to twenty-four-year-olds with a high school education was roughly U.S.$80 a month (John Knodel, *Gender and Schooling in Thailand* [New York: Population Council, Research Division Working Papers, 1994], 43).

21. Before IBC began broadcasting to the provinces in 1994, versions of cable television had existed outside the capital. Entrepreneurs, after placating local officials, would jerry-rig wires among subscribing homes to transmit national news and local programming (Hamilton, "The Mediascape of Modern Southeast Asia").

22. Ong, *Flexible Citizenship*, 21–22.

23. Yingyord, "The Shinawatras," 29.

24. Ibid.

25. Banyat and Nattaya, "Thaksin"; "Thaksin Tops PDP List in Public Wealth Declaration." Thaksin and Potjaman kept their finances separate, which allowed her to execute transactions or absorb profits that might have been more problematic for him.

26. This name change occurred after I had finished my fieldwork, so in my discussion I continue to use the name form "Shinawatra" because it is correct for the IBC period of my observations. Also, people continue informally to call the company Shinawatra.

27. On women's labor in the global factory in Southeast Asia, see, for example, Noeleen Heyzer, *Working Women in South-East Asia: Development, Subordi-*

nation and Emancipation (Philadelphia: Open University Press, 1986), 424–51; Mills, *Thai Women in the Global Labor Force*; Ong, *Spirits of Resistance and Capitalist Discipline: Factory Women in Malaysia* (Albany: State University of New York Press, 1987); and Aihwa Ong, "The Gender and Labor Politics of Postmodernity," *Annual Reviews of Anthropology* 20 (1991): 279–309.

28. See, for example, Mills, *Thai Women in the Global Labor Force*.

29. Several aristocratic Thais started advertising firms in the 1920s and after. However, from the 1960s until the 1980s, senior levels of leading multinational advertising companies (e.g., Cathay) were held by foreigners, mainly from the West. Since the 1980s, more senior posts have gone to Thais, who are now considered to have learned the industry. See Thananya Srestha, "One Hundred and Fifty Years of Selling," in *The Advertising Book*, no. 8 (Bangkok: AB Publications, 1994), 16–17. For examples of early Thai advertisements, see Anake Nawigamune, *Khosana Thai samai raek* (Advertising in Thailand) (Bangkok: Sangdad Publishers, 2535 B.E. [1992]).

30. Marketing, advertising, and market research grew rapidly during Thailand's economic boom years, when corporations increased their spending on advertising by about 20 percent annually in the late 1980s to early 1990s, and were a sector that drew large numbers of women professionals. After the 1997 economic crisis, the marketing industry was hard hit when businesses cut back on advertising, thus disproportionately affecting a female-heavy field.

31. Ong, *Flexible Citizenship*. Ong's suggestion that the paradigmatic flexible subjects, the overseas Chinese, are forging "a new translocal identity," often by perpetuating "kinship rituals and cultural values" taken out of long-standing contexts of ethnic Sino-Thai enclaves and codified for new locales and diffuse family relations. I have no information on whether or to what extent Thaksin and Potjaman continue ethnic Chinese practices or affiliations. However, commerce has codified the ethnic Chinese identity through retailing elements of Chinese rituals and by popularizing Chinese dynastic tales. See chapter 1; and Craig Reynolds, "Tycoons and Warlords: Modern Thai Social Formations and Chinese Historical Romance," in *Sojourners and Settlers: Histories of Southeast Asia and the Chinese*, ed. Anthony Reid (Honolulu: University of Hawaii Press, 1996), 115–147.

32. Royal offspring descend in rank each generation, eventually becoming commoners. In chatting about Wit, Kop asserted that he could not legitimately trace his royal status through a woman (a grandmother) but had to descend from a male (an arrangement that she considered unfair). Yet ranks of princes and princesses were graded according to their *mother's* rank in the harem.

33. On the presence of sexuality in workplaces, see Lisa Adkins, *Gendered Work: Sexuality, Family and the Labour Market* (Buckingham: Open University Press, 1995); and Rosemary Pringle, *Secretaries Talk: Sexuality, Power, and Work* (London: Verso, 1988).

34. Marc Askew, *Interpreting Bangkok: The Urban Question in Thai Studies* (Bangkok: Thai Studies Section, Chulalongkorn University Press, 1994).

35. On Thai views of homosexuality, see Peter A. Jackson, *Male Homosexuality in Thailand: An Interpretation of Contemporary Thai Sources* (New York: Global Academic Publishers, 1989); and Peter A. Jackson, "From *Kamma* to Unnatural Vice: Buddhism, Homosexuality and Intolerance in Thailand," paper presented at the School of Oriental and African Studies, University of London, July 1993.

36. The responses to homosexuality in the office represented a typically wide range. The out gay man Boon was integrated into the group that went out for lunch; in fact, he was the only person from another office to regularly accompany us out. Yet Kop saw homosexuality as a mental illness, a commonly held view that reflects years of Thai psychiatric and medical conceptions. At the same time, at one lunch, our group discussed the transgendered kathoey with an affectionate but perhaps condescending tone. Wit noted how a famous kathoey makeup artist was prettier than most women, but he also established a clear distance from her and from kathoey. The topic of lesbianism did not arise, and I did not raise it.

37. SC Matchbox was created in 1991 to design advertisements, mainly print and television, for Shinawatra divisions and also for outside firms (Thai Wah property developers, Spy Wine Cooler). Matchbox's logo spoofed a prominent Thai brand of matches, which had a Naga snake on its cover.

38. On Thais' and Southeast Asians' wide palate for media, which range from Chinese court dramas to Hong Kong and U.S. action films, see Hamilton, "The Mediascape of Modern Southeast Asia"; and Ong, *Flexible Citizenship*, 166–67.

39. Privileging status over money is not exceptional in Thai society, which is said to have allocated more prestige to the control of people or of the self (in terms of Buddhism) than to the accumulation of wealth and material goods. See Akin Rabibadana, "The Organization of Thai Society in the Early Bangkok Period, 1782–1873" (Cornell University, Southeast Asia Program, Data Paper 74, 1969); and S. J. Tambiah, *World Conqueror, World Renouncer: A Study of Buddhism and Polity in Thailand against a Historical Background* (Cambridge: Cambridge University Press, 1976). Of course, this prioritization has changed with a century of capitalist economic development of the Thai economy.

40. The terms *symbolic capital* and *cultural capital*, as well as *social capital*, are indebted to Pierre Bourdieu. *Cultural capital* tends to refer to certification, competencies, and a range of knowledge; *symbolic capital* is often glossed as prestige and authority conveyed through material objects and consumption. Both of these, for Bourdieu, are embedded in broader social and material systems and involve belief systems that obscure the actual economic bases and operations of these resources—that is, ideologies obscure the ways that symbolic and cultural capital are related to, and can be converted into, finance capital. Pierre Bourdieu, "The Forms of Capital," in *Handbook of Theory and Research for the Sociology of Education*, ed. J. G. Richardson (New York: Greenwood Press, 1986), 241–58.

41. Significantly, this redistribution of student orientation from government to business also coincided with the entrance of greater numbers of women into college, which prepared them to enter—and transform—academic, government, and business fields. In Thailand, families increasingly choose to educate their daughters as much as their sons past the minimum requirement of six years of grammar school (which most, but not all, children complete). These daughters have taken advantage of the examination system to prevail in many portions of the educational system. In the later 1980s, women began to outnumber men in tertiary education, constituting 56 percent of college and university students. Of the student body, female students represented 56 percent at universities, 66 percent at teaching colleges, and 91 percent at graduate nursing schools. Men outnumber women at vocational schools. See Knodel, *Gender and Schooling in Thailand*, 15–16. On changing higher education in Thailand, see, for example, Hewison, "Emerging Social Forces in Thailand," 144.

42. The first four television series are noted in Dole Anderson, *Marketing and Development: The Thailand Experience* (East Lansing: Michigan State University International Business and Economic Studies, 1970), 144. I learned of the other series in my research.

43. The company's television guide presumes a facility in English not only from workers but also from its Thai viewers. Such hybrid texts resemble the postcolonial vocabularies of the Philippines, Malaysia, and Indonesia, but given that Thailand was never a colony, it more represents the identifications of elites and modern Thai subjects in response to the global power of English and the West.

44. We worked with the backdrop of American films: *Basic Instinct* (which my colleague Kop called porno), *Back to School* (a group gathered to watch Rodney Dangerfield's comic moment on the diving board), and *Cape Fear* (which I found especially distracting but others ignored).

CHAPTER 5. THE AVON LADY,
THE AMWAY PLAN, AND THE MAKING
OF THAI ENTREPRENEURS

1. For the history and operations of direct sales in America, see: Mary Kay Ash, *Mary Kay* (New York: Harper Collins, 1981); Nicole Woolsey Biggart, *Charismatic Capitalism* (Chicago: University of Chicago, 1989); S. Butterfield, *Amway: Cult of Free Enterprise* (Boston: South End Press, 1985); Alison J. Clarke, *Tupperware: The Promise of Plastic in 1950s America* (Washington, D.C.: Smithsonian Institution Press, 1999); Rich DeVos, *Compassionate Capitalism* (New York: Penguin Books, 1993); Carol I. Keeley, "Avon," in *International Directory of Company Histories*, vol. 3 (Chicago: St. James Press, 1991), 15–16; *Phillips Case Narratives* (New York: C. W. Post Center, Long Island University, 1980), 2–31; James W. Robinson, *Empire of Freedom: The Amway Story and What It Means to You*, foreword by Richard L. Lesher (Rocklin, Calif.: Prima Publishing, 1997); Tupperware, "About Us," http://www.tupperware.com/about/index.html [accessed March 20, 1998]; and Ara Wilson, "The Empire of Direct Sales and the Making of Thai Entrepreneurs," *Critique of Anthropology* 19, no. 4 (1999): 401–22.

The global expansion of Amway, Avon, Tupperware, and other direct sales companies occurred largely as a response to flagging rates of growth in the United States. In the 1970s and 1980s, the American direct sales industry faced a crisis produced in part by the changing economic and gendered landscapes as married white women in particular entered the paid workforce in droves—that is, the loss of homemaker distributors and customers. See Wilson, "The Empire of Direct Sales."

2. Versions of direct sales include "network marketing" and "multilevel marketing." Such companies as Amway invite the distributors to recruit others and form their own network of subsidiary sellers, or "line." The established distributor receives a commission on the sales of the subdistributors and their subsequent recruits. The real income to be made in Amway derives from accumulating 6 to 9 percent commission from the sales volume accumulated by downline subdistributors—hence, from recruiting and motivating satellite sellers.

3. Suwanna Asavaroengchai, "Direct Sales under Suspicion," *Bangkok Post*, September 26, 1994, Outlook, 4.

4. Avon has had a presence in Thailand since the 1960s and launched full-scale business in 1978. Amway began operations in Thailand by extending distribution networks from the United States and Australia. Among the early proponents of Amway in Thailand was a heterosexual couple, a Euro-American

woman and her Thai husband. The wife's parents had sold Amway for over two decades in the United States. See Ara Wilson, "Women in the City of Consumption: Markets and the Construction of Gender in Bangkok, Thailand," Ph.D. diss., City University of New York Graduate School, 1997, chapter 6; and Wilson, "The Empire of Direct Sales."

5. By 1993, thirteen direct sales companies had joined forces to form an industry network, the Thai Direct Selling Association: Amway, Asian Home, Avon Cosmetic, Best Book, Forest Publication, Household System, Lucks Royal, Marketing Media Association, Mary Kay, Nutri, Thai Phola, Tupperware, and Phuen Satri (Ladies Friend). However, these are not the only companies in Thailand employing distributors (Suwanna, "Direct Sales under Suspicion"). Amway's general manager served as the association's president. During the boom years, direct sales grew from about U.S.$240 million in sales in 1993 (Nongsuda Tirawatanawit, "Amway Aiming for 35% Rise in Turnover," *Nation* [Bangkok], August 24, 1993, B3) to U.S.$400 million in 1994 (Suwanna, "Direct Sales under Suspicion") to U.S.$800 million in 1997 (Apisit Buranakanonda, "Opportunity Knocks for Some Extra Bucks," *Bangkok Post Business Post*, September 8, 1997, http://www.bkkpost.samart.co.th/news/BParchive/BP970908/0809 [accessed February 10, 1998]).

6. Rosalind C. Morris describes a spirit medium who converted his religious base into an Amway network. (See her "Modernity's Media and the End of Mediumship? On the Aesthetic Economy of Transparency in Thailand," *Public Culture* 12, no. 2 [2000]: 473–75.)

7. The pseudonym "Sila" replaces "Dean," which I assigned in my dissertation and one publication (Wilson: "Women in the City of Consumption"; and "Decentralization and the Avon Lady in Bangkok, Thailand," *Political and Legal Anthropology Review* 21, no. 1 [1998]: 77–83). "Sila" is her pen name.

8. The populist prowoman organizing of direct sales appeals to progressive women in other parts of the world. Anya Vanina, a Russian human rights activist, reports that the "tender care and value for people" expressed in a Mary Kay meeting and its emphasis on "financial independence, international sisterhood, and lifestyle" inspired her activism. Sabrina Tavernise, "A Russian Rights Crusader, Made by Mary Kay," *New York Times*, April 20, 2002, A4.

9. Generally, the products of direct sales companies such as Amway, Avon, and the Thai company Mistine use English words for product names and categories. This vocabulary is transliterated, rather than translated, into Thai. Of course the literal orthography is pronounced differently in Thai; thus, Amway's "colourful pencils," spelled in British English and Thai script, would be pro-

nounced "khunleufoon pensin." One of the Amway's colors is "lotus" (read: "lo-tut") rather than the Thai "dok bua," a common word for a pillar symbol of Ther-avada Buddhism.

10. Unlike other sellers I knew of, Suranee did not sell in her village. At that time, Amway was building a distribution center in her home province (Nong-suda, "Amway Aiming for 35% Rise").

11. Marjorie M. Muecke, "Make Money Not Babies: Changing Status of Northern Thai Women," *Asian Survey* 24, no. 4 (1984): 459–70.

12. For example, Suwanna, "Direct Sales under Suspicion."

13. See the introduction to this volume.

14. Charles Keyes, "Mother or Mistress but Never a Monk: Buddhist No-tions of Female Gender in Rural Thailand," *American Ethnologist* 11, no. 2 (1984): 223–39; Thomas Kirsch, "Text and Context: Buddhist Sex Roles/Culture of Gen-der Revisited," *American Ethnologist* 12, no. 3 (1985): 302–20.

15. See Deborah Kapchan, *Gender on the Market: Moroccan Women and the Revoicing of Tradition,* (Philadelphia: University of Pennsylvania Press, 1996).

16. Wilson, "The Empire of Direct Sales."

17. Tupperware, "About Us."

18. Butterfield, *Amway.*

19. However, a later Mistine television campaign adopted a soap opera story depicting a developing romance. Nonetheless, the mother still figured significantly.

20. See, for example, Apisit, "Opportunity Knocks for Some Extra Bucks."

21. See, for example, "Khreung samang direct sales reum sadud—tua theen theen phlik kolayuth nii talad wai" (Cosmetic direct sales falter—representatives adopt strategies to escape the dying market), *Krungthep turakij newspaper* (Bangkok business newspaper), March 5, 2541 B.E. (1998), no page number.

BIBLIOGRAPHY

Following Thai convention, Thai names are listed according to the given (first) name. When the year has been recorded following the Buddhist Era calendar used in Thailand (e.g., 2542 B.E.), the A.D. year follows in parentheses, as elsewhere in the book.

Abha Bhamorabutr. *The History of Bangkok.* Bangkok: Mr. Somsak Rangsiyopas, publisher; printed at Department of Corrections Press, 1982.

Abu-Lughod, Lila. "The Objects of Soap Opera: Egyptian Television and the Cultural Politics of Modernity." In *Worlds Apart: Modernity through the Prism of the Local,* ed. D. Miller, 189–210. New York: Routledge, 1995.

———. *Veiled Sentiments: Honor and Poetry in a Bedouin Society.* Berkeley: University of California Press, 1986.

Adkins, Lisa. "Cultural Femininization: 'Money, Sex and Power' for Women." *Signs* 6, no. 3 (2001): 679–95.

———. *Gendered Work: Sexuality, Family and the Labour Market.* Buckingham: Open University Press, 1995.

Akin Rabibadana. "Bangkok Slum: Aspects of Social Organization." Ph.D. diss., Cornell University, 1975.

———. "The Organization of Thai Society in the Early Bangkok Period, 1782–1873." Southeast Asia Program, Data Paper 74, Cornell University, 1969.

Alexander, Priscilla. "Prostitution: A Difficult Issue for Feminists." In *Sex Work: Writings by Women in the Sex Industry,* ed. F. Delacoste and P. Alexander, 184–214. Pittsburgh: Cleo Press, 1987.

Altman, Dennis. "Rupture or Continuity? The Internationalization of Gay Identities." *Social Text* 14, no. 3 (fall 1996): 77–94.

Amara Pongsapich. "Feminism Theories and Praxis: Women's Social Movement in Thailand." Paper presented at the Sixth International Conference on Thai Studies, Chiang Mai, Thailand, October 14–17, 1996.

———. "Methodological Problems in Research on Women in Thailand." *Journal of Social Research* (Thailand) 14, no. 2 (1992): 19–28.

———, ed. *Women's Issues: A Book of Readings*. Bangkok: Chulalongkorn University Social Research Institute (CUSRI), 1986.

Amphan Yosamornsuntorn. "Wages and Working Conditions in the Garment Industry." M.A. thesis, Thammasat University, Bangkok, 1986.

Anake Nawigamune. *Khosana Thai samai raek*. (Advertising in Thailand.) Bangkok: Sangdad Publishers, 2535 B.E. (1992).

Anderson, Benedict R. O'G. "The Idea of Power in Javanese Culture." In *Culture and Politics in Indonesia*, ed. C. Holt, 1–69.Ithaca, N.Y.: Cornell University Press, 1972.

———. *Imagined Communities: Reflections on the Origins of Nationalism*. London: Verso, 1992.

Anderson, Dole. *Marketing and Development: The Thailand Experience*. East Lansing: Michigan State University International Business and Economic Studies, 1970.

Ang, Ien. "To Be or Not to Be Chinese: Diaspora, Culture, and Postmodern Ethnicity." *Southeast Journal of Social Science* 21, no. 1 (1993): 1–17.

Apisit Buranakanonda. "Opportunity Knocks for Some Extra Bucks." *Bangkok Post Business Post*, September 8, 1997. http://www.bkkpost.samart.co.th/news/BParchive/BP970908/0809 [accessed February 10, 1998].

Appadurai, Arjun. "Disjuncture and Difference in the Global Cultural Economy." *Public Culture* 2, no. 2 (1990): 1–24.

———, ed. *The Social Life of Things*. Cambridge: Cambridge University Press, 1986.

The Architectural Pictures of Rattanakosin. Bangkok: Committee for the Rattanakosin Bicentennial Celebration, 1982.

Ardener, Edwin. "Belief and the Problem of Women." In *Perceiving Women*, ed. Shirley Ardener, 1–27. London: Maleby Press, 1975.

Arpapun Chaopunskul. "Here Comes Mistine." *Business Review*, August 1995, 96–97.

Asad, Talal, ed. *Anthropology and the Colonial Encounter*. New York: Humanities Press, 1973.

Ash, Mary Kay. *Mary Kay*. New York: Harper Collins, 1981.

Asian Women's Association. "Prostitution Tourism." *Asian Women's Liberation* 3, no. 6 (1980): 1–13.

Asia Watch, Women's Rights Project. *A Modern Form of Slavery: Trafficking of Burmese Women and Girls into Brothels in Thailand.* New York: Human Rights Watch, 1993.

Askew, Marc. *Interpreting Bangkok: The Urban Question in Thai Studies.* Bangkok: Chulalongkorn University Press, 1994.

———. "Sex Workers in Bangkok: Refashioning Female Identities in the Global Pleasure Space." In *Bangkok: Place, Practice and Representation,* 251–83. London: Routledge, 2002.

Atkinson, J., and S. Errington, eds. *Power and Difference: Gender in Island Southeast Asia.* Stanford: Stanford University Press, 1990.

"Bangkok's Major Shopping Complexes." *Business Review* (Thailand), March 1983, 25–29.

Banyat Tasaneeyavej and Nattaya Cheetchotiros. "Thaksin: I'll Step Down if Found Unfit." *Bangkok Post,* October 28, 1994, 2.

Bao, Jiemin. "Marriage among Ethnic Chinese in Bangkok: An Ethnography of Gender, Sexuality, and Ethnicity over Two Generations." Ph.D. diss., University of California, Berkeley, 1994.

———. "Reconfiguring Chineseness in Thailand: Articulating Ethnicity along Sex/Gender and Class Lines." In *Genders and Sexualities in Modern Thailand,* ed. Peter A. Jackson and. Nerida Cook, 63–77. Chiang Mai: Silkworm Books, 1999.

———. "Same Bed, Different Dreams: Ethnicized Sexuality and Gender among Elderly Chinese Immigrants in Bangkok." *positions* 4, no. 2 (1998): 475–502.

Barrett, Michele. "Ideology and the Cultural Production of Gender." In *Feminist Criticism and Social Change: Sex, Class and Race in Literature and Culture,* ed. Judith Newton and Deborah Rosentfelt, 65–85. New York: Methuen, 1985.

———. *Women's Oppression Today: The Marxist/Feminist Encounter,* revised ed. London: Verso, 1988.

"BBL, NFS Loan Fashion Island." *Nation* (Bangkok), September 19, 1994, B3.

"Beeppheen kaandamneunchiwit le pritikaam kaanboriphok khong gay kween nay Krungthepmahanakorn" (Lifestyle customs and consumption behaviors of gay queens in Bangkok). *Waansaaw brihaanthurakit* (Saturday business administration) 11, no. 44 (2530 B.E. [1987]): 51–66.

Bell, Laurie, ed. *Good Girls, Bad Girls: Feminists and Sex Trade Workers Face to Face.* Seattle: Seal Press, 1987.

Bencha Yoddumnern-Attig, Kerry Richter, Amara Soonthorndhada, Chanya Sethaput, and Anthony Pramualratana, eds. *Changing Roles and Statuses of Women in Thailand: A Documentary Assessment.* Nakhonpathom: Institute for Population and Social Research, Mahidol University, 1992.

Benson, Susan Porter. *Counter Cultures: Saleswomen, Managers, and Customers in American Department Stores, 1890–1940.* Urbana: University of Illinois, 1986.

Berlant, Lauren. "Intimacy: A Special Issue." In *Intimacy,* ed. Lauren Berlant, 1–8. Chicago: University of Chicago Press, 2000.

Bernstein, Ronald A. *Successful Direct Selling: How to Plan, Launch, Promote and Maintain a Profitable Direct-Selling Company.* Englewood Cliffs, N.J.: Prentice Hall, 1984.

Biggart, Nicole Woolsey. *Charismatic Capitalism.* Chicago: University of Chicago, 1989.

Bishop, Ryan, and Lillian Robinson. *Night Market: Sexual Cultures and the Thai Economic Miracle.* New York: Routledge, 1998.

Blackwood, Evelyn. "Senior Women, Model Mothers, and Dutiful Wives: Managing Gender Contradictions in a Minangkabao Village." In *Bewitching Women, Pious Men: Gender and Body Politics in Southeast Asia,* ed. Aihwa Ong and Michael Peletz, 124–58. Berkeley: University of California Press, 1995.

———. "*Tombois* in West Sumatra: Constructing Masculinity and Erotic Desire." *Cultural Anthropology* 13, no. 4 (November 1998): 491–521.

Blanc-Szanton, Cristina. "Collision of Cultures: Historical Reformulations of Gender in the Lowland Visayas, Philippines." In *Power and Difference: Gender in Island Southeast Asia,* ed. Jane M. Atkinson and Shelly Errington, 345–84. Stanford, Calif.: Stanford University Press, 1990.

———. "Gender and Inter-Generational Resource Allocation among Thai and Sino-Thai Households." In *Structure and Strategies: Women, Work and Family,* ed. Leela Dube and Rajni Paltriwala, 79–102. London: Sage Publications, 1990.

Bock, Carl. *Temples and Elephants: Travels in Siam in 1881–1882.* 1884. Reprint, Oxford: Oxford University Press, 1986.

Bohannan, Paul. "The Impact of Money on an African Subsistence Economy." *Journal of Economic History* 19 (1959): 491–503.

Boserup, Ester. *Woman's Role in Economic Development.* New York: St. Martin's Press, 1970.

Botan [Supha Lusiri]. *Letters from Thailand.* Trans. Susan Fulop. Bangkok: Editions Duang Kamol, 1982.

Bourdieu, Pierre. *Distinction: A Social Critique of the Judgement of Taste*. Cambridge, Mass.: Harvard University Press, 1984.

———. "The Forms of Capital." In *Handbook of Theory and Research for the Sociology of Education*, ed. J. G. Richardson, 241–58. New York: Greenwood Press, 1986.

———. *The Logic of Practice*. Cambridge: Polity, 1990.

Bowie, Katherine A. "The Alchemy of Charity: Of Class and Buddhism in Northern Thailand." *American Anthropologist* 100, no. 2 (1998): 469–81.

———. "Trade and Textiles in Northern Thailand: A Historical Perspective." In *Textiles of Asia: A Common Heritage*, ed. Somsak Prangwatthanakun, 180–96. Bangkok: Office of the National Cultural Commission, 1993.

Brenner, Suzanne A. *The Domestication of Desire: Women, Wealth, and Modernity in Java*. Princeton: Princeton University Press, 1998.

———. "Why Women Rule the Roost: Rethinking Javanese Ideologies of Gender and Self-Control." In *Bewitching Women, Pious Men: Gender and Body Politics in Southeast Asia*, ed. Aihwa Ong and Michael Peletz, 19–50. Berkeley: University of California Press, 1995.

Briggs, Charles L. *Learning How to Ask: A Sociolinguistic Appraisal of the Role of the Interview in Social Science Research*. London: Cambridge University Press, 1986.

Brummelhuis, H., and J. Kemp, eds. *Strategies and Structures in Thai Society*. South and Southeast Asia Publication no. 31. Amsterdam: Antropologisch-Sociologisch Centrum, University of Amsterdam, 1984.

Bunsri Funeral Commemoration. "'Mae' Bunsri Chirathivat" (Mother Bunsri Chirathivat). Dated 2541 B.E. (1998). Photocopied manuscript from Chulalongkorn University Library, Bangkok.

Busarin Treerapongpichit. "Printemps Sales Suffer as Seacon Draws the Crowds." *Nation* (Bangkok), October 3, 1994, B12.

Business Research, Ltd. *Bangkok Profile: Selected Characteristics in Bangkok and Thonburi*. Bangkok: Business Research Ltd., 1966.

Butler, Judith. *Gender Trouble: Feminism and the Subversion of Identity*. New York: Routledge, 1990.

———. "Gender Trouble, Feminist Theory, and Psychoanalytic Discourse." In *Feminism/Postmodernism*, ed. Linda J. Nicholson, 324–40. New York: Routledge, 1990.

Butterfield, S. *Amway: Cult of Free Enterprise*. Boston: South End Press, 1985.

Campbell, Burham O., Andrew Mason, and Ernesto M. Pernia, eds. *The Eco-*

nomic Impact of Demographic Change in Thailand 1980–2015: An Application of the HOMES Household Forecasting Model. Honolulu: East-West Center, 1993.

Central Department Store. Yuwade Bhicharnchitr, "Greeting." http://ltsc2.com-line.co.th/central/greeting.htm [accessed May 15, 1999].

————. "History." http://www.central.co.th/web/html/aboutus/history.htm [accessed November 4, 2001].

"Central Department Store Co. Ltd." *Business Review,* September 1985, 125–26.

"Central song hua hawk radom tun khayaay sakhaa" (Central spearheading branch expansion investment). *Phujatkaan* (Manager), November 11, 1994, 1.

Chandruang, K. *My Boyhood in Siam.* New York: Day Company, 1940.

Charin Chamsakorn. "Klong Lod Market." *Nation* (Bangkok), July 25, 1994, A2.

Chavivun Prachuabmohh. "The Role of Religion and Economics in Decision Making: The Case of Thai/Malay Women." In *Anuson: Walter Vella,* ed. Ronald D. Renardo, 295–315. Chiang Mai, Thailand: Walter F. Vella Fund, Payap University, 1986.

"Chiiwit khon tham direct sales" (Life of direct sellers). *Phujatkaan Raisapdaa* (Manager weekend), September 30–October 6, 2538 B.E. (1995), 16–19.

Clark, Danae. "Commodity Lesbianism." *Camera obscura* 25/26 (1991): 180–201.

Clarke, Alison J. *Tupperware: The Promise of Plastic in 1950s America.* Washington D.C.: Smithsonian Institution Press, 1999.

Cohen, Eric. "Lovelorn Farangs: The Correspondence between Foreign Men and Thai Girls." *Anthropological Quarterly* 59, no. 3 (1986): 115–27.

————. "Open-Ended Prostitution as a Skilful Game of Luck." In *Tourism in South-East Asia,* ed. M. Hitchcock, V. King, and M. Parnwell, 155–78. London: Routledge, 1982.

————. "Sensuality and Venality in Bangkok: The Dynamics of Cross-Cultural Mapping of Prostitution." *Deviant Behavior* 8 (1987): 223–34.

Colomina, Beatriz, ed. *Sexuality and Space.* Princeton, N.J.: Princeton University Press, 1992.

Cook, Nerida. " 'Dutiful Daughters,' Estranged Sisters: Women in Thailand." In *Gender and Power in Affluent Asia,* ed. Krishna Sen and Maila Stivens, 250–90. New York: Routledge, 1998.

Cook, Nerida, and Peter A. Jackson. "Introduction." In *Genders and Sexualities in Modern Thailand,* ed. Peter A. Jackson and Nerida Cook, 1–27. Chiang Mai, Thailand: Silkworm Books, 1999.

Crawfurd, John. *Journal of an Embassy from the Governor-General of India to the Courts of Siam and Cochin China.* 2 vols. 1830. 2nd ed., Oxford in Asia Historical Reprints. Kuala Lumpur, Malaysia: Oxford University Press, 1967.

Creighton, M. R. "Maintaining Cultural Boundaries in Retailing: How Japanese Department Stores Domesticate Things Foreign." *Modern Asian Studies* 25, no. 4 (1992): 675–709.

Cushman, Jennifer W. *Family and State, the Formation of a Sino-Thai Tin-Mining Dynasty, 1792–1932.* Singapore: Oxford University Press, 1991.

———. "Siamese State Trade and the Chinese Go-Between, 1767–1855." *Journal of Southeast Asian Studies* 12, no. 1 (March 1981): 46–61.

DaGrossa, Pamela S. "Kamphaeng Din: A Study of Prostitution in the All-Thai Brothels of Chiang Mai City." *Crossroads* 4, no. 2 (1989): 1–7.

Darunee Tantiwiramanond and Sashi Pandey. "The Status and Role of Thai Women in the Pre-Modern Period: A Historical and Cultural Perspective." *Sojourn* 2, no. 1 (1992): 125–49.

Davidson, Julie O'Connell. "British Sex Tourists in Thailand." In *(Hetero)Sexual Politics*, ed. Mary Maynard and June Purvis, 42–64. London and Bristol, Pa.: Taylor & Francis, 1995.

Delacoste, Frederique, and Priscilla Alexander, eds. *Sex Work: Writings by Women in the Sex Industry.* Pittsburgh: Cleo Press, 1987.

de Lauretis, Teresa. *Technologies of Gender.* Bloomington: University of Indiana Press, 1987.

D'Emilio, John. "Capitalism and Gay Identity." In *Powers of Desire: The Politics of Sexuality*, ed. Ann Snitow, Christine Stansell, and Sharon Thompson, 100–113. New York: Monthly Review Press, 1983.

———. *Sexual Politics, Sexual Communities: The Making of a Homosexual Minority in the United States, 1940–1970.* Chicago: University of Chicago Press, 1983.

"Department Stores and Shopping Centres: The List Grows Longer." *Business Review* (Thailand), March 1984, 9–24.

"Department Stores Getting into High Gear." *Business in Thailand*, February 1987, 83–91.

DeVos, Rich. *Compassionate Capitalism.* New York: Penguin Books, 1993.

Dharani Kothandapani. "Location Is Gaysorn Plaza's Prime 'Anchor.'" *Bangkok Post*, July 27, 1984, 50.

di Leonardo, Micaela. "The Female World of Cards and Holidays: Women, Families, and the Work of Kinship." *Signs* 12, no. 3 (1987): 440–53.

———. "Introduction." In *Gender at the Crossroads of Knowledge: Feminist Anthropology in the Postmodern Era*, ed. M. di Leonardo, 1–35. Berkeley: University of California Press, 1991.

Donner, Wolf. *The Five Faces of Thailand: An Economic Geography.* St. Lucia, Queensland: University of Queensland Press, 1978.

Douglas, Mary. *Purity and Danger: An Analysis of the Concepts of Pollution and Taboo.* London: Routledge and Kegan Paul, 1966.

Douglas, Mary, and B. Isherwood. *The World of Goods.* New York: Basic Books, 1978.

Duangporn Prinyanut. "Store Wars: The Sequel." *Nation, Year in Review* (Bangkok), December 1992, 71.

Eberhardt, Nancy, ed. *Gender, Power, and the Construction of the Moral Order: Studies from the Thai Periphery.* Monograph Series no. 4. Madison: University of Wisconsin Center for Southeast Asian Studies, 1988.

Ebihara, May. "Khmer Village Women in Cambodia: A Happy Balance." In *Many Sisters: Women in Cross-Cultural Perspective*, ed. C. Matthiasson. New York: Free Press, 1974.

Eckardt, James. "Malls: Lost in Space." *Manager* (Thailand), March 1995, 15.

Elliot, David. "The Socio-Economic Formation of Modern Thailand." *Journal of Contemporary Asia* 8, no. 1 (1978): 21–50.

Embree, John. "A Loosely Structured Social System." *American Anthropologist* 52 (1950): 181–93.

Enloe, Cynthia H. *Bananas, Beaches, and Bases: Making Feminist Sense of International Politics.* Berkeley: University of California, 1989.

Evers, Hans-Deiter, ed. *Loosely Structured Social Systems: Thailand in Comparative Perspective.* New Haven, Conn.: Yale University Southeast Asian Studies Cultural Report Series, 1969.

"Expanding or Just Staying Competitive." *Business Review* (Thailand), January 1987, 91.

Faderman, Lillian. *Odd Girls and Twilight Lovers: A History of Lesbian Life in Twentieth-Century America.* New York: Penguin, 1991.

Fawcett, J. T., Siew-Ean Khoo, and Peter C. Smith, eds. *Women in the Cities of Asia.* Boulder, Colo.: Westview Press, 1984.

Featherstone, Mike. *Consumer Culture and Postmodernism.* London: Sage Publications, 1991.

Fernandes, Leela. "Nationalizing 'the Global': Media Images, Cultural Politics, and the Middle Class in India." *Media, Culture and Society* 22, no. 5 (2000): 611–28.

Fischer, Michael M.J. "Emergent Forms of Life: Anthropologies of Late or Postmodernities." *Annual Reviews of Anthropology* 28 (1999): 455–78.

Ford, Nicholas, and S. Kaetsawang. "The Socio-Cultural Context of the Transmission of HIV in Thailand." *Social Science and Medicine* 33, no. 4 (1991): 405–14.

Ford, Nicholas, and Sirinan Kittisuksathit. *Youth Sexuality in Thailand.* Nakhon Pathom, Thailand: Mahidol University Press, 1996.

"For the Love of God" (interview with Anchalee Jongkhadeekit). *Nation* (Bangkok), February 11, 1997. http://www.nationgroup.com [accessed February 20, 1997].

Foster, Brian L. *Commerce and Ethnic Differences: The Case for the Mons in Thailand.* Athens, Ohio: Ohio University Center for International Studies, Southeast Asian Program, 1982.

Freeman, Carla. *High Tech and High Heels in the Global Economy: Women, Work, and Pink Collar Identities in the Caribbean.* Durham, N.C.: Duke University Press, 2000.

"From Gay to Tom-Dee: The Strange World." *Phuean Chiwit* 2, no. 6 (1984): 19. (In Thai.)

"Fun for All Members of the Family." *Business Review* (Thailand). March 1984, 18.

Ganjanapan, Anan. "The Idiom of Phii Ka: Peasant Conception of Class Differentiation in Northern Thailand." *Mankind* 74, no. 4 (1984): 325–29.

Geertz, Clifford. *Negara: The Theatre State in Nineteenth Century Bali.* Princeton, N.J.: Princeton University Press, 1980.

———. "Person, Time and Conduct in Bali." Yale Southeast Asia Program, Cultural Report Series no. 14. 1966. Reprinted in *The Interpretation of Cultures*, 360–411. New York: Basic Books, 1973.

Gibson-Graham, J. K. *The End of Capitalism (as We Knew It).* London: Blackwell Publishers, 1996.

Giddens, Anthony. *The Transformation of Intimacy: Sexuality, Love and Eroticism in Modern Societies.* Stanford, Calif.: Stanford University Press, 1992.

Girling, J. E. *Thailand: Society and Politics.* Ithaca, N.Y.: Cornell University Press, 1981.

———. "Thailand in Gramscian Perspective." *Pacific Affairs* 57, no. 3 (1984): 385–403.

Goldberg, Carey. "Sex Slavery, Thailand to New York" *New York Times*, September 11, 1995, B1, B6.

Gramsci, Antonio. *Selections from the Prison Notebook.* Ed. and trans. Quentin Hoare and Geoffrey Nowell Smith. New York: International Publishers, 1971.

Graves, William. "Bangkok, City of Angels." *National Geographic* 114, no. 1 (July 1973): 96–129.

Grewal, Inderpal, and Caren Kaplan, eds. *Scattered Hegemonies: Postmodernity and Transnational Feminist Practices.* Minneapolis: University of Minnesota Press, 1994.

Gungwu, Wang. "Sojourning: The Chinese Experience in Southeast Asia." In *Sojourners and Settlers: Histories of Southeast Asia and the Chinese in Honour of Jennifer Cushman*, ed. Anthony Reid, with assistance of Kristine Alilunas Rodgers, 1–14. St. Leonards, NSW, Australia: Allen & Unwin, 1996.

Guy, Clifford. *The Retail Development Process: Location, Property, and Planning*. London: Routledge, 1994.

Hainsworth, G. D., ed. *Southeast Asia: Women, Changing Social Structure and Cultural Continuity*. Ottawa: University of Ottawa Press, 1981.

Halberstam, Judith. *Female Masculinity*. Durham, N.C.: Duke University Press, 1998.

Hall, Stuart. "Introduction: Who Needs 'Identity'?" In *Questions of Cultural Identity*, ed. Stuart Hall and Paul DuGay, 1–17. London: Sage Publications, 1996.

Hamilton, Annette. "The Mediascape of Modern Southeast Asia." *Screen* 33, no. 1 (1992): 81–92.

———. "Wonderful, Terrible: Everyday Life in Bangkok." In *A Companion to the City*, ed. Gary Bridge and Sophie Watson, 460–71. Oxford: Blackwell Publishers, 2000.

Hanks, Lucien M. "Merit and Power in the Thai Social Order." *American Anthropologist* 64, no. 6 (1962): 1247–61.

Hanks, Lucien M., and Jane Richardson Hanks. "Thailand: Equality Between the Sexes." In *Women in the New Asia*, ed. Barbara Ward, 424–51. Paris: UNESCO, 1963.

Harlow, Tim. "Changing Patterns of Bangkok Retailing." *Property Review*, March–May 1992, 14–17.

Harris, Andrew. *Bangkok after Dark*. New York: MacFadden Books, 1968.

Harrison, Rachel. "The Madonna and the Whore: Self/'Other' Tensions in the Characterization of the Prostitute by Thai Female Authors." In *Genders and Sexualities in Modern Thailand*, ed. Peter A. Jackson and Nerida Cook, 168–90. Chiang Mai, Thailand: Silkworm Books, 1999.

Harvey, David. *The Condition of PostModernity*. Oxford: Basil Blackwell, 1989.

Hennessy, Rosemary. *Profit and Pleasure: Sexual Identities in Late Capitalism*. New York: Routledge, 2000.

Hewison, Kevin. *Bankers and Bureaucrats: Capital and Role of the State in Thailand*. Southeast Asian Studies Monograph Series no. 34. New Haven, Conn.: Yale University Press, 1990.

———. "Emerging Social Forces in Thailand: New Political and Economic Roles." In *The New Rich in Asia: Mobile Phones, McDonalds, and Middle-Class*

Revolution, ed. Richard Robison and David S. G. Goodman, 137–60. New York: Routledge, 1996.

———. "Industry Prior to Industrialisation: Thailand." Paper presented at the conference Industrializing Elites in Southeast Asia, Sukhothai, Thailand, December 1–12, 1986.

———. "The Structure of Bangkok Capital in Thailand." *Southeast Asian Journal of Social Science* 16, no. 1 (1988): 81–91.

Heyzer, Noeleen. *Working Women in South-East Asia: Development, Subordination and Emancipation*. Philadelphia: Open University Press, 1986.

Hill, Ann Maxwell. *Merchants and Migrants: Ethnicity and Trade among Yunnanese Chinese in Southeast Asia*. Yale University Southeast Asia Studies Monograph no. 47, 1998.

"Home Shopping to Make Local Debut." *Thailand Times*, September 2, 1994, 12.

Hong, Lysa. *Thailand in the Nineteenth Century*. Singapore: Institute of Southeast Asian Studies, 1984.

Hussain, Zakir. *The Silent Minority: Indians in Thailand*. Bangkok: Chulalongkorn University Social Research Institute (CUSRI), 1982.

International Broadcasting Corporation Limited. *Annual Report*. Bangkok, 1992.

International Broadcasting Corporation Public Company Limited. *Annual Report*. Bangkok, 1993.

Ingersoll, Jasper. "Merit and Identity in Village Thailand." In *Change and Persistence in Thai Society*, ed. G. W. Skinner and A. T. Kirsch, 219–51. Ithaca, N.Y.: Cornell University Press, 1975.

Ingram, James C. *Economic Change in Thailand since 1850*. Stanford, Calif.: Stanford University Press, 1955.

Insor, D. *Thailand: A Political, Social, and Economic Analysis*. London: Allen & Unwin, 1963.

Irvine, W. "Decline of Village Spirit Cults and the Growth of Urban Spirit Mediumship: The Persistence of Spirit Beliefs, the Position of Women and Modernization." *Mankind* 14, no. 4 (1984): 315–24.

Jackson, Peter A. "From *Kamma* to Unnatural Vice: Buddhism, Homosexuality and Intolerance in Thailand." Paper presented at the School of Oriental and African Studies, University of London, July 1993.

———. *Male Homosexuality in Thailand: An Interpretation of Contemporary Thai Sources*. New York: Global Academic Publishers, 1989.

Jackson, Peter A., and Gerard Sullivan. "A Panoply of Roles: Sexual and Gender Diversity in Contemporary Thailand." In *Lady Boys, Tom Boys, Rent Boys: Male and Female Homosexualities in Contemporary Thailand*, ed. Peter A. Jackson and Gerard Sullivan, 1–28. Binghamton, N.Y.: Harrington Park Press, Haworth Press, 1999.

Jameson, Frederic. "Postmodernism, or The Cultural Logic of Late Capitalism." *New Left Review* 146 (1984): 53–92.

Janssen, Peter. "Robinson Department Store: Joining forces." *Asia Magazine.* http://web3.asia1.com.3g/times [accessed October 6, 1999].

Jones, G., ed. *Women in the Urban and Industrial Workforce.* Canberra: Australian National University, 1984.

June Nualtaranee. "Household Consumption and Savings: Random Walk Hypothesis." Master's thesis, Thammasat University, Bangkok, 1992.

Juranee Taesamran. "New Retail Method Will Force Giants to Increase Efficiency." *Nation* (Bangkok), October 3, 1994, B12.

Kanokwan Tarawan. "Thailand." In *Unspoken Rules: Sexual Orientation and Women's Human Rights*, ed. Rachel Rosenbloom, 203–8. San Francisco: International Gay and Lesbian Human Rights Commission, 1995.

Kapchan, Deborah. *Gender on the Market: Moroccan Women and the Revoicing of Tradition.* Philadelphia: University of Pennsylvania Press, 1996.

Kaplan, Caren. "A World without Boundaries: The Body Shop's Trans/National Geographics." *Social Text* 43 (fall 1995): 45–66.

Kasmir, Sharryn, and Ara Wilson. "Introduction." *Critique of Anthropology* 19, no. 4 (1999): 376–78.

Katz, Jonathan Ned. "The Invention of Heterosexuality." *Socialist Review* 20, no. 1 (1990): 7–34.

———. *The Invention of Heterosexuality.* New York: Dutton, 1995.

Keeley, Carol I. "Avon." In *International Directory of Company Histories*, vol. 3: 15–16. Chicago: St. James Press, 1991.

Kemp, Jeremy. "The Manipulation of Personal Relations: From Kinship to Patron-Clientage." In *Strategies and Structures in Thai Society*, ed. H. Brummelhuis and J. Kemp, 55–70. South and Southeast Asia Publication no. 31. Amsterdam: Antropologisch-Sociologisch Centrum, University of Amsterdam, 1984.

Kennedy, Elizabeth Lapovsky, and Natalie Davis. *Boots of Leather, Slippers of Gold: The History of a Lesbian Community.* New York: Routledge, 1993.

Keyes, Charles. "Ambiguous Gender: Male Initiation in a Buddhist Society." In *Gender and Religion: On the Complexity of Symbols*, ed. C. Bynum and P. Rich, 66–96. Boston: Beacon Press, 1986.

———. "Mother or Mistress but Never a Monk: Buddhist Notions of Female Gender in Rural Thailand." *American Ethnologist* 11, no. 2 (1984): 223–39.

———. *Thailand: Buddhist Kingdom as Modern Nation-State*. Boulder, Colo.: Westview Press, 1987.

Key Statistics of Thailand. Bangkok: National Identity Office, Office of the Prime Minister, 1993.

"Khreung samang direct sales reum sadud—tua theen theen phlik kolayuth nii talad wai" (Cosmetic direct sales falter—representatives adopt strategies to escape the dying market). *Krungthep turakij newspaper* (Bangkok business newspaper), March 5, 2541 B.E. (1998), no page number.

Kirkup, James. *Cities of the World: Bangkok*. London: Phoenix House, 1968.

Kirsch, Thomas. "Buddhism, Sex-Roles and Thai Society." *Women of Southeast Asia*, ed. Penny Van Esterik, 16–41. Northern Illinois University Occasional Paper no. 9. Dekalb, Ill.: Center for Southeast Asian Studies, 1982.

———. "Text and Context: Buddhist Sex Roles/Culture of Gender Revisited." *American Ethnologist* 12, no. 3 (1985): 302–20.

Kittiwut Jod Tywaditep, Eli Coleman, and Pacharin Dumronggittigule. "Thailand (Muang Thai)." In *The International Encyclopedia of Sexuality*, vol. 3, ed. Robert T. Francoeur, 1192–265. New York: Continuum, 1997.

Klausner, William J. *Reflections in a Log Pond*. Bangkok: Suksit Siam, 1972.

Knodel, John. *Gender and Schooling in Thailand*. New York: Population Council, Research Division Working Papers, 1994.

———. *Thailand's Reproductive Revolution: Rapid Fertility Decline in a Third World Setting*. Madison: University of Wisconsin Press, 1987.

Kohut, John. "A Cut-Price, Cutthroat Challenge." *Asia Inc.*, July 1996. http://www.asia_inc.com/index.php?articleID = 1025 [accessed November 11, 2001].

Kondo, Dorinne. *Crafting Selves: Power, Gender, and Discourses of Identity in a Japanese Workplace*. Chicago: University of Chicago Press, 1990.

Korff, Rudiger. *Bangkok and Modernity*. Bangkok: Chulalongkorn University Social Research Institute (CUSRI), 1989.

Krier, Jennifer. "Narrating Herself: Power and Gender in a Minangkabao Woman's Tale of Conflict." In *Bewitching Women, Pious Men: Gender and Body Politics in Southeast Asia*, ed. Aihwa Ong and Michael Peletz, 51–75. Berkeley: University of California Press, 1995.

Krirkkiat Phipatheritham and Kunio Yoshihara. *Business Groups in Thailand*. Singapore: Institute in Southeast Asian Studies, 1983.

Kung-Nguan Sae-aua. "MBK to Go Ahead with Listing: Chanut." *Nation* (Bangkok), October 13, 1994, B13.

Kwanchai Rungfapaisarn. "Bt 300m Set for Major Facelift to Central/Lardprao." *Nation* (Bangkok), November 23, 1994, B2.

Laderman, Carol C. "Putting Malay Women in Their Place." In *Women of Southeast Asia*, ed. Penny Van Esterik, 79–99. Northern Illinois University Occasional Paper no. 9. Dekalb, Ill.: Center for Southeast Asian Studies, 1982.

Lamsang Naamfeng. "Bantheuk wai nai Praew" (Notes in Praew). *Praew* 9, no. 216 (2531 B.E. [1988]): 180–81, 184–85; reprinted in Bunsri Funeral Commemoration, 73–75.

Landon, Kenneth P. *The Chinese in Thailand.* New York: Institute of Pacific Relation, 1941.

———. *Siam in Transition.* Chicago: University of Chicago Press, 1939.

Leach, William R. *Land of Desire: Merchants, Power, and the Rise of a New American Culture.* New York: Pantheon, 1993.

Leonowans, Anna. *The English Governess at the Siamese Court.* New York: Roy Publishers, 1954.

Lévi-Strauss, Claude. *The Elementary Structures of Kinship.* Revised ed. Ed. Rodney Needham. Trans. James Harle Bell and John Richard von Sturmer. Boston: Beacon Press, 1969.

Lim, Linda. "Women Workers in Multinational Corporations: The Case of the Electronics Industry in Malaysia and Singapore." Michigan Occasional Papers in Women's Studies, Women's Studies Program, University of Michigan, Ann Arbor, 1978.

Lindenbaum, Shirley. "Culture, Structure and Change: Sex Research after Modernity." In *Conceiving Sexuality: Approaches to Sex Research in a Postmodern World*, ed. Richard G. Parker and John H. Gagnon, 1–25. New York: Routledge, 1995.

Lyttleton, Chris. "The Good People of Isan: Commercial Sex in Northeast Thailand." *Australian Journal of Anthropology* 5, no. 3 (1994): 257–79.

"Ma Bulakun, Mr." In *Khrai pen khrai nai Prathet Thai 2506 (Who's Who in Thailand 1963)*, vol. 2: 245. Bangkok: 2506 B.E. (1963). Athens, Ohio: Ohio University Library, Center for International Collections. Microfiche.

McClintock, Anne. "Sex Workers and Sex Work: Introduction." *Social Text* 37 (winter 1993): 1–10.

McCracken, Grant. *Culture and Consumption: New Approaches to the Symbolic Character of Goods and Activities.* Bloomington: Indiana University Press, 1988.

McDonald, Duff J. "Beat the U.S. Market without Leaving the U.S." *Money* (February 1997): 41–42.

McDonnell, Etain, and Karuna Buakumsri. "Prostitutes in Japan." *Friends of Women Newsletter* 4, no. 2 (December 1993): 13–17.

Mackie, Jamie. "Changing Patterns of Chinese Big Business in Southeast Asia."

In *Southeast Asian Capitalists*, ed. Ruth McVey, 161–90. Ithaca, N.Y.: Cornell University Press, 1992.

"Mahbunkhrong Sirichai tong pheung 'Philip Cox'" (Mahbunkhrong Sirichai promotes "Philip Cox"). *Phujatkaan raisapdah* (Manager weekend), July 4–10, 2537 B.E. (1994).

Malinowski, Bronislaw. *Argonauts of the Western Pacific*. 1922. New York: Dutton, 1961.

Manderson, Lenore. "Public Sex Performances in Patpong and Explorations of the Edges of Imagination." *Journal of Sex Research* 29 (1992): 451–75.

———. "The Pursuit of Pleasure and the Sale of Sex." In *Sexual Nature, Sexual Culture*, ed. Paul R. Abramson and Steven D. Pinkerton, 305–29. Chicago: University of Chicago Press, 1995.

Manderson, Lenore, and Margret Jolly, eds. *Sites of Desire, Economies of Pleasure: Sexualities in Asia and the Pacific*. Chicago: University of Chicago Press, 1997.

Martin, Emily. *Flexible Bodies: Tracking Immunity in American Culture from the Days of Polio to the Age of AIDS*. Boston: Beacon Press, 1994.

Massey, Doreen B. *Space, Place and Gender*. Minneapolis: University of Minnesota Press, 1994.

Matthaei, Julie, and Theresa Amott. "Race, Gender, and Work: The History of Asian and Asian American Women." *Race & Class* 31, no. 3 (1990): 61–80.

Matthana Chetamee. "Withi chiwit le chiwit khrawpkhrua khong ying rak ying" (Lifestyle and family life among women who love women). Master's thesis, Thammasat University, Bangkok, 2539 B.E. (1996).

Mauss, Marcel. *The Gift*. New York: Norton, 1967.

Mayfield, Frank M. *The Department Store Story*. New York: Fairchild Publications, 1949.

"MBK Cuts 625m Baht off Sirichai's Rent." *Bangkok Post*, October 15, 1994, Business, 17.

Midyear Report. Bangkok: The Nation, June 1994.

Miller, Daniel. *Capitalism: An Ethnographic Approach*. New York: Berg Publishers, 1997.

———. *A Theory of Shopping*. Ithaca, N.Y.: Cornell University Press, 1998.

———, ed. *Worlds Apart: Modernity through the Prism of the Local*. New York: Routledge, 1995.

Mills, Mary Beth. "Attack of the Widow Ghosts: Gender, Death, and Modernity in Northeast Thailand." In *Bewitching Women, Pious Men: Gender and Body Politics in Southeast Asia*, ed. Aihwa Ong and Michael Peletz, 244–73. Berkeley: University of California Press, 1995.

———. *Thai Women in the Global Labor Force: Consuming Desires, Contested Selves.* New Brunswick, N.J.: Rutgers University Press, 1999.

———. "We Are Not Like Our Mothers: Migrants, Modernity and Identity in Northeast Thailand." Ph.D. diss., University of California, Berkeley, 1993.

Moerman, M. "Chiangkham's Trade in the 'Old Days.'" In *Change and Persistence in Thai Society,* ed. William Skinner and A. Thomas Kirsch, 151–71. Ithaca, N.Y.: Cornell University Press, 1975.

Mohanty, Chandra Talpade, Ann Russon, and Lourdes Torres, eds. *Third World Women and the Politics of Feminism.* Bloomington: Indiana University Press, 1991.

Montgomery, Heather. "Children, Prostitution, and Identity: A Case Study from a Tourist Resort in Thailand." In *Global Sex Workers: Rights, Resistance, and Redefinition,* ed. Kamala Kempadoo and Jo Doezema, 139–50. New York: Routledge, 1998.

Moore, Henrietta L. *Feminism and Anthropology.* Minneapolis: University of Minnesota Press, 1988.

Morris, Meaghan. "Things to Do with Shopping Centres." In *Grafts: Feminist Cultural Criticism,* ed. Susan Sheridan, 193–225. London: Verso, 1988.

Morris, Rosalind C. "All Made Up: Performance Theory and the New Anthropology of Sex and Gender." *Annual Reviews of Anthropology* 25 (1995): 567–92.

———. "Modernity's Media and the End of Mediumship? On the Aesthetic Economy of Transparency in Thailand." *Public Culture* 12, no. 2 (2000): 457–75.

———. "Three Sexes and Four Sexualities: Redressing the Discourses on Gender and Sexuality in Contemporary Thailand." *positions* 2, no. 1 (1994): 15–43.

M.S.S. Tour Trans Co., Ltd. http://www.google.com/search?q = cache: 2XK4xw3I4A4:www.awebspace.com/mss/bkk/croc.html+%22floating+market%22+history&hl = en [accessed October 10, 2001].

Muecke, Marjorie M. "Health Care Systems as Socializing Agents: Childbearing in the North Thai and Western Ways." *Social Science and Medicine* 10 (1976): 377–83.

———. "Make Money Not Babies: Changing Status of Northern Thai Women." *Asian Survey* 24, no. 4 (1984): 459–70.

———. "Mother Sold Food, Daughter Sells Her Body: The Cultural Continuity of Prostitution." *Social Science and Medicine* 35, no. 7 (1992): 891–901.

Nakagawa, Takio. "Asian Retailing Revolution and Japanese Companies: The Thailand Case." International Economic Conflict Discussion Paper no. 34, Tokyo, 1987.

Napat Sirisambhand. "Gender Relations and Changing Rural Society." *Journal of Social Research* (Thailand) 14, no. 2 (1991): 19–28.

Napat Sirisambhand and Christina Szanton. *Thailand's Street Food Vending: The Sellers and Consumers of "Traditional Fast Foods."* Women's Studies Programme, Social Research Institute, Chulalongkorn University, Bangkok, 1986.

Nash, June, and Patricia Fernandez-Kelly, eds. *Women, Men, and the International Division of Labor.* Albany, N.Y.: State University of New York Press, 1983.

"News for Nang and Nangsao." *Bangkok World,* June 16, 1963, 10.

Newton, Esther. *Mother Camp: Female Impersonators in America.* Chicago: University of Chicago Press, 1972.

Nicholson, Linda. "Feminism and Marx: Integrating Kinship with the Economic." In *Feminism as Critique: On the Politics of Gender,* ed. Seyla Benhabib and Drucilla Cornell, 16–33. Minneapolis: University of Minnesota Press, 1987.

Nithi Aeuwsrivongse. "The Early Bangkok Period: Literary Change and Its Social Causes." *Asian Studies Review* 18, no. 1 (July 1994): 69–76.

———. "Ruang po po, pleuay pleuay" (Prudish pornography). *Silapa Watanatham* (Art and culture) 16 (2538 B.E. [1995]): 94–106.

Nongsuda Tirawatanawit. "Amway Aiming for 35% Rise in Turnover." *Nation* (Bangkok), August 24, 1993, B3.

Nuntawan Polkwamdee. "MBK Combatants Fail to Find Common Ground." *Bangkok Post,* August 8, 1994, B3.

O'Connor, Richard Allan. "Urbanism and Religion: Community, Hierarchy and Sanctity in Urban Thai Buddhist Temples." Ph.D. diss., Cornell University, 1978.

Odzer, Cleo. "Patpong Prostitution: Its Relationship to, and Effect on, the Position of Women in Thai Society." Ph.D. diss., New School for Social Research, New York, 1990.

———. *Patpong Sisters: An American Woman's View of the Bangkok Sex World.* New York: Blue Moon Books, Arcade Publishing, 1994.

O'Merry, Rory. *My Wife in Bangkok.* Berkeley, Calif.: Asia Press, 1990.

Ong, Aihwa. "Center, Periphery and Hierarchy: Gender in Southeast Asia." In *Gender and Anthropology,* ed. Sandra Morgen, 294–312. Washington, D.C.: American Anthropological Association, 1989.

———. "Colonialism and Modernity: Feminist Re-presentations of Women in Non-Western Societies." *Inscriptions* 3–4 (1988): 79–93.

———. *Flexible Citizenship: The Cultural Logics of Transnationality.* Durham, N.C.: Duke University Press, 1999.

———. "The Gender and Labor Politics of Postmodernity." *Annual Reviews of Anthropology* 20 (1991): 279–309.

———. "Industrialization and Prostitution in Southeast Asia." *Southeast Asia Chronicle* 96 (1985): 2–6.

———. *Spirits of Resistance and Capitalist Discipline: Factory Women in Malaysia.* Albany: State University of New York Press, 1987.

———. "State versus Islam: Malay Families, Women's Bodies, and the Body Politic in Malaysia." *American Ethnologist* 17, no. 2 (1990): 258–76.

Ong, Aihwa, and Michael Peletz, eds. *Bewitching Women, Pious Men: Gender and Body Politics in Southeast Asia.* Berkeley: University of California Press, 1995.

Ong, Aihwa, and Donald Nonini, eds. *Ungrounded Empires: The Cultural Politics of Modern Chinese Transnationalism.* New York: Routledge, 1997.

Orathai Ard-Am and Chanya Sethaput, eds. *Sopheni dek nai sankhom Thai* (Child prostitution in Thailand). Bangkok: Mahidol University, Institute of Population and Social Research, 2537 B.E. (1994).

Parissara Liewkeat. "Theorizing 'Women,' Practicing Prostitution: U.S. and Thai Feminists Discursive Practices." Master's thesis, Ohio State University, 1996.

Pasuk Phongpaichit. *From Peasant Girl to Bangkok Masseuse.* Geneva: ILO Report, 1980.

Pasuk Phongpaichit and Chris Baker. *Thailand: Economy and Politics.* New York: Oxford University Press, 1995.

———. *Thailand's Boom and Bust.* Chiang Mai: Silkworm Books, 1998.

Peiss, Kathy. *Cheap Amusements: Working Women and Leisure in Turn-of-the-Century New York.* Philadelphia: Temple University Press, 1988.

Pheterson, Gail. "The Social Consequences of Unchastity." In *Sex Work: Writings by Women in the Sex Industry,* ed. F. Delacoste and P. Alexander, 215–30. Pittsburgh: Cleo Press, 1987.

———, ed. *A Vindication of the Rights of Whores.* Seattle: Seal Press, 1988.

Phillips, H. P. "The Culture of Siamese Intellectuals." In *Change and Persistence in Thai Society,* ed. G. W. Skinner and T. Kirsch, 324–79. Ithaca, N.Y.: Cornell University Press, 1975.

———. *Thai Peasant Personality.* Berkeley: University of California Press, 1966.

Phillips Case Narratives. New York: C. W. Post Center, Long Island University, 1980.

Polanyi, Karl. "The Economy as Instituted Process." In *Trade and Market in the Early Empires,* ed. Karl Polanyi, Conrad M. Arensberg, and Harry W. Pearson, 240–70. Glencoe, Ill.: Free Press and Falcon's Wing Press, 1957.

————. *The Great Transformation: The Political and Economic Origins of Our Time.* Boston: Beacon Press, 1957 (originally published 1944).

Pongsak Ruamsak. "Twilight Descends on Old Market." *Nation* (Bangkok), August 21, 1994, C1.

Potter, Sulamith. *Family Life in a Northern Thai Village.* Berkeley: University of California Press, 1977.

Pred, Allan, and Michael J. Watts. *Reworking Modernity: Capitalisms and Symbolic Discontent.* New Brunswick, N.J.: Rutgers University Press, 1992.

Preecha Kuwinpant. *Marketing in North-Central Thailand: A Study of Socio-Economic Organization in a Thai Market Town.* Bangkok: Chulalongkorn University Social Research Institute (CUSRI), 1980.

Pringle, Rosemary. *Secretaries Talk: Sexuality, Power, and Work.* London: Verso, 1988.

Prügl, Elisabeth. *The Global Construction of Gender: Home-Based Work in the Political Economy of the 20th Century.* New York: Columbia University Press, 1999.

Puar, Jasbir Kaur. "Introduction." *GLQ: A Journal of Lesbian and Gay Studies* 8, nos. 1 & 2 (December 2002): 1–6

Purcell, Victor. *The Chinese in Southeast Asia.* 1951. 2nd ed. Kuala Lumpur: Oxford, 1980.

Reid, Anthony, ed., with assistance of Kristine Alilunas Rodgers. *Sojourners and Settlers: Histories of Southeast Asia and the Chinese in Honour of Jennifer Cushman.* St. Leonard, NSW: Allen & Unwin, 1996.

"Retailing." *Business in Thailand,* March 1981, 33–37.

Reynolds, Craig. "On the Gendering of Nationalist and Postnationalist Selves in Twentieth Century Thailand." In *Genders and Sexualities in Modern Thailand,* ed. Peter A. Jackson and Nerida Cook, 261–74. Chiang Mai: Silkworm Books, 1999.

————. "Predicaments of Modern Thai History." *Southeast Asia Research* 2, no. 1 (1994): 64–90.

————. "Tycoons and Warlords: Modern Thai Social Formations and Chinese Historical Romance." In *Sojourners and Settlers: Histories of Southeast Asia and the Chinese in Honour of Jennifer Cushman,* ed. Anthony Reid, 115–47. St. Leonard, NSW: Allen & Unwin, 1996.

Robinson, James W. *Empire of Freedom: The Amway Story and What It Means to You.* Foreword by Richard L. Lesher. Rocklin, Calif.: Prima Publishing, 1997.

Rosaldo, M. Z. *Knowledge and Passion: Ilongot Notions of Self and Social Life.* Cambridge: Cambridge University Press, 1980.

Rose, Emily. "Now on Internet: E-mail Order Brides." *San Francisco Examiner*, November 28, 1995, A15.

Rubin, Gayle. "Thinking Sex: Notes for a Radical Theory of the Politics of Sexuality." In *Pleasure and Danger*, ed. Carole S. Vance, 267–319. Boston: Routledge, Kegan and Paul, 1984.

———. "The Traffic in Women: Notes on the Political Economy of Sex." In *Towards an Anthropology of Women*, ed. Rayna Rapp [Reiter], 157–210. New York: Monthly Review Press, 1975.

"Sampeng." *Khao sot* (Fresh news), Special Issue 11 (April 1982): 7–34.

Samrit Funeral Commemoration. "Chirathivat Samrit." Nangseu thi raleuk ngansob (Samrit Chirathivat, Funeral/cremation remembrance book), 3 P.Y. 2535 (November 3, 1992), unpaginated photocopied manuscript from Chulalongkorn University Library, Bangkok. (Page numbers added by author.)

Santi Chatterji. "Central's Plaza." *Business in Thailand*, March 1980, 33–36.

Sassen, Saskia. *Globalization and Its Discontents*. New York: New Press, 1998.

Sawitree, Dabbhasuta. "The Relations between Thai, Chinese, and Western Communities in Bangkok 1855–1910." Master's thesis, Chulalongkorn University, Bangkok, 1983.

"Scents and Sensibility." *Economist*, July 13, 1996, 57–58.

Scott, James C. *The Moral Economy of the Peasant: Rebellion and Subsistence in Southeast Asia*. New Haven, Conn.: Yale University Press, 1976.

Sedgewick, Eve Kosofsky. *Epistemology of the Closet*. Berkeley: University of California Press, 1990.

Sen, Krishna, and Maila Stivens, eds. *Gender and Power in Affluent Asia*. London: Routledge, 1998.

Shideler, Jack. "Versioning a High Art." *Bangkok World*, January 13, 1963, 2–3, 8.

Shinawatra Computer & Communications Group. A special publication of the Bangkok Post, 1991, 9.

Siegal, J. T. *Solo in the New Order: Language and Hierarchy in an Indonesian City*. Princeton, N.J.: Princeton University Press, 1986.

Singh, Devika. "Gender Benders: The Role of Masculinity in Thai Lesbianism." Unpublished paper, Summer in Thailand Program, Chiang Mai, 1993.

Sinnott, Megan. "Masculinity and *Tom* Identity in Thailand." In *Lady Boys, Tom Boys, Rent Boys: Male and Female Homosexualities in Contemporary Thailand*, ed. Peter A. Jackson and Gerard Sullivan, 97–120. Binghamton, N.Y.: Harrington Park Press, Haworth Press, 1999.

Siriporn Skrobanek. "In Pursuit of an Illusion: Thai Women in Europe." *Southeast Asia Chronicle* 96 (1985): 7–12.

Siriporn Skrobanek, Nattaya Boonpakdi, and Chutima Janthakeero. *The Traffic in Women: Human Realities of the International Sex Trade*. London: Zed Books, 1997.

Siskind, Janet. "Kinship and Mode of Production." *American Anthropologist* 80 (1978): 860–72.

Skinner, G. W. *Chinese Society in Thailand*. London: Oxford University Press, 1957.

———. *Leadership and Power in a Chinese Community in Thailand*. Ithaca, N.Y.: Cornell University Press, 1958.

Skinner, G. W., and T. Kirsch, eds. *Change and Persistence in Thai Society*. Ithaca, N.Y.: Cornell University Press, 1975.

Stanley, Allessandra. "New Face of Russian Capitalism: Avon and Mary Kay Create Opportunities for Women." *New York Times Business Day*, August 14, 1996, D1, D16.

Stansell, Christine. *City of Women: Sex and Class in New York 1789–1860*. New York: Alfred A Knopf, 1982.

Sternstein, Larry. *Bangkok Portrait*. Bangkok: Bangkok Metropolitan Organization, Committee on the Rattanakosin Bicentennial, 1982.

Stivens, Maila. "Theorising Gender, Power, and Modernity." In *Gender and Power in Affluent Asia*, ed. Krishna Sen and Maila Stivens, 1–34. London: Routledge, 1998.

Stoler, Ann Laura. "Carnal Knowledge and Imperial Power: Gender, Race and Morality in Colonial Asia." In *Gender at the Crossroads of Knowledge*, ed. Micaela di Leonardo, 51–101. Berkeley: University of California Press, 1992.

———. "Class Structure and Female Autonomy in Rural Java." *Signs* 3, no. 1 (autumn 1977): 74–89.

———. "Making Empire Respectable." *American Ethnologist* 16, no. 4 (1989): 622–33.

"Strategies of the Discounters Push Department Stores to High-end Niches." *Nation* (Bangkok), October 3, 1994, B12.

Strathern, Marilyn. *The Gender of the Gift*. Berkeley: University of California, 1988.

———. "Subject or Object? Women and the Circulation of Valuables in Highland New Guinea." In *Women and Property, Women as Property*, ed. R. Hirschon, 158–75. London: Croom Helm, 1981.

"Suan sanuk boom" (Amusement park boom). *Weekend* (Thailand), February 11–17, 2538 B.E. (1995), 38–41.

Suchart Prasith-rathsint and S. Piampiti, eds. *Women in Development: Implications for Population Dynamics in Thailand*. Bangkok: NIDA, 1982.

Suehiro, Akira. *Capital Accumulation in Thailand 1855–1985.* Tokyo: Centre for East Asian Cultural Studies, 1989.

———. "Capitalist Development in Postwar Thailand: Commercial Bankers, Industrial Elite, and Agribusiness Group." In *Southeast Asian Capitalists*, ed. Ruth McVey, 35–63. Ithaca, N.Y.: Cornell University Press, 1992.

———. "Family Business Reassessed: Corporate Structure and Late-Starting Industrialization in Thailand." *Developing Economies* 31, no. 4 (December 1993): 378–407.

Sukanya Hantrakul. "Prostitution in Thailand." In *Development and Displacement: Women in Southeast Asia*, ed. G. Chandler, N. Sullivan, and J. Branson, 115–36. Monash Papers on Southeast Asia no. 18. Melbourne, Australia: Center for Southeast Asian Studies, Monash University, 1988.

Sumalee Bumroongsook. *Love and Marriage: Mate Selection in Twentieth-Century Central Thailand.* Bangkok: Thai Studies, Chulalongkorn University, 1995.

Supakana Sopittakamol. "Costly Promotions Push Up Sales." *Bangkok Post*, July 19, 1993, 51.

———. "Major Changes in the Market." *Bangkok Post*, July 19, 1993, 50.

Supakana Soppitakamol and Kirssana Pansoonthorn. "Downtown Retail Projects to Prosper." *Bangkok Post*, July 28, 1994, 30.

Suphaphan Plengmaneepun. "Satun Woman Shakes Up Telecommunications Industry." *Bangkok Post*, October 10, 1994, 31.

Surapongshai, Vinit. "Advertising in a Changing Thai Society." *Business Review* (Thailand), December 1990, 60.

Suteera Thomson and Maytinee Bhongsvej. *Profile of Women in Thailand.* Prepared for the UN Economic and Social Commission for Asia and the Pacific. Bangkok: Gender and Development Research Institute, 1995.

Suvanna Kriengkraipetch. "Folksong and Socio-Cultural Change in Village Life." *Asian Review* 2 (1988): 111–31.

Suwanna Asavaroengchai. "Direct Sales under Suspicion." *Bangkok Post*, September 26, 1994, Outlook, 4.

Tambiah, S.J. *The Buddhist Saints of the Forest and the Cult of the Amulets.* Cambridge: Cambridge University Press, 1984.

———. "The Galactic Polity: The Structure of Traditional Kingdoms in Southeast Asia." *Annals of the New York Academy of Sciences* 293 (1977): 69–97.

———. *World Conqueror, World Renouncer: A Study of Buddhism and Polity in Thailand against a Historical Background.* Cambridge: Cambridge University Press, 1976.

Tannenbaum, Nicola. "Buddhism, Prostitution, and Sex: Limits on the Academic Discourse on Gender in Thailand." In *Genders and Sexualities in Modern Thailand*, ed. Peter A. Jackson and Nerida Cook, 243–60. Chiang Mai: Silkworm Books, 1999.

Tanom Pipityakorn. "MBK Rental Deal Good for Both Sides." *Bangkok Post*, July 13, 1995, 33.

Tate, D. J. M. *The Making of Modern South-East Asia*. Vol. 2 of *The Western Impact*. Kuala Lumpur: Oxford University Press, 1979.

Taussig, Michael. *The Devil and Commodity Fetishism in South America*. Chapel Hill: University of North Carolina, 1980.

Tavernise, Sabrina. "A Russian Rights Crusader, Made by Mary Kay." *New York Times*, April 20, 2002, A4.

Terry, Jennifer. *An American Obsession: Science, Medicine, and Homosexuality in Modern Society*. Chicago: University of Chicago Press, 1999.

Thailand Development Research Institute. "Thailand Economic Information Kit June 1992." Bangkok, 1992.

Thailand Government Public Relations Department, National News Bureau. "Thaksin Shinawatra." http://www.thaimain.org/cgibin/newsdesk_perspect.cgi?a = 276&t = index_2.html [accessed on October 24, 2001].

Thailand in the 80s. Bangkok: National Identity Office, Office of the Prime Minister, 1984.

Thailand in the 90s. Bangkok: National Identity Office, Office of the Prime Minister, 1992.

"Thaksin: I'll Step Down if Found Unfit." *Bangkok Post*, October 28, 1994, 2.

"Thaksin Tops PDP List in Public Wealth Declaration." *Bangkok Post*, November 19, 1994, 1.

Thamsook Numnonda. "When Thailand Followed the Leader," trans. the Bangkok Post. In *Review of Thai Social Sciences: A Collection of Articles by Thai Scholars*, vol. 3: 197–223. Bangkok: Social Science Association of Thailand, 1977.

Thananya Srestha. "One Hundred and Fifty Years of Selling." In *The Advertising Book*, no. 8: 16–17. Bangkok: AB Publications, 1994.

Thitsa, Khin. "Nuns, Mediums and Prostitutes in Chiengmai: A Study of Some Marginal Categories of Women." Women and Development in Southeast Asia, Occasional Paper no. 1, University of Kent at Canterbury, 1983.

Thompson, E. P. *Customs in Common*. New York: New Press, 1993.

Thomson, Sheila Sukonta. *Thai Women in Local Politics: Democracy in the Making*. Bangkok: Gender and Development Research Institute and Friedrich Ebert Stiftung, 1995.

Thongchai Winichakul. *Siam Mapped: A History of the Geo-Body of a Nation.* Hawaii: University of Hawaii Press, 1992.

Thorbek, Susanne. *Voices from the City: Women of Bangkok.* London: Zed Books, 1987.

Took Took Thongthiraj. "Toward a Struggle against Invisibility: Love between Women in Thailand." *Amerasia* 20, no. 1 (1994): 45–58.

"Top Companies 1985: Central Department Store Co., Ltd." *Business Review* (Thailand), September 1985, 125–26.

Trinh T. Minh-ha. *Woman, Native, Other: Writing Postcoloniality and Feminism.* Bloomington: Indiana University Press, 1989.

Truong, Thanh-Dam. *Sex, Money and Morality: Prostitution and Tourism in South-East Asia.* London: Zed Books, 1990.

Tsing, Anna. *In the Realm of the Diamond Queen.* Princeton, N.J.: Princeton University Press, 1993.

Tupperware. "About Us." http://www.tupperware.com/about/index.html [accessed March 20, 1998].

Turton, Andrew. "Architectural and Political Space in Thailand." In *Natural Symbols in Southeast Asia*, ed. G. B. Milner, 113–32. London: School of Oriental and African Studies, 1978.

Ubonrat Siriyuvasak. *The Dynamics of Audience Media Activities: An Ethnography of Women Textile Workers.* Department of Mass Communication, Publication no. 7, Chulalongkorn University, Bangkok, 1989.

Udom Kerdpibule. *Market Structure and Competition in Bangkok Wholesale Market.* Center for Applied Economics, Research Report no. 3, Kasetsart University, Bangkok, 1976.

"Update." *Business Review* (Thailand), August 1994, 79.

Van Beek, Steve. *Bangkok.* Hong Kong: Insight CityGuides, 1988.

Vance, Carol. "Anthropology Rediscovers Sexuality: A Theoretical Comment." *Social Science and Medicine* 33, no. 8 (1990): 875–84.

Van Esterik, Penny. "Deconstructing Display: Gender and Development in Thailand." Thai Studies Project/WID Consortium paper no. 2. York University, Toronto, 1989.

———. "Foreign Bodies, Diseased Bodies, No Bodies: Thai Prostitution and Gender Identity." Paper presented at the SSRC Conference on Sexuality and Gender in East and Southeast Asia, University of California, Los Angeles, December 1990.

———. *Materializing Thailand.* Oxford: Berg Publishers, 2000.

———. "The Politics of Beauty in Thailand." In *Beauty Queens on the Global Stage:*

Gender, Contests, and Power, ed. Colleen Cohen, Richard Wilk, and Beverly Stoeltje, 203–16. New York: Routledge, 1995.

———, ed. *Women of Southeast Asia.* Northern Illinois University Occasional Paper no. 9. Dekalb, Ill.: Center for Southeast Asian Studies, 1982.

Van Fleet, Sara. "Prime-Time Dramas: Television, Gender and Desire in Thailand's Urban North." Unpublished ms. in author's possession, University of Washington, 1996.

Veena Thoopkrajae, Busrin Treerapongpichit, and Nattha Komolvadhin. "ATM Spreads Out Risks via Franchising, Realty." *Nation* (Bangkok), December 5, 1994, B1.

Virada Somswasdi and Sally Theobald, eds. *Women, Gender Relations and Development in Thai Society.* Vols. 1 and 2. Chiang Mai: Women's Studies Center, Faculty of Social Sciences, 1997.

Vitit Muntarbhorn, Wimolsiri Jamnarnvej, and Tanawadee Boonlue. "UNESCO Status of Women: Thailand." RUSHAP Series on Monographs and Occasional Papers, UNESCO, Social and Human Sciences in Asia and the Pacific, Bangkok, 1990.

Wakin, Eric. *Anthropology Goes to War: Professional Ethics and Counterinsurgency in Thailand.* Madison: University of Wisconsin, Center for Southeast Asian Studies, 1992.

Walker, Dave, and Richard S. Erlich. *"Hello My Big Big Honey": Love Letters to Bangkok Bar Girls.* Bangkok: Dragon Dance Publications, 1992.

Walker, Marilyn. "A World of Everything: The Thai Supermarket as Image and Practice." Paper presented at Northwest Regional Consortium for Southeast Asian Studies, October 1992.

Walkowitz, Judith R. *City of Dreadful Delight: Narratives of Sexual Danger in Late Victorian London.* Chicago: University of Chicago, 1992.

———. *Prostitution and Victorian Society: Women, Class, and the State.* Cambridge: Cambridge University Press, 1980.

Walters, Suzanna Danuta. *Material Girls: Making Sense of Feminist Cultural Theory.* Berkeley: University of California, 1995.

Wanjiku Kaime-Atterhog, Orathai Ard-Am, and Chanya Sethaput. "Child Prostitution in Thailand: A Documentary Assessment" (also published in Thai: "Dek nai turakit phetphanit nai Sangkom Thai"). In *Sopheni dek nai sankhom Thai* (Child prostitution in Thailand), ed. Orathai Ard-Am and Chanya Sethaput, 37–72. Salaya, Thailand: Mahidol University, Institute of Population and Social Research, 1994.

Wathinee Boonchalakski and Phillip Guest. *Prostitution in Thailand.* Salaya,

Thailand: Mahidol University, Institute for Population and Social Research, 1994.

Weeks, Jeffrey. *Sexuality and Its Discontents: Meanings, Myths, and Modern Sexualities*. London: Routledge, 1985.

Weisman, Jan Robyn. "Tropes and Traces: Hybridity, Race, Sex and Responses to Modernity in Thailand." Ph.D. diss., University of Washington, Seattle, 2000.

Wells, Troth, and Foo Gaik Sim. *Till They Have Faces: Women as Consumers*. Kuala Lumpur, Malaysia: International Organization of Consumers—Regional Office for Asia and the Pacific Unions and Isis International, 1987.

White, Luise. *The Comforts of Home: Prostitution in Colonial Nairobi*. Chicago: University of Chicago Press, 1990.

Whittaker, Andrea. *Intimate Knowledge: Women and Their Health in North-East Thailand*. St. Leonards, NSW, Australia: Allen & Unwin, 2000.

Wilson, Ara. "American Catalogues of Asian Brides." In *Anthropology for the Nineties*, ed. Johnnetta B. Cole, 114–25. New York: Free Press, 1988.

———. "Bangkok, The Bubble City." In *Wounded Cities: Destruction and Reconstruction in a Globalized World*, ed. Jane Schneider and Ida Susser, 203–26. Oxford: Berg Publishers, 2003.

———. "Decentralization and the Avon Lady in Bangkok, Thailand." *Political and Legal Anthropology Review* 21, no. 1 (1998): 77–83.

———. "The Empire of Direct Sales and the Making of Thai Entrepreneurs." *Critique of Anthropology* 19, no. 4 (1999): 401–22.

———. "Women in the City of Consumption: Markets and the Construction of Gender in Bangkok, Thailand." Ph.D. diss., City University of New York Graduate School, 1997.

Wilson, Constance. "Bangkok in 1883: An Economic and Social Profile." *Journal of Siam Society* 77, no. 1 (1989): 49–58.

———. "Economic Activities of Women in Bangkok, 1883." *Journal of the Siam Society* 78, no. 1 (1990): 85–87.

Wilson, Elizabeth. *The Sphinx of the City: Urban Life, the Control of Disorder, and Women*. Berkeley: University of California Press, 1991.

Wohl, Victoria. *Intimate Commerce: Exchange, Gender, and Subjectivity in Greek Tragedy*. Austin: University of Texas Press, 1997.

Wright, Arnold, ed. *Twentieth Century Impressions of Siam: Its History, People, Commerce, Industries, and Resources*. 1908. Reprint, Bangkok: White Lotus Press, 1994.

Wyatt, David K. "Family Politics in 19th Century Thailand." *Journal of Southeast Asian History* 9, no. 2 (September 1968): 208–28.

———. *Thailand: A Short History.* New Haven, Conn.: Yale University Press, 1982.

Yanagisako, S., and J. Collier. "Toward a Unified Analysis of Gender and Kinship." In *Gender and Kinship: Toward a Unified Analysis*, ed. J. Collier and S. Yanagisako, 14–50. Stanford, Calif.: Stanford University Press, 1987.

Yingyord Manchuvisith. "The Shinawatras." *The Nation Mid-year Review: Thai Tycoons—Winners & Losers in the Economic Crisis* (Bangkok: The Nation, July 1998), 27–29.

Ywin, Kenneth. "Mail Order Giant Looks to Thailand." *Nation* (Bangkok), April 4, 1994, B1–2.

———. "Showing the Unsafe of 'Safe' Products via Distributors." *Nation* (Bangkok), November 4, 1993, B-3.

Zola, Émile. *The Ladies' Paradise.* 1883. Originally published serially in France as *Au bonheur des dames*, 1882.

INDEX

advertising, 122; at IBC Cable TV, 146, 155–56; Thai and foreigners in, 145, 228n29

Alien Business Law, 50, 65

Alien Registration Act, 49

Amagram (Amway magazine), 176–77

American School (in Bangkok), 104

Amway, 9, 24, 163; distributor of, 164, 165, 166, 175–76, 185–88; entrepreneurial self-help discourse of, 177–79; motivational meeting of, 184–85; "The Plan" of, 176, 178, 184; promotion of marriage by, 186–87; stratification of distributors by, 175–76; training, 176–78. *See also* direct sales; distributor

Anand Panyacharun (prime minister), 65

Anchalee (singer), 128–30

An Fong Lao (store), 34–35

Anjaree (lesbian group), 24, 111, 128, 131, 220n28

anthropology: definitions of economy by, 11; globalization and, 27

Apasara Hongsakula (Miss Universe), 61, 66

Asia, 124, 149; globalization in, 138, 140–41

Assumption Commercial College, 41

Australia, 42

Avon, 9, 24, 163, 171, 179, 231n4; business system of, 172–73; catalogues of, 169–70; decline in Thailand, 188; distributor of, 164, 184; entry of into Thailand, 165, 168; training of, 169, 172. *See also* Avon Lady; direct sales; distributor

Avon Lady, 24, 168–71, 187, 191; image of, 169, 172, 183–84, 186, 188; training of, 169–70; tom as, 169, 171–73. *See also* distributor

Bangkok: advertising in, 122; capitalist development in, 32, 35; department store development in, 30, 53–54; foreign residents in, 15–17, 32, 200n18; global capitalism's impact in, 9, 22, 195; growth of shopping malls in, 103–6; map of, 10; migrant workers to, 21, 76, 90–91, 174; modern markets in, 9, 22–24; modern urbanity of, 5; as a multicultural city, 16; 1997 economic crisis in, 2, 64, 188, 192, 197n2; prostitution industry for foreigners

Text: 10/15 Janson
Display: Janson
Compositor: Integrated Composition Systems
Printer: Friesens Corporation